Presented to Purchase College
by
Gary Waller, PhD Cambridge

State University of New York
Distinguished Professor

Professor
of Literature & Cultural
Studies, and Theatre &
Performance, 1995-2019
Provost 1995-2004

SIR PHILIP SIDNEY

AN ANNOTATED BIBLIOGRAPHY
OF MODERN CRITICISM, 1941–1970

University of Missouri Studies LVI

SIR PHILIP SIDNEY

AN ANNOTATED BIBLIOGRAPHY
OF MODERN CRITICISM, 1941–1970

MARY A. WASHINGTON

University of Missouri Press
Columbia, 1972

FOR JAMES V. HOLLERAN

Contents

Introduction

Although this work is a continuation of Samuel A. Tannenbaum's *Sir Philip Sidney* (*A Concise Bibliography*), published in 1941, the organization is different, and it contains annotations for most of the works listed. Tannenbaum's bibliography, which covers the period from Sidney's death through 1940, is divided into sections for Sidney's works, for selections from his works, for poems in praise of Sidney, for biography and criticism, and finally a section for modern fiction based on Sidney's life or his works.

The present bibliography is a guide to Sidney criticism from 1941 through 1970. It consists of sections for general criticism, for biographical materials, for each of Sidney's major works, for the minor works, and final sections for foreign studies and for reprints of books and articles noted in Tannenbaum's bibliography. While I have not tried to find all book reviews, those I noticed I have listed below the annotations of the books reviewed. A few book reviews that also contain Sidney criticism are entered as separate items.

I have annotated all U.S. dissertations dealing with Sidney and have derived many of the annotations from abstracts of the dissertations. Because most foreign theses and dissertations are not available through interlibrary loan and are not abstracted, I have listed them, unannotated, in a separate section and have named the book in which the reference to each entry occurred.

The section dealing with the life of Sidney includes references to poems dedicated to Sidney, as well as works for which Sidney's life may have been a source. I have not, as Tannenbaum did, listed modern works of fiction based on Sidney's life—although a few of the biographies nearly cross the borderline into fiction.

Another section is for books listed by Tannenbaum but reprinted during the period covered by this bibliography. Many of the standard books about Sidney have been reprinted recently; these I have noted briefly. A few articles and mentions of Sidney that Tannenbaum did not list are entered according to subject matter. I did not attempt to check the period prior to 1941, but when I found an article not listed by Tannenbaum, I did incorporate it in the appropriate section of my own work.

The material peripheral to Sidney criticism and much of the material dealing equally with two or more of Sidney's works appears in the general section. I wanted to place major critical works under one of the sections for a specific work; thus, of necessity, I had to select the work for which I believe the criticism to be most valuable. The Index provides cross references to other works to which the entry applies.

The annotations—descriptive rather than critical—indicate the way in which each work applies to Sidney criticism. In those in which Sidney criticism is not central, I have attempted to explain the relationship between the comments about Sidney and the thesis of the work.

Although I have analyzed periodicals that might contain material about Sidney, primarily I have collected bibliography listings of Sidney studies. Many of the entries in this bibliography are not, probably, vital for most Sidney scholarship, yet many of them appeared in the sources listed. Only modern fiction and a very few erroneous entries have intentionally been omitted from these sources.

Finally, I want to thank the many people who have helped me. Specifically, I would like to acknowledge the outstanding work of Mrs. Ann-Todd Rubey, Humanities Librarian, and her staff at the University of Missouri—Columbia. Many other librarians and libraries were very generous in allowing me to borrow or photocopy material. Merrill Library and Learning Resouces Center at Utah State University has also been helpful.

Professors Leon T. Dickenson, Donald K. Anderson, Jr., and William M. Jones, all of the University of Missouri—Columbia, have generously given their time and attention. I also want to thank Mrs. Ann Holleran, who checked many of the bibliographies used in compiling this work, and Professor Eugene Washington of Utah State University, who offered thoughtful criticism and helped with translations of some of the articles.

My greatest debt is to Professor James V. Holleran of the University of Missouri—Columbia. His assistance has been of such value that it is impossible to express the extent of my obligation. Perhaps his persistent encouragement is the thing for which I am most grateful.

I, of course, am responsible for any errors in fact or judgment in this work.

M.A.W.
Logan, Utah
November, 1971

Abbreviations Used in This Text *

ACF · Annali di Ca' Foscari (Venice)

AHR · American Historical Review

Archiv · Archiv für das Studium der Neueren Sprachen und Literaturen

AUL · Annali dell' Università di Lecce

AUMLA · Journal of the Australasian Universities Language and Literature Association

BC · Book Collector

BHR · Bibliothèque d'Humanisme et Renaissance

BJA · British Journal of Aesthetics (London)

BJRL · Bulletin of the John Rylands Library

BLR · Bodleian Library Record

BNYPL · Bulletin of the New York Public Library

CE · College English

CJ · Classical Journal

CL · Comparative Literature

CollG · Colloquia Germanica, Internationale Zeitschrift für Germanische Sprach- und Literaturwissenschaft

ConTM · Concordia Theological Monthly

DA · Dissertation Abstracts

DDAAU · Doctoral Dissertations Accepted by American Universities

DR · Dalhousie Review

DSPS · Duquesne Studies, Philological Series

DUJ · Durham University Journal

DVLG · Deutsche Vierteljahrsschrift für Literaturwissenschaft und Geistesgeschichte

EA · Etudes Anglaises

EALN · Early American Literature Newsletter

EDH · Essays by Divers Hands

EF · Etudes Françaises

EIC · Essays in Criticism (Oxford)

ELH · Journal of English Literary History

ELN · English Language Notes (U. of Colorado)

EM · English Miscellany

ES · English Studies

ESA · English Studies in Africa (Johannesburg)

ESQ · Emerson Society Quarterly

Expl · Explicator

---

* The abbreviations are based on the Master List and Table of Abbreviations in the PMLA Bibliography of June, 1969.

FeL · Filologia e Letteratura

HLB · Harvard Library Bulletin

HLQ · Huntington Library Quarterly

HRDP · Harvard University and Radcliffe College. Doctors of Philosophy with the Titles of Their Theses

HSE · Hungarian Studies in English (L. Kossuth U., Debrecen)

HudR · Hudson Review

Index · Index to American Doctoral Dissertations (Ann Arbor, Mich.)

ISLL · Illinois Studies in Language and Literature

JEGP · Journal of English and Germanic Philology

JHI · Journal of the History of Ideas

JWCI · Journal of the Warburg and Courtauld Institute

KR · Kenyon Review

Lang&S · Language and Style

LSE · Lund Studies in English

MLJ · Modern Language Journal

MLN · Modern Language Notes

MLQ · Modern Language Quarterly

MLR · Modern Language Review

MP · Modern Philology

N&Q · Notes and Queries

NEQ · New England Quarterly

NM · Neuphilologische Mitteilungen

NS · Die Neueren Sprachen

NYTB · New York Times Book Review

PAPS · Proceedings of the American Philosophical Society

PBSA · Papers of the Bibliographical Society of America

PLL · Papers on Language and Literature

PMASAL · Papers of the Michigan Academy of Science, Arts, and Letters

PMLA · Publications of the Modern Language Association of America

PoetryR · Poetry Review (London)

PQ · Philological Quarterly (Iowa City)

PTRSC · Proceedings and Transactions of the Royal Society of Canada

PULC · Princeton University Library Chronicle

QJS · Quarterly Journal of Speech

QQ · Queen's Quarterly

RenD · Renaissance Drama (Northwestern U.)

RenP · Renaissance Papers

RenQ · Renaissance Quarterly

RES · Review of English Studies

RHL · Revue d'Histoire Littéraire de la France

RLMC · Riv. di Letteratura Moderne e Comparate (Florence)

RQ · Riverside Quarterly (U. of Saskatchewan)

RUS · Rice University Studies

SAQ · South Atlantic Quarterly

SatR · Saturday Review

SB · Studies in Bibliography: Papers of the Bibliographical Society of the University of Virginia

SCN · Seventeenth-Century News

SEL · Studies in English Literature, 1500–1900

ShS · Shakespeare Survey

SJH · Shakespeare-Jahrbuch (Heidelberg)

SJW · Shakespeare-Jahrbuch (Weimar)

SN · Studia Neophilologica

SNL · Satire Newsletter (State U. College, Oneonta, N.Y.)

SP · Studies in Philology

SQ · Shakespeare Quarterly

SR · Sewanee Review

SRen · Studies in the Renaissance

SSL · Studies in Scottish Literature (U. of South Carolina)

SSLL · Stanford Studies in Language and Literature

TA · Theater Annual

TLS · [London] Times Literary Supplement

TQ · Texas Quarterly (U. of Texas)

TSLL · Texas Studies in Literature and Language

UMCMP · University of Michigan Contributions in Modern Philology

UTQ · University of Toronto Quarterly

UTS · University of Texas Studies in English

VMKVA · Verslagen en Mededelingen van de Koninklijke Vlaamse Academie voor Taal- en Letterkunde

WBEP · Wiener Beitrage zur Englischen Philologie

WHR · Western Humanities Review

ZAA · Zeitschrift für Anglistik und Amerikanistik (East Berlin)

I

General

⋙ 1. ADOLPH, ROBERT. *The Rise of Modern Prose Style.* Cambridge, Mass. The MIT Press, 1968. 372 pp.

Combines the objectivity of linguistics with the subjectivity of literary criticism to examine changes in prose style. Sidney's writing is "conscious artifice" and follows classical prose (pp. 157–58). *Arcadia* is more active than later fiction, but has less characterization (pp. 266–67).

⋙ 2. AKRIGG, G. P. V. "The Renaissance Reconsidered." *QQ*, 52 (1945), 311–19.

The Renaissance was a rebirth of classical studies. It was characterized by awareness, individualism, social mobility, and idealism. Sidney exemplifies Renaissance idealism.

⋙ 3. BABIN, MARÍA TERESA. "Garcilaso de la Vega y Sir Philip Sidney." *La Nueva Democracia*, 33 (1953), 63–75.

Compares Sidney and Garcilaso to establish a common denominator for the Renaissance. While both men were inspired by love, Sidney's poetry reflects Platonism more than Garcilaso's does. Both men used the theme of passion against reason, but Garcilaso resolved the conflict in favor of reason. Sidney's tone is more romantic than Garcilaso's. Compares image patterns.

⋙ 4. BAKER, HERSCHEL. *The Dignity of Man: Studies in the Persistence of the Idea of Human Dignity in Classical Antiquity, the Middle Ages and the Renaissance.* Cambridge, Mass.: Harvard University Press, 1947. 365 pp.

Believes that Renaissance men held approximately the same idea of human nature as those of the late Middle Ages did. Sidney illustrated the "purest form of the ethics of gentility" (pp. 296–97).

Rev.: *Booklist*, 44 (November 1, 1947), 82; *Manchester Guardian*, September 28, 1948, p. 3; Douglas Bush, *JEGP*, 47 (1948), 196–98; Crane Briton, *Isis*, 39 (1948), 199–200.

◄§ 5. BALDWIN, THOMAS WHITFIELD. *On the Literary Genetics of Shakspere's Plays, 1592–1594.* Urbana: University of Illinois Press, 1959. ix, 562 pp.

Examines the plays written between 1592 and 1594 in relation to contemporary methods of composition. Cites *The Faerie Queene* and *Arcadia* as sources for *Selimus* (pp. 223–24).

Rev.: R. F. Hill, *Theatre Notebook*, 14 (1960), 136–37; J. C. Maxwell, *N&Q*, n.s., 7 (1960), 354–55; Sylvan Barnet, *MP*, 58 (1960), 57–59.

◄§ 6. ———. *On the Literary Genetics of Shakspere's Poems and Sonnets.* Urbana: University of Illinois Press, 1950. xi, 399 pp.

Concerns Shakespeare's use of the Ovidian tradition. Traces the source of several of Shakespeare's sonnets to *Arcadia*, specifically to Cecropia's arguments for procreation (pp. 194–203).

Rev.: Virgil K. Whitaker, *SQ*, 2 (1951), 137–39.

◄§ 7. BARKER, SIR ERNEST. *Traditions of Civility: Eight Essays.* Cambridge: University Press, 1948. viii, 369 pp.

Gives Sidney's education as an example of 16th-century education (pp. 124–58). See also Index.

◄§ 8. BERGER, HARRY, JR. "The Renaissance Imagination: Second World and Green World." *The Centennial Review*, 9 (1965), 36–78.

Distinguishes between Abrams' "second world" and Fry's "green world." The second world may be taken to be the field of the work of art. Examines the relations among artist, object, and viewer in this second world, taking the Renaissance use of perspective as an example. The green world may be taken to be the imaginary world inside the work of art, as Arcadia, or Utopia. The customary pattern of withdrawal to and return from the green world was, in the Renaissance, extended to the second world. As the viewer withdrew to the art object, he withdrew to a source of both delight and profit.

◄§ 9. BLACK, J. B. *The Reign of Elizabeth, 1558–1603.* Oxford: Clarendon Press, 1959. xxvi, 539 pp.

[First published, 1936.] Emphasizes the social and cultural aspects of Elizabethan life. Only Sidney, Spenser, and Shakespeare tried to give real experience in their sonnets (p. 289). The "golden period" of Elizabethan literature began with Sidney's *Astrophel and Stella* and *Arcadia* (p. 290).

◄§ 10. BOLGAR, R. R. *The Classical Heritage and Its Beneficiaries.* Cambridge: University Press, 1954. vii, 591 pp.

Sidney, Spenser, and Elyot made classical material available through their imitations (p. 328).

Rev.: *SCN*, 14 (1955), 11.

◄§ 11. BROOKE, TUCKER. "The Renaissance." In *A Literary History of England*, Albert C. Baugh, ed., pp. 315–696. New York: Appleton-Century-Crofts, Inc., 1948.

[2d edition, published in 1967, includes recent scholarship in a supplement.] Sidney's character is as interesting as his works. He influenced such writers as Spenser and Edward Dyer. Sidney tried to rewrite *Arcadia* following classical studies he had made for the *Defence*. In the New *Arcadia* Sidney tried to change a romance into an epic. The *Defence of Poesie* is romantic in its protest against dogma. All of Sidney's major works seem genuine rather than strictly traditional.

◄§ 12. BROOKS, ALDEN. *Will Shakspere and the Dyer's Hand.* New York: Charles Scribner's Sons, 1943. xx, 704 pp.

Attempts to show that Shakespeare, the man, was not the writer of Shakespeare's plays. Suggests that Edward Dyer may have written many of them and that he is the friend mentioned in Sidney's Sonnet 21 (pp. 534–38). *Venus and Adonis* may be in part an elegy for Sidney (pp. 630–32).

Rev.: Theodore Spenser, *Nation*, 156 (1943), 315.

◄§ 13. BRUNO, GIORDANO. *The Expulsion of the Triumphant Beast*, trans. by Arthur D. Imerti, ed. New Brunswick, N.J.: Rutgers University Press, 1964. ix, 324 pp.

Examines the evidence for Bruno's influence upon Sidney; quotes from Bruno regarding Sidney (pp. 10–11).

Rev.: Sears Jayne, *Shakespeare Studies*, 1 (1965), 318–21.

◄§ 14. BUSH, DOUGLAS. *English Poetry: The Main Currents from Chaucer to the Present.* New York: Oxford University Press, 1952. 222 pp.

Sidney's sonnets are marked by artistic control (pp. 28–30). See also Index.

Rev.: *EA*, 6 (1953), 372; *SAQ*, 52 (1953), 489–90.

⁊ 15. ———. *Prefaces to Renaissance Literature*. Cambridge, Mass.: Harvard University Press, 1965. viii, 110 pp.

Contains five essays. Several of the essays deal with Sidney: in "Humanism and the Critical Spirit," Sidney is said to follow Aristotelian aesthetics (p. 18); in "The Classics and Imaginative Literature," Sidney is cited in relation to the convention of cataloguing a woman's beauties (p. 35). The essay "English Poetry: Time and Man" contains several references to the *Defence*, and cites "Leave me, O love . . ." as an example of the theme of *contemptus mundi* (p. 81).

Rev.: Kenneth S. Rothwell, *CE*, 27 (1966), 650; Roland M. Frye, *ELN*, 4 (1966), 136–37; R. F. Hill, *MLR*, 61 (1966), 662–63; *TLS*, August 19, 1965, p. 716; Charles Daves, *SCN*, 23 (1965), 32–33; Carl Meyer, *ConTM*, 36 (1965), 453.

⁊ 16. ———. *The Renaissance and English Humanism*. Toronto: University of Toronto Press, 1939. 139 pp.

Believes that in *Arcadia* Sidney contrasts chance and nature with providence and Christian ethics (p. 87). See also Index.

Rev.: B. F. C. Davis, *MLR*, 36 (1941), 256–58.

⁊ 17. CARRÉ, MEYRICK H. *Phases of Thought in England*. Oxford: Clarendon Press, 1949. xix, 392 pp.

Surveys patterns of thought in England from the beginnings of Christianity to the 20th century. Chapter 6 pertains to Bruno and to Sidney's interest in Neo-Platonism (pp. 178–223).

⁊ 18. CARROLL, WILLIAM MEREDITH. *Animal Conventions in English Renaissance Non-Religious Prose* (1550–1600). New York: Bookman Associates, 1954. 166 pp.

Studies the source and persistence of animal conventions and includes a catalogue of conventional animal images. Contains examples from Sidney's works.

Rev.: A. Lytton Sells, *JEGP*, 55 (1956), 537–40.

⁊ 19. CLEMENTS, ROBERT J. *Critical Theory and Practice of the Pléiade*. Cambridge, Mass.: Harvard University Press, 1942. 281 pp.

Relates to traditional critical theory the theory of the Pléiade regarding such topics as sincerity in poetry and the conflict between art and nature. Sidney's *Defence* was one of the Renaissance works to take up the questions of whether poetry should be sweet or useful and whether sweet poetry could be dangerous (p. 126).

⋙ 20. ──────. *Picta Poesis: Literary and Humanistic Theory in Renaissance Emblem Books.* Rome: Edizionidi Storia e Letteratura, 1960. 248 pp., 13 pls.

Relates emblem literature to Renaissance literary theory and uses emblemata to interpret literature. Quotes Blunt's translation of Estienne, that Sidney's motto *Sine refluxu* refers to the Caspian Sea. Several references to the *Defence.*

⋙ 21. Close, A. J. "Commonplace Theories of Art and Nature in Classical Antiquity and in the Renaissance." *JHI*, 30 (1969), 467–86.

Examines the various Renaissance assumptions concerning the relation between practical art and nature. Nature in the Renaissance might be a principle of generation, or a causative power in the universe, or matter, or the physical force of things, or a simple reference to the natural world. Sidney advanced the theories that art imitates nature and that art is based on experience (the study of nature). Other writers advanced theories that art perfects nature, that art makes use of nature's material, that art has its beginning in nature, that art is inferior to nature, and that nature is an artist. Many of these commonplaces were used to develop prescriptive treatises.

⋙ 22. Collins, Joseph B. *Christian Mysticism in the Elizabethan Age, With Its Background in Mystical Methodology.* Baltimore: Johns Hopkins Press, 1940. xiv, 251 pp.

Breton, chiefly influenced by Gascoigne, was also influenced by Sidney, Spenser, Southwell, and Drayton (p. 177).

⋙ 23. Courthope, William J. *The Renaissance and the Reformation: Influence of the Court and the University.* Vol. II of A *History of English Poetry.* London: Macmillan Company, 1962. 429 pp.

[First printing, 1897.] Emphasizes Sidney's friendship with Languet and Spenser (pp. 203–33 *passim*). Includes a plot summary of *Arcadia*, followed by the criticism that Sidney was more concerned with expression than with content (p. 220). Suggests that *Astrophel and Stella* does not express real love (pp. 226–33).

⋙ 24. Craig, Hardin. *The Enchanted Glass: The Elizabethan Mind in Literature.* Oxford: Blackwell, 1950. ix, 293 pp.

Studies Renaissance belief in relation to such subjects as philosophy and astrology. The allusions to astrology in *Arcadia* probably are intended to be serious (pp. 33–35). Pyrocles' disguise illustrates a violation of nature (pp. 154–56). Describes the rhetoric of *A Discourse to the Queenes Majesty* (pp. 164–67).

Rev.: *TLS*, November 10, 1950, p. 706.

&§ 25. ———. *The Literature of the English Renaissance, 1485–1660.* Book II of *A History of English Literature,* Hardin Craig, ed. New York: Oxford University Press, 1950. xiii, 697 pp.

Describes the relationship between Castiglione's writings and Sidney's (p. 199). Compares Sidney's sonnets to Spenser's sonnets (pp. 240–44). See also Index.

Rev.: D. A. Stauffer, *CE,* 12 (1950–1951), 298–99.

&§ 26. ———. *New Lamps for Old: A Sequel to the Enchanted Glass.* Oxford: Basil Blackwell, 1960. 244 pp.

Even though Sidney was an Aristotelian, he admired the ballad. He was a better critic than his age allowed him to be (pp. 175–76). See also Index.

Rev.: *TLS*, August 4, 1961, p. 485.

&§ 27. CRAIGIE, SIR WILLIAM A. *The Critique of Pure English from Caxton to Smollett.* Society for Pure English Tracts 65. Oxford: Clarendon Press, 1946. 171 pp.

Contains comments upon the burlesque Latin in *The Lady of May* (p. 132). Contains an excerpt from Heylin's *Extraneus Vapulans* referring to Sidney's *Defence* (p. 154).

Rev.: *TLS*, November 2, 1946, p. 539.

&§ 28. CURTIUS, ERNST ROBERT. *European Literature and the Latin Middle Ages,* trans. by Willard R. Trask. New York: Pantheon Books, 1953. xv, 662 pp.

Most European literature through the Middle Ages may be interpreted in light of Greek rhetorical theory. All works including in their title the word *Defence* are related to the "apelenctic" form of the *protreptikos,* or the form in which the detractors of an art or a science were exposed (pp. 548–49). See also Index.

Rev.: *TLS*, December 4, 1953, p. 786.

⋙ 29. DAICHES, DAVID. *A Critical History of English Literature.* New York: Ronald Press Company, 1960. 2 vols.

Relates the October eclogue of *Shepheardes Calender* to the *Defence* (p. 127). Sidney enlarged the possibilities of the sonnet form, but Shakespeare did not (p. 205).

Rev.: Robert Hillyer, *NYTB*, April 9, 1961, p. 18.

⋙ 30. DAY, MARTIN S. *History of English Literature to 1660.* Garden City, N.Y.: Doubleday and Company, 1963. 467 pp.

Lists Sidney's arguments in the *Defence* (p. 219). See also Index.

⋙ 31. DEAN, LEONARD F. "Bodin's *Methodus* in England Before 1625." *SP*, 39 (1942), 160–66.

Writes that Sidney, as well as Spenser, Harvey, and Nashe, used Bodin's book. Sidney referred to it in a letter of October 18, 1580.

⋙ 32. DELATTRE, FLORIS, AND CAMILLE CHEMIN. *Les Chansons Élizabéthaines.* Paris: Librairie Marcel Didier, 1948. 459 pp.

Gives extensive literary history and the French translation of many Elizabethan poems, including some of Sidney's.

Rev.: G. A. Bonnard, *ES*, 33 (1952), 72–76.

⋙ 33. DORAN, MADELEINE. *Endeavors of Art: A Study of Form in Elizabethan Drama.* Madison: University of Wisconsin Press, 1954. xv, 482 pp.

Examines the form of Elizabethan drama in a context of assumptions regarding the relation of art and nature, the moral aim of art, the critical theory of the drama, and verisimilitude; also in relation to the traditional forms of writing. Contrasts Sidney's prose in *Arcadia* with Lyly's euphuism. Sidney's style is studied and is free of ornamentation (pp. 65–66). Also contains frequent references to the *Defence*.

Rev.: Marvin T. Herrick, *JEGP*, 53 (1954), 472–73.

⋙ 34. ELLRODT, ROBERT. *Neoplatonism in the Poetry of Spenser.* Travaux d'humanisme et Renaissance, XXXV. Geneva: Librairie E. Droz, 1960. 247 pp.

Re-examines the extent of Spenser's Platonism, Neo-Platonism, and the extent to which he uses traditional Christian themes. Spenser wrote *Astrophel*, thinking Lady Sidney to be Stella (p. 23n). Sidney was more influenced by Cicero's translation of Plato's *Phaedrus* than by the original (p. 97).

35. ENTWISTLE, WILLIAM J., AND ERIC GILLET. *The Literature of England, A.D. 500–1942*. London: Longmans, 1943.
xii, 292 pp.

Sidney's life was more successful than Spenser's. Sidney's *Defence* offers principles for composition without the trivial details
given in Puttenham's *Art of English Poesie* (Chapter IV).

36. EVANS, B. IFOR. *A Short History of English Literature*.
New York: Penguin Books, 1940. 215 pp.

Arcadia may be the first novel in English (p. 128). Describes
Arcadia and *Euphues* (p. 131). See also Index.

37. EVANS, MAURICE. *English Poetry in the Sixteenth Century*, 2d ed., rev. London: Hutchinson, 1967. 184 pp.

[First edition, 1955.] Reviews English poetry from Skelton
through Donne. Writes that Sidney's sonnets were the most influential in the period. Even though the biographical element is important, Sidney's purpose was to create literature. The sonnets
have a three-part structure, with divisions after the first song and
after the eighth song (pp. 98–108). The poetry of *Arcadia* is experimental and helped to free English poetry from older forms (p.
90).

38. FORD, BORIS, ed. *The Age of Shakespeare*. Vol. 2 of *The
Pelican Guide to English Literature*. London: Penguin
Books, 1955. 480 pp.

Stella represents a Platonic idea of goodness (pp. 92–94). The
descriptions in *Arcadia* are one of its most pleasing parts (pp. 120–
24). Contrasts the Elizabethan novel with modern novels (pp.
122–23). See also Index.

39. FRIEDERICH, WERNER P., AND D. H. MALONE. *Outline of
Comparative Literature from Dante Alighieri to Eugene
O'Neill*. University of North Carolina Studies in Comparative Literature 11. Chapel Hill: University of North Carolina Press, 1954. 451 pp.

Describes the effects of one literature upon another, and the
spread of literary ideas. Suggests that Sidney's *Defence* is for the
most part borrowed from Minturno's *L'Arte Poetica* (p. 28). Describes Petrarchism and Sidney's use of it (pp. 56–59). *Arcadia* was
second only to *Diana* in influence (p. 73).

⊷§ 40. "The Gentleman Poet." *TLS*, January 25, 1963, p. 58.
Reviews Ringler's edition of Sidney's poems. Includes an assessment of Sidney's position in English literature.

⊷§ 41. GRIERSON, HERBERT JOHN CLIFFORD, AND J. C. SMITH. A *Critical History of English Poetry*. London: Chatto and Windus, 1944. viii, 527 pp.
See Chapter III, "Spenser, Sidney and Their Circle." Sidney's sonnets are next in rank to Shakespeare's (pp. 76–78). *Arcadia* contains some good poems (p. 78).

⊷§ 42. GUFFEY, GEORGE R., comp. *Elizabethan Bibliographies Supplements VII: Samuel Daniel 1942–1965, Michael Drayton 1941–1965, Sir Philip Sidney 1941–1965*. London: Nether Press, 1967. 52 pp.
Lists in chronological order critical articles about Sidney, Daniel, and Drayton. Articles on Sidney are numbered 194–510.

⊷§ 43. HAGSTRUM, JEAN H. *The Sister Arts: The Tradition of Literary Pictorialism and English Poetry from Dryden to Gray*. Chicago: University of Chicago Press, 1958. 337 pp., 32 pls.
Uses the methods of literary history to analyze the pictorialism of poetry. Refers to Sidney's "speaking picture" (p. 64*n*). Greene's romances may have influenced Sidney's formalistic imagery (pp. 78–79).
Rev.: Alan D. McKillop, *MLQ*, 20 (1959), 198–99.

⊷§ 44. HAMILTON, A. C. "The Modern Study of Renaissance English Literature: A Critical Survey." *MLQ*, 26 (1965), 150–83.
Traces changes in Renaissance criticism from historical criticism to an interest in the work itself, and expresses the need for a poetic synthesis. Believes that Sidney is central to his age. Writes that an important crux for *Astrophel and Stella* is the degree of autobiography (p. 177). *Arcadia* is judged the best piece of prose fiction written in the 16th or 17th century.

◦§ 45. HARDISON, O. B., JR. *The Enduring Monument: A Study of the Idea of Praise in Renaissance Literary Theory and Practice.* Chapel Hill: University of North Carolina Press, 1962. 240 pp.

Relates the theory of praise and blame to specific Renaissance literature. Takes the word "works" in paragraph 17 of the *Defence* to mean "moral effects," and "parts" to mean "genres"; believes Sidney's *Defence* is part of the epideictic tradition (pp. 42–67).

Rev.: J. P. Pritchard, *Books Abroad*, 37 (1963), 334.

◦§ 46. HAYDN, HIRAM COLLINS. *The Counter-Renaissance.* New York: Charles Scribner's Sons, 1950. xvii, 705 pp.

The Counter Renaissance was a revolt against reason, uniting the empirical scientists and the Puritans. Sidney held both humanistic views and views characteristic of the Counter Renaissance (pp. 652–53). Sidney may have been influenced by "naturalistic humanism" (p. 67). See also Index.

Rev.: Hans Kohn, *NYTB*, April 23, 1950, p. 18; John Herman Randall, *SatR* (June 24, 1950), 21.

◦§ 47. HAYWARD, JOHN. *English Poetry: A Catalogue of First and Early Editions of Works of the English Poets from Chaucer to the Present Day Exhibited by the National Book League at 7 Albemarle Street, London, 1947.* National Book League: Cambridge University Press, 1947. 141 pp.

Lists Sidney's works contained in the library (p. 111).

◦§ 48. HENINGER, S. K., JR. *A Handbook of Renaissance Meteorology with Particular Reference to Elizabethan and Jacobean Literature.* Durham, N.C.: Duke University Press, 1960. xii, 269 pp.

To understand Elizabethan writing one must understand Elizabethan concepts of meteorology. Meteorology to the Elizabethans meant any process that occurred in the air. Includes chapters on meteorology in Spenser, Marlowe, Jonson, Chapman, Donne, and Shakespeare. Indicates that Sidney followed Bartholomaeus when he wrote of the sweetness of rain (p. 52). See also Index.

Rev.: M. Mincoff, *ES*, 42 (1961), 250–51; R. H. Syfret, *RES*, n.s., 12 (1961), 288–89; Michael Macklem, *JEGP*, 59 (1960), 730–31.

ஞ§ 49. Hobsbaum, Philip, ed. *Ten Elizabethan Poets: Wyatt, Chapman, Marston, Stanyhurst, Golding, Harington, Raleigh, Greville, Sidney, Spenser.* London: Longmans, 1969. vii, 199.

Includes poems from each poet and an introduction. Finds Sidney inferior to Greville; *Astrophel and Stella* contains few poems that rise above convention (pp. 16–17). The "drab" poets are in the main line of English poetry.

ஞ§ 50. Hollander, John. *The Untuning of the Sky: Ideas of Music in English Poetry 1500–1700.* Princeton, N.J.: Princeton University Press, 1961. xii, 467 pp.

Uses a framework of practical and of speculative music to analyze poetry. Analyzes an image from "As I my little flock on Ister bank" and finds that in the fifth stanza, music has the ethical function of creating harmony between reason and feeling (pp. 126–27). Finds that Sidney frequently used the word "music" to mean poetry (p. 141).

Rev.: Willa McClung Evans, *JEGP*, 61 (1962), 151–55.

ஞ§ 51. Howell, Wilber Samuel. *Logic and Rhetoric in England, 1500–1700.* Princeton, N.J.: Princeton University Press, 1956. vii, 411 pp.

William Temple, a Ramist, was Sidney's private secretary while in the Netherlands, and he inscribed the 1584 edition of *dialecticae libri duo* to Sidney (pp. 204–5). Fraunce, another Ramist, used Sidney's works to illustrate rhetorical methods. In doing so, he followed Ramus' advice to derive principles from the actual practice of writers (p. 258).

Rev.: *SCN*, 14 (1956), 5; Donald C. Bryant, *QJS*, 42 (1956), 304–6.

ஞ§ 52. Hughey, Ruth, ed. *The Arundel Harington Manuscript of Tudor Poetry.* Columbus: Ohio State University Press, 1960. 2 vols.

Contains the text of poems in the Arundel Harington MS. Includes many of Sidney's poems: "The Fyre to see my woes for anger burnethe" (67), "O deer lyfe when shall yt bee" (71), "Since, shunninge payne, I ease can never fynde" (176), "Locke up faire liddes the treasure of my harte" (191), "All thy scence my swetenes gained" (192), "Ringe out the bells lett morninge shewes be spred" (196), "Loving in trewth, and fayn my love in verse to show" (223), "Unto the Caitife wretch, whome long affliction holdeth" (229). Gives variant readings and bibliographic detail in footnotes. Reviews the evidence for identifying Stella as Lady Rich (pp. 352–55).

◄§ 53. HUNTER, G. K. "Drab and Golden Lyrics of the Renaissance." In *Forms of Lyric*, Reuben A. Brower, ed., pp. 1–18. Selected Papers from the English Institute. New York: Columbia University Press, 1970.
[See 617.] Winters seems to judge "drab" lyrics better than "golden" ones because they are more realistic. Yet both schools produced good poems. "Ye goatherd gods . . ." is rhetorical rather than realistic, but it is a good poem. The poets between Wyatt and Sidney developed a realistic persona, but with Sidney the lyric became symbolic and represented a created world, not reality.

◄§ 54. ———. *John Lyly: The Humanist as Courtier*. Cambridge, Mass.: Harvard University Press, 1962. ix, 376 pp.
Examines Lyly's work to show that it has intrinsic merit. Contains a stylistic comparison of Lyly's *Euphues* and of Sidney's *Arcadia*. Lyly may be the forerunner of Congrevian elegance, while Sidney is "the patron of bourgeois idealism" (pp. 286–89).

◄§ 55. INGLIS, FRED. *The Elizabethan Poets: The Making of English Poetry from Wyatt to Ben Jonson*. London: Evans Brothers Limited, 1969. 168 pp.
Contains a chapter entitled "Courtesy and Meditation: Edmund Spenser, Sir Philip Sidney and his circle, and Robert Southwell." Finds Sidney to be inferior to Greville as a poet. Sidney's poems are trivial. He was, however, important as an experimental poet.

◄§ 56. JACKSON, WILLIAM A., AND EMMA V. UNGER. *The Carl H. Pforzheimer Library, English Literature 1475–1700*. New York: Privately printed, 1940. 3 vols.
The library contains a copy of the Olney edition of *Apologie for Poetrie* published in 1595 (p. 937), a copy of the Ponsonby edition of *Arcadia* published in 1590 (p. 938), and a copy of the 4th edition of *Countesse of Pembrokes Arcadia* published in 1605 (p. 939). See also pp. 963–66.

◄§ 57. JAYNE, SEARS. "Ficino and the Platonism of the English Renaissance." *CL*, 4 (1952), 214–38.
Re-examines the influence that Ficino had upon the Platonism of the Renaissance. Probably Boethius' and Augustine's Platonism

influenced English thought before Ficino's birth. Even though few English writers read Ficino, the writings of Colet, Spenser, Ralegh, Chapman, and Burton show evidence of direct influence. They may have had the French poets and the Italian popularizers as their sources. The period of Platonic poetry was derived from Ficino's treatment of Plato as a philosopher of love and beauty. He added personal love to the Medieval ladder stretching from God to man. The Renaissance poets celebrated three types of love: courtly, Christian, and Neo-Platonic. French poets were a source for combining Petrarchism and Neo-Platonism, but Spenser, Sidney, Greville, and Chapman appear to have gone beyond their French sources. While Platonic love appears in the plays of Fletcher and Chapman, Ficino's greatest influence was upon the theory of love and beauty used by the English poets.

◄§ 58. JORGENSEN, PAUL A. "Elizabethan Literature Today: A Review of Recent Scholarship." *TSLL*, 1 (1960), 562–78.
Reviews modern editions of Elizabethan writers and modern studies of textual editing. Suggests the need for an edition of Sidney's works.

◄§ 59. KERMAN, JOSEPH. *The Elizabethan Madrigal: A Comparative Study*. New York: American Musicological Society, 1962. xxii, 318 pp.
Compares English to Italian madrigals. Part I gives background; Part II, the Elizabethan madrigal. Has a chapter on Thomas Morley. Finds few of Sidney's poems in madrigal books. Some few, however, were sources for John Ward's *Madrigals*, 1613 (p. 19).
Rev.: Frank Howes, *BJA*, 4 (1964), 84–85.

◄§ 60. KERMODE, J. F. *English Pastoral Poetry from the Beginnings to Marvell*. New York: Barnes and Noble, 1952. 256 pp.
Contains an Introduction and examples of pastoral verse. Includes Sidney's "Dorus his Comparisons," "Sestina," "The Shepheard to his Chosen Nimph," "Astrophell to his Stella," and "Espilus and Therion." Describes the pastoral and its function in Elizabethan poetry.

◄§ 61. KOLLER, KATHRINE. "Abraham Fraunce and Edmund Spenser." *ELH*, 7 (1940), 108–20.
Indicates the influence of the Areopagus upon Fraunce. Fraunce, a friend of the Sidney family, was interested in Ramus. Fraunce

followed the Ramist doctrine that poets be used as models for reasoning. He took Sidney and Spenser as his models for *Lawiers Logike* and *The Arcadian Rhetorike*.

᳥§ 62. LANGDALE, ABRAM BARNETT. *Phineas Fletcher: Man of Letters, Science, and Divinity.* New York: Columbia University Press, 1937. vi, 230 pp.
Sidney may have influenced the structure, characters, and incidents in Fletcher's *Sicelides* (pp. 122–24). See also Index.

᳥§ 63. LEGOUIS, EMILE. *A Short History of English Literature,* trans. by V. F. Boyson and J. Coulson. Oxford: Clarendon Press, 1934. 404 pp.
Sidney's major innovation was to import Italian descriptive writing. *Arcadia* may best be described as a romance that deals with chivalry and love (pp. 85–88).

᳥§ 64. MACCAFFERY, W. T. "Places and Patronage in Elizabethan Politics." In *Elizabethan Government and Society, Essays Presented to Sir John Neale,* S. T. Bindoff, J. Hurstfield, and C. H. Williams, eds., pp. 95–126. London: Athlone Press, 1961.
Elizabeth's government rested partially upon gifts of office, prestige and wealth. The Sidney interest in Queen's Park of Otford is an example of local appointments (pp. 123–24).

᳥§ 65. MARENCO, FRANCO. "Sir Philip Sidney: Studi, 1965–66." *FeL,* 13 (1967), 216–24.
Describes Sidney criticism in 1965 and 1966.

᳥§ 66. MAXWELL, MARJORIE E. "The Renowned Sir Philip Sidney: An Anniversary Tribute." *Time and Tide,* 35 (1954), 1680–81.
Reviews Sidney's life and work.

᳥§ 67. MILES, JOSEPHINE. *Renaissance, Eighteenth-Century, and Modern Language in English Poetry: A Tabular View.* Berkeley: University of California Press, 1960. iii, 73 pp.
Tabulates word usage of 200 poets from Chaucer to modern times. Table I lists the numbers of nouns, verbs, and adjectives found in a selection from each poet. In 4,410 lines from Sidney are 1,030 adjectives, 2,909 nouns, and 1,290 verbs. In Table II, a list of repeated words, under Sidney are the words, "good" "eye"

"heart," and "love." Table III indicates the proportion of nouns to adjectives in different periods. Table IV deals with the poetic line. Table V deals with word use.

Rev.: Arthur M. Axelrad, *SCN*, 19 (1961–1962), 6–7.

⌘§ 68. MILL, ADAIR. "*Tottel's Miscellany* and *England's Helicon.*" *Ingiliz Filolojisi Dergisi* (Studies by Members of the English Department, University of Istanbul), 3 (1952), 42–60.

Contrasts the poetry of *Tottel's Miscellany* with that of *England's Helicon* to show the difference between early poets, such as Wyatt and Surrey, and late poets, such as Sidney and Spenser. The latter group used greater variety in line length because of their interest in music. The latter group was interested in the sound of their poems.

⌘§ 69. MILLER, AUDREY BERRYMAN. "Themes and Techniques in Mid-Tudor Lyric Poetry: An Analytical Study of the Short Poem from Wyatt to Sidney." Ph.D. diss., Northwestern University, 1949. Northwestern University, Graduate School, *Summaries of Doctoral Dissertations Submitted to the Graduate School of Northwestern University in Partial Fulfillment of the Requirements for the Degree of Doctor of Philosophy*, 17 (June–September, 1949), 35–41.

Investigates themes, techniques, and trends as represented in 1,100 short poems. Finds that during the mid-Tudor period about half the poems written have the theme of love. Toward the end of this period other themes became more popular. Investigates the meaning of the terms "Petrarchan" and "classical."

⌘§ 70. MILLER, EDWIN HAVILAND. *The Professional Writer in Elizabethan England: A Study of Non-Dramatic Literature.* Cambridge, Mass.: Harvard University Press, 1959. 282 pp.

Analyzes Elizabethan writers in terms of their society and profession, their audience and patrons. Lists Sidney among the patrons of Richard Robinson's book *Eupolemia. Amadis de Gaule* was a source for *Arcadia* (p. 82). See also Index.

Rev.: Robert L. Tener, *SNL*, 12 (1962), 10; G. R. Hibbard, *MLR*, 56 (1961), 246–47; Jean Robertson, *RES*, n.s., 12 (1961), 73–75; Harold Jenkins, *MLN*, 76 (1961), 53–55.

◄§ 71. MORRIS, HELEN. *Elizabethan Literature.* Home University Library of Modern Knowledge 233. London: Oxford University Press, 1958. 239 pp.

Includes chapters on Elizabethan thought, language, poetry, prose, and drama. Contains a description of the plot and theme of *Arcadia* (pp. 60–64) and of *Astrophel and Stella* (pp. 64–66), as well as an outline of the *Defence* (pp. 30–33).

Rev.: *Listener,* 60 (1958), 891.

◄§ 72. MUIR, KENNETH. "Sir Philip Sidney and the Sonneteers." In *Introduction to Elizabethan Literature,* pp. 34–63. New York: Random House, 1967.

Although Sidney's taste was broad, the men who tried to follow his precepts in the *Defence* wrote Senecan dramas and ignored the great contemporary plays (pp. 37–38). *Arcadia* contains good descriptive passages and good argumentative speeches (p. 41). It is both didactic and amusing (p. 40). *Astrophel and Stella* gives the impression of sincerity (p. 47).

◄§ 73. MUNDAY, ANTHONY. *Zelauto: The Fountaine of Fame,* Jack Stillinger, ed. Carbondale: Southern Illinois University Press, 1963. xxix, 204 pp.

Contains text of *Zelauto,* textual notes, and an Introduction. Both Sidney and Munday used the chivalric romance for themes and incidents (p. xvi).

◄§ 74. NICOLSON, MARJORIE. "The Discovery of Space." In *Medieval and Renaissance Studies,* O. B. Hardison, ed., pp. 40–59. Proceedings of the Southeastern Institute of Medieval and Renaissance Studies, Summer, 1965. Chapel Hill: University of North Carolina Press, 1966.

The 17th-century concept of space separates the modern world from that preceding it. The discoveries of Copernicus and Galileo added a new concept to literary imagination. Giordano Bruno used this concept of an infinite universe in his philosophy. While Sidney may have attended the dinner Bruno describes in the *Ash Wednesday Supper,* Bruno did not influence him greatly. Henry More and Milton were among the first English writers to use the concept of infinite space.

◦§ 75. O'Brien, Gordon Worth. *Renaissance Poetics and the Problem of Power*. Chicago: Institute of Elizabethan Studies, 1956. xxvi, 147 pp.

Studies the relation between Christian humanism and Renaissance literature. Both Sidney in the *Defence* and Chapman in *To the Trulie Learned and My Worthy Frende Ma Mathew Royden* based their views of poetry upon Christian humanism. Both assumed man to be potentially equal to the diety (pp. xiv–xxvi). Chapter II deals with Sidney's translation of Mornay's *Christian Religion*.

Rev.: Jackson I. Cope, MLN, 72 (1957), 364–69.

◦§ 76. O'Connor, John J. *Amadis de Gaule and Its Influence on Elizabethan Literature*. New Brunswick, N.J.: Rutgers University Press, 1970. 308 pp.

Amadis is a story of war and of love and is also a courtesy book. It was translated by Anthony Munday and Nicholas de Herberay. Sidney used it freely in *Astrophel and Stella* and in *Arcadia*. Arlanges' chanson probably is the source for the eighth song from *Astrophel and Stella* (p. 151). Books XI and VIII were both important sources for *Arcadia* (pp. 183–201). Sidney may have taken the comic tone from *Amadis*.

◦§ 77. Oruch, Jack Bernard. "Topography in the Prose and Poetry of the English Renaissance, 1540–1640." Ph.D. diss., Indiana University, 1964. DA, 25 (1964), 2966.

A number of "antiquarian scholars," such as Sidney, described real places in their literature. The dissertation traces the development of this topographical prose and compares the methods used.

◦§ 78. Osgood, Charles Grosvenor. *Poetry as a Means of Grace*. Princeton, N.J.: Princeton University Press, 1941. 131 pp.

Divided into essays on Dante, Spenser, Milton, and Johnson. Indicates that *Arcadia* is old fashioned and is read primarily in the classroom (p. 11). See also Index.

◦§ 79. Phillips, James E. "Daniel Rogers: A Neo-Latin Link Between the Pléiade and Sidney's 'Areopagus.'" In *Neo-Latin Poetry of the Sixteenth and Seventeenth Centuries*, pp. 5–28. Los Angeles: William Andrews Clark Memorial Library, 1965.

The Areopagus was probably a group of writers interested in new literary and philosophical ideas, not a formal academy. Sidney,

Spenser, Harvey, and Dyer were interested in the intellectual developments in France. Rogers associated with members of the Pléiade in the 1560's, then met Sidney when he returned to London in 1570. Rogers may have introduced a new concern for Neo-Platonism and Christian unity to the Sidney group. Both the Pléiade and the Areopagus probably were drawn together for a worthier motive than that of versification.

◄§ 80. POGGIOLI, RENATO. "The Oaten Flute." *HLB*, 11 (1957), 147–84.

The pastoral is in the lyric mode. Its theme is that peace and morality are best found away from civilization, but its ethical code is negative, proscribing greed and presuming that nature will supply necessities. The pastoral tends to reconcile innocence and happiness. Sidney suggested that the pastoral may deal with the failure of justice for the lowly. The function of the pastoral is to compensate for the renunciation imposed by the social order. A humanistic outlook, material progress, scientific spirit, and artistic realism have distroyed the pastoral as an art form.

◄§ 81. PRAZ, MARIO. *The Flaming Heart: Essays on Crashaw, Machiavelli, and Other Studies in the Relations Between Italian and English Literature from Chaucer to T. S. Eliot.* Anchor Books. Garden City, N.Y.: Doubleday and Co., 1958. x, 390 pp.

Traces the relationship between English and Italian literature from Chaucer to T. S. Eliot. Examines the relation of Petrarch to Sidney (pp. 272–76). Sidney's poetry illustrates the late arrival of the sonnet in England. It is anti-Petrarchan as was Du Bellay's ode, *Contre les Petrarquistes.* But Sidney's anti-Petrarchist strain is mixed with Petrarchisms. Sidney is not an imitator alone; his poetry has psychological subtlety and genuine passion.

Rev.: Chandler B. Beall, *CL*, 10 (1958), 358–60.

◄§ 82. ———. *Storia della Letteratura Inglese.* Florence: G. C. Samsoni, 1951. 435 pp.

Describes Sidney's life and works. *Arcadia* was begun because Sidney was in disgrace at court. *Astrophel and Stella* was influenced by the anti-Petrarchism of Du Bellay (pp. 56–58).

☙§ 83. PROUTY, C. T. *George Gascoigne: Elizabethan Courtier, Soldier, and Poet.* New York: Columbia University Press, 1942. xii, 351 pp.

The biography of a man whom later Elizabethans read. Sidney's and Spenser's work is dependent upon the imitations and translations of such men as Gascoigne.

☙§ 84. PURCELL, J. M. [Review Article.] *PQ*, 11 (1932), 218–20.

Reviews Denkinger's *Immortal Sidney*, Wilson's *Sir Philip Sidney*, Wilson's edition of *Astrophel and Stella*, and Zandvoort's *Sidney's Arcadia.* Finds both biographies follow tradition and are unsatisfactory. Zandvoort's study is valuable, showing as it does that the New *Arcadia* is an advance over the Old.

☙§ 85. REBORA, PIETRO. "Aspetti dell'Umanismo in Inghilterra." *La Rinascita*, 2 (1939), 366–414.

Gives a historical account of humanism in England. Considers Sidney and Spenser to have spoken with the voice of the Italian Renaissance (pp. 405ff.).

☙§ 86. REESE, MAX MEREDITH. *Shakespeare: His World and His Work.* London: Edward Arnold and Company, 1953. 589 pp.

Contains a review of the sonnet tradition and Petrarchan conventions (pp. 412–15). The *Defence* helped playwrights correct vulgarity and carelessness of style (pp. 65–68).

☙§ 87. REEVES, JAMES. *A Short History of English Poetry: Thirteen Forty-Nineteen Forty.* London: Heinemann, 1961. 228 pp.

Sidney's best poetry is in *Astrophel and Stella.* He achieves in it real feeling with free movement of verse. His rhythm and diction enforce the idea. Sidney, as other Renaissance poets, is noticeable for his use of wit (pp. 48–51).

☙§ 88. RIBNER, IRVING. *The English History Play in the Age of Shakespeare.* Princeton, N.J.: Princeton University Press, 1957. xii, 354 pp.

One of the motifs in *Arcadia* is the effect of a weak king upon a nation (p. 245). Considers briefly Shakespeare's use of *Arcadia* in *King Lear* (pp. 250–51).

89. Rowse, A. L. *The England of Elizabeth: The Structure of Society.* New York: Macmillan Company, 1951. xv, 546 pp.
Examines the structure of Elizabethan society. Sidney, Drake, Walsingham, Greville, Sir William Mohun, and Sir William Courtenay were on the committee to confirm Ralegh's letter patent for colonization of America (p. 307). See also Index.

90. ———. *The Elizabethans and America.* New York: Harper and Brothers, 1959. 222 pp.
Lists Sidney as a member of the Virginia Council (p. 70). Suggests that the shipwreck in *Arcadia* may have been influenced by Sidney's interest in the voyages to the New World (pp. 189–90).

91. ———. *The Expansion of Elizabethan England.* New York: St. Martin's Press, 1955. xiii, 450 pp.
Studies English expansion and the resulting problems with Spain and the Netherlands. Sidney contributed money to Frobisher's first voyage in search of a passage to China (pp. 192–93).

92. ——— *Sir Walter Ralegh, His Family and Private Life.* New York: Harper and Brothers, 1962. 348 pp.
Sets Ralegh in the perspective of his family. Describes the relationship between Lord and Lady Rich (pp. 124–25). See also Index.

93. ———. *Christopher Marlowe: His Life and Work.* New York: Harper and Row, 1964. viii, 220 pp.
Uses Sidney as an example of the value set upon individual achievement (p. 67). Suggests that Watson's sonnet cycle has been underestimated compared with Sidney's (p. 113).

94. Rubel, Veré L. *Poetic Diction in the English Renaissance from Skelton through Spenser.* New York: Modern Language Association, 1941. xiii, 312 pp.
Analyzes the language and rhetoric of English poetry from Skelton through Spenser. Finds an unbroken continuity in the development of diction and an increasing use of rhetoric. Compares Sidney's critical theories with Puttenham's and Webbe's (p. 104). Identifies the many rhetorical figures used in Sidney's classical verse (pp. 123–26). Sidney used archaisms in *Arcadia*

(pp. 152–58). The sonnets contain more compounds than the prose (pp. 203–12).

◄§ 95. RUTHVEN, K. K. *The Conceit*. London: Methuen and Company, Ltd., 1969. 70 pp.

Although Elizabethans used the word "conceit" as a synonym for thought, occasionally they used the word in the modern sense of device or invention. The metaphor might be either perceptual or ornamental. Of the various types of conceits, Sidney used such sonneteering conceits as the jealousy of the lover (p. 21). He also used heraldic conceits (p. 31).

◄§ 96. SAMPSON, GEORGE. *The Concise Cambridge History of English Literature*. Cambridge: University Press, 1941. 1094 pp.

Sidney's is the first real sonnet sequence (p. 515). The *Defence* is not good criticism, for when Sidney wrote there was no large body of English poetry (p. 155). The idea for *Arcadia* comes from Sannazaro's *Arcadia* and Montemayor's *Diana* (p. 162).

◄§ 97. SATTERTHWAITE, ALFRED W. *Spenser, Ronsard and Du Bellay: A Renaissance Comparison*. Princeton, N.J.: Princeton University Press, 1960. 282 pp.

Examines Spenser's relation to Ronsard and Du Bellay against the background of the Renaissance. Mentions Sidney in relation to the Areopagus and quantitative verse (pp. 52–53). Mentions that Spenser's "The Ruines of Time" concludes with an allegory of Sidney's life (pp. 93–94). Sidney may have misrepresented Plato's *Ion* in his *Defence* (p. 186n). See also Index.

◄§ 98. SCHRICKX, W. *Shakespeare's Early Contemporaries: The Background of the Harvey-Nashe Polemic and* Love's Labour's Lost. Antwerp: De Nederlandshe Boekhandel, 1956. 291 pp.

Reviews Nashe's role in the publication of *Astrophel and Stella* and of *Arcadia*. Nashe wrote the preface to the 1591 edition of the sonnets. He attacked Sandford's edition of *Arcadia* in *Lenten Stuffe* (pp. 157–60). See also Index.

Rev.: S. K. Heninger, Jr., *MLR*, 72 (1957), 437–39.

꽃§ 99. SELLS, A. LYTTON. *The Italian Influence in English Poetry from Chaucer to Southwell*. Bloomington: Indiana University Press, 1955. 346 pp.
Contains a chapter on Sidney (pp. 129–49). The pastoral romance came from Italy to England. Sidney's *Arcadia* shows Italian influence. The metaphors are similar to Tasso's. The prose of the *Defence* is superior to that of *Arcadia*. Stella is idealized, not real.
Rev.: H. H. Blanchard, *MLN*, 71 (1956), 515–18.

꽃§ 100. SMITH, LACEY BALDWIN. *The Elizabethan Epic*. London: Jonathan Cape, 1966. 286 pp.
Studies the forces that made Elizabethan England great. Takes Sidney's death as an example of the exaggerated actions of the time (p. 211). See also Index.

꽃§ 101. SQUIRE, SIR JOHN. "Sidney's Influence on Elizabethan Literature." *The Illustrated London News*, November 13, 1954, p. 338.
Reviews Buxton's *Sir Philip Sidney and the English Renaissance*. Includes pictures of Sidney, Languet, Mary Sidney, and John Buxton.

꽃§ 102. STERNBERG, JOACHIM. *Untersuchungen zur Verwendung des antiken Mythus in der Dichtung Sir Philip Sidneys als ein Beitrag zur Interpretation*. Bonn, 1969. 382 pp.
Listed in *The National Union Catalog: A Cumulative Author List Representing Library of Congress Printed Cards and Titles Reported by Other American Libraries* (1971).

꽃§ 103. TANNENBAUM, SAMUEL A. *Sir Philip Sidney (A Concise Bibliography)*. Elizabethan Bibliographies 23. New York: Privately printed, 1941. 69 pp.
Covers period from first editions of works through 1940. Includes a selected list of editions and criticism.

꽃§ 104. THOMSON, J. A. K. *The Classical Background of English Literature*. London: Allen and Unwin, 1948. 272 pp.
Surveys classical literature and its influence on English writers. Finds little classical about *Arcadia* except the characters' names (p. 182). Sidney's quantitative verse is bad poetry (pp. 181–83).

105. THOMSON, PATRICIA. *Elizabethan Lyrical Poets*. London: Routledge and Kegan Paul, 1967. 219 pp.

Includes poems from eight poets and an Introduction. Writes that Spenser and Sidney were the first important Elizabethan lyricists. Both men were interested in variety of metrical forms. One of Sidney's innovations in *Astrophel and Stella* was a picture of Cupid as a "roaring boy."

106: ———. "The Literature of Patronage, 1580–1630." *EIC*, 2 (1952), 267–84.

Studies the changes in patronage and the effects on such poets as Spenser. Mentions Gosson, Sidney, and *The School of Abuse*.

107. TILLOTSON, GEOFFREY. *Essays in Criticism and Research*. Cambridge: University Press, 1942. 215 pp.

Believes that the Elizabethans enjoyed functional and decorative art equally. Sidney's "Virtue, beauty, and speech did strike, wound, charm" exemplifies formal decoration. See also Index.

108. TILLYARD, E. M. W. *The English Renaissance: Fact or Fiction?* Baltimore: Johns Hopkins Press, 1952. 118 pp.

Takes Sidney as the central Elizabethan writer. Discusses *Astrophel and Stella* as a combination of Medieval and new (pp. 65–68). The *Defence* is Medieval in argument but original in manner (pp. 86–90). *Arcadia* and *The Faerie Queene* differ from *Piers Plowman* in their shift from the divine to the mundane (pp. 106–14).

Rev.: M. Poirier, *EA*, 5 (1952), 355.

109. TUCKER, MARTIN. *Mouton's Library of Literary Criticism of English and American Authors Through the Beginning of the 20th Century*. Vol. I. New York: Frederick Ungar Company, 1966. 768 pp.

Includes comments regarding Sidney and his works by Spenser, Walsingham, Nashe, Harvey, Walpole, and Lowell (pp. 111–18).

110. TUVE, ROSEMOND. "A Critical Survey of Scholarship in the Field of English Literature of the Renaissance." *SP*, 40 (1943), 204–55.

Mentions Myrick's *Sir Philip Sidney as a Literary Craftsman*, and Gilbert's *Literary Criticism: Plato to Dryden* (p. 233). Suggests that Sidney scholarship should also consider genres (pp. 235n, 227n).

111. UNTERMEYER, LOUIS. *Lives of the Poets: The Story of One Thousand Years of English and American Poetry.* New York: Simon and Schuster, 1959. 757 pp.
Gives a brief summary of *Astrophel and Stella* and *Apologie for Poetrie* (pp. 67–70).

112. VAN TIEGHEM, PAUL. *Histoire Litteraire de L'Europe et de Renaissance a nos Jours.* Paris: Librairie Armand Colin, 1946. 426 pp.
Sannazaro's *Arcadia* set the pattern for future pastoral romances like Sidney's *Arcadia* (p. 31). See also Index.

113. WARD, A. C. *Chaucer to Shakespeare.* Vol. I of *Illustrated History of English Literature.* London: Longmans, Green, 1953. xv, 244 pp.
Sidney's *Astrophel and Stella* is "gentleman's poetry" and lacks force (pp. 136–37). *Arcadia* is interesting because of Sidney's character (p. 158).

114. WASHINGTON, MARY ALDRIDGE. "A Bibliography of Criticism of Sir Philip Sidney, 1940–1965." Ph.D. diss., University of Missouri, 1969. *DA*, 30 (1970), 5007A.
Incorporated in this bibliography.

115. WASSERMAN, EARL R. *Elizabethan Poetry in the Eighteenth Century.* ISLL, 32. Urbana: University of Illinois Press, 1947. 291 pp.
Even though the Augustans tended to look upon the Elizabethan period as one of ignorance, Elizabethan literature still exerted influence. Quotes from Sheridan's letter to Grenville, recommending *Arcadia* (p. 35). Studies the influence of the Elizabethans on William Thompson (p. 105). Percy's *Reliques* created a taste for Elizabethan lyrics (p. 165). An appendix, "The Popularity of Elizabethan Prose Fiction in the Eighteenth Century" (pp. 253–59), examines the changes Mrs. Stanley made in her edition of *Arcadia.* She omitted the poems and changed grammar and style in nearly every sentence.

116. WINTERS, YVOR. *Forms of Discovery.* Chicago: Alan Swallow, 1967. 377 pp.
Poetry is the best medium for understanding human experience. In Chapter I, "Aspects of the Short Poem in the English Renaissance," writes that the Petrarchan school produced no important

poems before Sidney and Spenser. All the early good poems came from the school of Wyatt and Surrey. The defect in the plain school is a "certain harshness and monotony" (p. 27). Sidney's "Highway, since you my chief Parnassus be" illustrates the Petrarchan quality (pp. 30–31). The technique of the poem is good, but the content is trivial. "Leave me, O love . . ." is a second-rate poem although the rhythm is beautiful (p. 34).

Rev.: Arvid Løsnes, *ES*, 50 (1969), 314–17.

⋘ 117. YATES, FRANCES A. *The Art of Memory*. Chicago: University of Chicago Press, 1966. 400 pp.

Traces the art of memory from the classical period through the 16th century. Suggests that Sidney may have learned the theory of *ut pictura poesis* from Dee (pp. 263–64). Dicson, a "master of the art of memory," attended Sidney (p. 272). Bruno, as well as Ramus, influenced Sidney (pp. 282–84).

Rev.: *TLS*, November 10, 1966, p. 1025.

⋘ 118. ———. *Giordano Bruno and the Hermetic Tradition*. Chicago: University of Chicago Press, 1964. xiv, 466 pp.

Places Bruno in the Hermetic tradition. Sidney learned Hermeticism from Mornay's *A Woorke concerning the trewnesse of the Christian Religion* (pp. 178–79). Sidney also knew Dee's version of Hermeticism (pp. 187–88). See also Index.

⋘ 119. Z. "Sir Philip Sidney: 1554 – November 30 – 1954." *ES*, 35 (1954), 262–63.

Reviews the 20th-century interest in Sidney. Quotes C. S. Lewis to show that after 400 years Sidney is still an important figure in English literature.

II

Life

❧ 120. BAUGHAN, DENVER EWING. "A Compliment to Sidney in *Hamlet*." *N&Q*, 177 (1939), 133-36.
Believes that "Lamound" or "Lamond" in *Hamlet* (IV,iii,91) is a reference to Sidney and a tribute to his horsemanship. It may have been "Le Mort" originally.

❧ 121. BENHAM, W. GURNEY. [Letter answering 180.] *N&Q*, 180 (1941), 444-45.
Replies to Newdigate's "Mourners at Sir Philip Sidney's Funeral." Identifies Edward Jobsone as one of the mourners.

❧ 122. BENNETT, A. L. "The Principal Rhetorical Conventions in the Renaissance Personal Elegy." *SP*, 51 (1954), 107-26.
[See 123.] Studies standard devices of *topoi* used in the Renaissance elegy. Some elegies written about Sidney are used as examples.

❧ 123. ———. "The Renaissance Personal Elegy and the Rhetorical Tradition." Ph.D. diss., University of Texas, 1952. *DDAAU*, 1951-1952, No. 19.
This study of the elegy discusses some of those written for Sidney. In *Astrophel* Spenser noted the chief periods of Sidney's life: his birth, childhood, youth, service to his prince, and his death (p. 207). Explicates Ralegh's epitaph to Sidney and identifies rhetorical figures.

❧ 124. BEVAN, BRYAN. "Sir Philip Sidney." *Contemporary Review*, 186 (1954), 346-49.
Sketches Sidney's adult life in order to make him appear more human.

❧ 125. BOAS, FREDERICK S. *Sir Philip Sidney, Representative Elizabethan: His Life and Writings*. London: Staples Press, 1956. 204 pp.
In the first and last chapters, deals with Sidney's life. Other chapters are critical studies of his works in the light of his life and Elizabethan custom. Gives the background for the *Defence* and suggests that Sidney's standards for drama are "perverted."

Philisides and Mira episode in *Arcadia* could refer to one of Sidney's early love affairs. *Astrophel and Stella* combines biography and fantasy. The first thirty sonnets were probably written after Penelope's marriage.

Rev.: M. Poirier, *EA*, 9 (1956), 149–50; *TLS*, December 9, 1955, p. 744.

126. BOND, WILLIAM H. "The Epitaph of Sir Philip Sidney." *MLN*, 58 (1943), 253–57.
The epitaph above Sidney's grave is an adaptation of one by Du Bellay.

127. ———. "A Letter of Languet about Sidney." *HLB*, 9 (1955), 105–9.
Prints and translates a letter of March 12, 1575, from Hubert Languet to Dr. Glauburg regarding Sidney. Contains a brief account of Languet, of his relationship to Sidney, and of the circumstances of the letter.

128. ———. "The Reputation and Influence of Sir Philip Sidney." Ph.D. diss., Harvard University, 1941. Harvard University, Graduate School of Arts and Sciences, *Summaries of Theses Accepted in Partial Fulfilment of the Requirements for the Degree of Doctor of Philosophy* (1941), 329–32.
The abstract summarizes the first section of the dissertation: a history of Sidney's life and reputation, and a sampling of allusions to Sidney from 1586 through 1700. Sidney exemplified the Elizabethan ideal and was often cited to show that literary activity was not degrading. But Sidney was imitated so frequently that the whole romance genre became debased, and Milton could attack *Eikon Basilike* because it contained a prayer from *Arcadia*. By the end of the 17th century Sidney's reputation had diminished. When his works were republished early in the 19th century, however, both Lamb and Southey admired them. Since the middle of the 19th century, his reputation has not changed.

129. ———. "Two Ghosts: Herbert's *Baripenthes* and the Vaughan-Holland Portrait of Sidney." *The Library*, 24 (1944), 175–81.
Of the many tributes to Sidney following his death, two have been lost. Sir William Herbert's poem *Baripenthes* was registered at the Stationer's company on January 16, 1587. A copy existed in

1834. Joseph Hunter's *Chorus vatum anglicanorum* contains an account of the poem and an excerpt. The lost portrait was registered on March 30, 1622, by Henry Holland. A copy of *Arcadia* in the Huntington Library contains a picture of Sidney that may be the Vaughan portrait.

◄§ 130. BUCHAN, A. M. "The Political Allegory of Book IV of *The Faerie Queene*." *ELH*, 11 (1944), 237–48.
Explains the episode of the rivers in canto xi in relation to the general theme of concord. Penshurst was situated on the Medway. The marriage of the Thames and Medway symbolizes political harmony.

◄§ 131. BUXTON, JOHN. "The Sidney Exhibition."
BLR, 5 (1956), 125–29.
Lists the objects displayed: manuscripts of Sidney's works, other works connected with Sidney, and contemporary objects, such as gloves and watches.

◄§ 132. ———. *Sir Philip Sidney and the English Renaissance*.
London: Macmillan Company, 1954. 284 pp.
Focuses upon Sidney's literary influence, rather than his life or work. Attributes the growth of English poetry in the 1580's and 1590's to such patrons as the Sidneys. Gives an account of Bruno's relationship with Sidney. Concludes with an account of other patrons: the countess of Pembroke, the countess of Bedford, and William, 3d earl of Pembroke. Does not stress a biographical interpretation of the sonnets. Believes that the interest in quantitative verse was caused by the desire to set verses to music. Considers the 1593 edition of the *Arcadia* superior to the 1590.
Rev.: R. W. Zandvoort, *ES*, 36 (1955), 37–38; Marcus S. Goldman, *JEGP*, 56 (1957), 131; George A. Bonnard, *Erasmus*, 9 (1956), 591–94.

◄§ 133. ———, AND BENT JUEL-JENSEN. "Bibliographical Notes."
The Library, 25 (1970), 45–46.
Reprints the passport Sidney used on his Continental tour. The passport indicates that Sidney must have obtained an extension of his alloted time on the Continent. He did not return to England until May 31, 1575. The passport was given to New College, Oxford, by John Lavicount Anderdon in 1851.

✒§ 134. CAMPBELL, LILY B. "Sidney as 'The Learned Soldier.'"
    HLQ, 7 (1944), 175–78.
Reprints the opening paragraphs of Dudley Digges' apology for
the military written in 1604. Digges calls Sidney "a man of armes
by nature" and wishes that he had left the defense of poetry "to
some more private spirit."

✒§ 135. CARRÉ, MEYRICK H. "Visitors to Mortlake: The Life and
    Misfortunes of John Dee." *History Today*,
    12 (1962), 640–47.
Lists Sidney as a visitor to Dr. Dee. Includes a portrait of
Sidney.

✒§ 136. CARSANIGA, GIOVANNI M. "The Truth in John Ford's
    The Broken Heart." *CL*, 10 (1958), 344–48.
Believes with Stuart P. Sherman [*PMLA*, 24 (1909)] that *The
Broken Heart* is about Sidney and Stella. Sherman suggested
Arcadia as a source for the setting and for King Amyclas. Carsaniga
suggests that the oracle and moralizing names also come from
Arcadia. Another source may be an account of a murder com-
mitted by Simone Turchi in 1551. Orgylus' character is not based
on Astrophel.

✒§ 137. CHECKSFIELD, M. M. "Sir Philip Sidney." In *Portraits of
    Renaissance Life and Thought*, pp. 192–214. London:
    Longmans, 1964.
Sidney embodied Castiglione's ideal gentleman in an English
form. He was noble, cultured, and skilled in sports. He, as
Castiglione, was politically active.
Rev.: *TLS*, November 19, 1964, p. 1032.

✒§ 138. COHEN, EILEEN ZELDA. "Gentle Knight and Pious Serv-
    ant: A Study of Sidney's Protestantism." Ph.D. diss., Uni-
    versity of Maryland, 1965. *DA*, 26 (1966), 7312.
Sidney was an Anglican, not a Puritan. Reviews scholarship on
his religion. Sidney found allies for his foreign policy among the
Puritans, but his writings indicate him to be a religious moderate.

✒§ 139. COPE, JACKSON I. "Jonson's Readng of Spenser: The
    Genesis of a Poem." *EM*, 10 (1959), 61–66.
Spenser's "The Ruins of Time," an elegy for Sidney and
Leicester. may be the source for Jonson's verses for the countess
of Rutland.

◄§ 140. CROWDER, RICHARD. " 'Phoenix Spenser' a Note on Anne Bradstreet." *NEQ*, 17 (1944), 310.

Concerns Anne Bradstreet's error in assuming that three elegies for Sidney, first published in *The Phoenix Nest*, later with *Astrophel*, were written by Spenser.

◄§ 141. CUMMINGS, L. "Spenser's *Amoretti*, VIII: New Manuscript Versions." *SEL*, 4 (1964), 125–35.

Studies variations of *Amoretti*, VIII, also suggests a closer relationship between Sidney and Spenser than Ringler suggests existed. Shows that Greville, who wrote poems in competition with Sidney and Dyer, also wrote a poem rivaling Spenser's *Amoretti*, VIII.

◄§ 142. DOBBS, M. HOPE. [Letter answering 180.] *N&Q*, 180 (1941), 463–64.

[See 121.] The picture on the frontispiece of Pollard's edition of *Astrophel and Stella* is of Lant, not Sidney. Identifies Sir Thomas Perrot in Sidney's funeral procession as the son of Sir John Perrot.

◄§ 143. DUNCAN-JONES, KATHERINE. "Sidney's Personal Imprese." *JWCI*, 33 (1970), 321–24.

Describes the imprese Sidney probably designed and judges it to be skillfully done.

◄§ 144. ESPLIN, ROSS STOLWORTHY. "The Emerging Legend of Sir Philip Sidney, 1586–1652." Ph.D. diss., University of Utah, 1970.

Traces the growth of the legend of Sir Philip Sidney from the elegies published following his death to Fulke Greville's partially apochryphal biography published in 1652. Finds that the legend contains some truth but much fiction. Many of Sidney's real accomplishments are ignored by the legend.

◄§ 145. EWING, S. BLAINE. "A New Manuscript of Greville's *Life of Sidney*." *MLR*, 49 (1954), 424–27.

Describes a manuscript of Greville's *Life of Sidney* that was discovered in the public library at Shrewsbury. It contains some variant readings and two unique transition passages, one of which indicates that Sidney was instrumental in forming Spanish policy. The structure of this manuscript differs from that of the other two.

✍§ 146. FALLS, CYRIL. "Sir Philip Sidney and His Age." *The Illustrated London News*, July 10, 1954, p. 54.

Written during the Sidney exhibition at Tunbridge Wells, it contains a picture of a helmet carried at Sidney's funeral. Suggests that Victorian hero worship has raised a barrier between the 20th century and Sidney. Sidney's ideals were not those that Victorian critics claimed for him.

✍§ 147. FARMER, NORMAN, JR. "Fulke Greville and Sir John Coke: An Exchange of Letters on a History Lecture and Certain Latin Verses on Sir Philip Sidney." *HLQ*, 33 (1970), 217–36.

Contains the text of letters exchanged by Greville and Coke. Greville asked Coke's advice regarding the appointment of a history lecturer at Cambridge and regarding verses to be placed on Sidney's tomb. Coke's reply quotes parts of the proposed verses. Greville's letter indicates his belief that history can be a guide to virtue. In his biography of Sidney, Greville recommends Sidney's life as such a guide. One of Sidney's letters indicates a similar view of history.

✍§ 148. ———. "Fulke Greville and the Poetic of Plain Style." *TSLL*, 11 (1969), 657–70.

Reconstructs Greville's critical theory of the plain style from his life of Sidney and "A Treatie of Humane Learning." The *Life* was intended to be a preface to an edition of Greville's dramas. Those qualities for which Sidney is praised are those which Greville believed characterized a poet. Greville used a plain style in his dramas.

✍§ 149. FERGUSON, ARTHUR B. *The Indian Summer of English Chivalry*. Durham, N.C.: Duke University Press, 1960. 260 pp.

Believes that Sidney and Spenser turned the tale of chivalry into a humanistic romance (p. 94). While Sidney tried to follow the chivalric ideal, he viewed the life of a soldier as only one of many roles (p. 105).

✍§ 150. FERRUOLO, ARNOLFO. "Sir Philip Sidney e Giordano Bruno." *Convivium* (Bologna), Raccolta nuova (1948), 686–99.

Reviews the relationship between Bruno and Sidney. Bruno dedicated *Spaccio della bestia trionfante* and the *Eroici furori* to Sidney, but nothing certain is known of conversations between the two. Sidney's writings do not refer to Bruno. However, the writings of the two are similar.

᪄§ 151. Freeman, John. *Literature and Locality.* London: Cassell, 1963. 401 pp.

Includes a description of Penshurst, Kenilworth and Wilton.

᪄§ 152. Gál, István. "Sir Philip Sidney's Guidebook to Hungary." *HSE*, 4 (1969), 53–64.

In several letters Sidney mentions facts from Pietro Bizarri's *Pannonicum Bellum*, a book given him by Languet. This book describes the war between Hungary and Turkey in 1566. The letters are addressed to Leicester (November 27, 1574), to Burghley (December 17, 1574, February 8, 1577, and March 22, 1577), and to Walsingham (March 22, 1579, and May 3, 1577).

᪄§ 153. Galimberti, Alice. *Edmondo Spenser, "L'Ariosto Inglese."* Turin: Giuseppe Gambino, 1938. xiv, 237 pp.

Contains an appendix on the friendship between Spenser and Sidney and between patron and artist in general (pp. 183–91). Not much evidence for assuming a close relationship between Spenser and Sidney.

᪄§ 154. Godshalk, William Leigh. "A Sidney Autograph." *BC*, 13 (1964), 65.

Sidney's autograph appears on the title page of a copy of Guicciardini's *La Historia D'Italia.* The date, Junij 20, 1574, places him in Padua at that time.

᪄§ 155. Great Britain, Historical Manuscripts Commission. *Report on the Manuscripts of Lord de L'Isle and Dudley, Preserved at Penshurst Place.* London: Her Majesty's Stationery Office, 1925–1966. 6 vols.

Volume I contains the general accounts of Sir Philip Sidney. Other volumes are concerned with Robert Sidney.

᪄§ 156. Howell, Roger. *Sir Philip Sidney: The Shepherd Knight.* Boston: Little, Brown, 1968. viii, 308 pp.

Considers Sidney as courtier, as writer, and as man of action. Sidney was not an important political or military leader but was important as the symbol of an Elizabethan ideal. Sidney's first diplomatic mission for Elizabeth was his trip as ambassador to the

Emperor Rudolph; however, Sidney's attempts to arouse interest in a Protestant league did not please Elizabeth (p. 41). Suggests that Fox Bourne's account of Sidney's relation to Gray and Scotland is incorrect (p. 106). Criticizes Sidney's major works (pp. 154–204). *Arcadia* is unlikely to please a modern reader (p. 165). *Astrophel and Stella* was written in 1582 (pp. 185–87). It can be approached as a study of the psychological states of Sidney-Astrophel (pp. 193–204). Sidney influenced the development of historical writing by explaining the nature of history and by showing that it can teach men how to behave politically (pp. 219–20).

Rev.: *TLS*, April 25, 1968, p. 416; *Spectator*, March 15, 1968, p. 337.

◄§ 157. Jenkins, Elizabeth. *Elizabeth and Leicester*. London: V. Gollancz, 1961. 384 pp.

In a study of the relationship between Elizabeth and Leicester, includes Sidney's relations with Leicester. Mentions that Helen's coach in *Arcadia* indicates the interest in black and white color patterns that marked the late 1570's and the 1580's (pp. 220–21). Includes the background for *The Lady of May* (p. 226) and the *Defence of Leicester* (pp. 294–96).

◄§ 158. John, Lisle C. "The Date of Marriage of Penelope Devereux." *PMLA*, 49 (1934), 961–62.

Places the marriage later than generally assumed on evidence found in a letter from Richard Brakinbury to the earl of Rutland. The marriage may have been at Allhallowtide, not in March of 1581.

◄§ 159. ———. "Elizabethan Letter Writer." *PQ*, 24 (1945), 106–13.

Richard Brakinbury, an usher at court for forty years, mentions in a letter of September 18, 1581, that Lady Penelope Devereux will marry Lord Rich about the time of Allhallows. Sidney's sonnets, if they were written after her marriage, must have been written late in 1581 or in 1582.

◄§ 160. ———. "The First Edition of the Letters of Hubert Languet to Sir Philip Sidney." *JEGP*, 48 (1949), 361–66.

Contrary to S. A. Pears, the first edition of the letters was printed in 1633 at Frankfort by William Fitzer, not in 1646 at Leyden by Elzevirs. Gives a biographical sketch of Fitzer and a description of the 1633 edition.

161. ———. "Sir Stephen Le Sieur and Sir Philip Sidney."
MLQ, 17 (1956), 340–51.
Stephen Le Sieur, Sidney's secretary, was the Stephen mentioned in Sidney's will and in one of Sidney's letters. He was employed by the Sidneys by January 13, 1579. Sidney mentioned him in a letter to Robert on October 18, 1580. When Le Sieur was imprisoned at Dunkirk, Sidney wrote Walsingham asking for aid. Some of Le Sieur's letters from prison are in *State Papers, Foreign*, 1585, 1586, 1587, 1588. One letter is to Sidney. Le Sieur, according to Fitzer's dedication, preserved Languet's letters to Sidney.

162. JOHNSON, FRANCIS R. *Astronomical Thought in Renaissance England: A Study of the English Scientific Writings from 1500–1645*. Baltimore: Johns Hopkins Press, 1937. 357 pp.
Describes the relationship between Dee and Sidney (p. 139). Mentions Temple's work with Sidney (p. 190). See also Index.

163. JOHNSON, STANLEY D. "The Literary Patronage of Sir Philip Sidney and His Family." Ph.D. diss., Yale University, 1943. DDAAU, 10 (1943), 94.
Surveys the patronage of individual members of the Sidney family. Studies Sidney's friendships with Théophile de Banos, Ramus, Languet, Henri Estienne, and Paul Schede (Melissus), as well as with Spenser and William Temple. Lists books from the *Short Title Catalogue* dedicated to a member of the Sidney family.

164. JUDSON, ALEXANDER C. *Sidney's Appearance: A Study in Elizabethan Portraiture*. Indiana University Publications, Humanities Series 41. Bloomington: Indiana University Press, 1958. xiv, 98 pp., 32 pls.
Contains thirty-two plates and an appendix that estimates the authenticity of each portrait. The text includes a chapter on Sidney's interest in painting. Concludes that the Van de Passe engraving, the Elstracke engraving, the Zuccaro portrait, the Knole House portrait, and the Impresa portrait are authentic. The Windsor Castle miniature, the Laurence Currie miniature, and the West Park drawing probably are not *ad vivum* likenesses.
Rev.: T. J. B. Spencer, MLR, 55 (1960), 140–41.

☙ 165. JUEL-JENSEN, BENT. [Correspondence.]
   PBSA, 63 (1969), 121.
   [See 211.] Replies to Woodward that William Dugard, not
Fuller, is the probable author of the biography of Sidney con-
tained in the 1655 edition of *Arcadia*.

☙ 166. KELLOGG, ELIZABETH ROCKEY. *Sir Philip Sidney: Impres-
sions of a Remarkable Character*. Cincinnati, Ohio: C. J.
Krehbiel Company, 1960. 124 pp.
   A biography written in the style of fiction.

☙ 167. ———. *Study for a Portrait of Sir Philip Sidney*. Cincinnati, Ohio: Privately printed, 1959. 112 pp.
   A biography written in the style of fiction. Begins with Sidney's
boyhood.

☙ 168. KOSZUL, ANDRE. "Argentoratensia Britannica—Les Sidney et Strasbourg—I. Philip Sidney." *Bulletin de la Faculté
des Lettres de Strasbourg*, 17 (1938–1939), 37–44.
   Reconstructs Sidney's Continental tour from his arrival at Paris
through his stay in Strasbourg. Takes up his acquaintance with
Languet and Henri Estienne.

☙ 169. LANHAM, RICHARD A. "Sidney: The Ornament of his
Age." *Southern Review: An Australian Journal of Literary
Studies*, 2 (1967), 319–40.
   Writes that the facts of Sidney's life need to be reinterpreted
in light of the realization that both Languet and Greville were
interested parties. The Sidney myth began at his death, not before. Sidney's life was uneventful; possibly his idealism may have
made the Queen hesitate to use him. Only Greville records the
incident of the drink of water given the soldier.

☙ 170. LANSDALE, NELSON. "Penshurst Place." *SatR* (February
18, 1956), 46.
   Contains a picture and a description of Penshurst Place.

☙ 171. McLANE, PAUL E. *Spenser's* Shepheardes Calender: A
Study in Elizabethan Allegory. Notre Dame, Ind.: Uni-
versity of Notre Dame Press, 1961. 370 pp.
   Deals with political, religious, and personal allegory in *The
Shepheardes Calender*. The political allegory may involve the
Alençon marriage in which Sidney's letter played a part (pp. 24–

26). The tennis-court quarrel with Oxford may be a source of the fable of the Oak and the Briar (pp. 67–71). Richard Davies, not Sidney, is the probable source for Diggon Davie (pp. 220–34). Fulke Greville may be E. K. (p. 281).

Rev.: Joan Grundy, *MLR*, 57 (1962), 409–10; *TLS*, January 5, 1962, p. 10.

◄§ 172. ———. "The Death of a Queen: Spenser's Dido as Elizabeth." *HLQ*, 18 (1954), 1–11.

Dido in the November eclogue of *The Shepheardes Calender* may represent Queen Elizabeth. That she is "dead" means that she is separated from the Leicester-Sidney group because of their opposition to the marriage with Alençon. Does not believe that Dido can be identified as an illegitimate daughter of Leicester, nor as Ambrosia Sidney, nor as Susan Watts.

◄§ 173. MOHL, RUTH. *Studies in Spenser, Milton, and the Theory of Monarchy.* New York: King's Crown Press, 1949. viii, 144 pp.

Sidney may be the Diggon Davie of *The Shepheardes Calender.* Many details concerning the shepherd would fit Sidney's life. If Diggon is Sidney, then the allegorical form allows Sidney's views to be expressed more frankly than Sidney could write them (pp. 23–30).

Rev.: *QQ*, 57 (1950), 580–82.

◄§ 174. MORRIS, HARRY. "Richard Barnfield, 'Amyntas,' and the Sidney Circle." *PMLA*, 74 (1959), 318–24.

The name "Amyntas" is used in Elizabethan literature either as a reference to a contemporary, or as an appropriate name for any shepherd, or as a reference to poetry containing that name. Barnfield wrote the first twelve poems of *Greenes Funeralls,* and the "Amyntas" he mentioned is Watson, a member of the Sidney circle. The "Amyntas" in *The Faerie Queene* (VI,45,7–9) refers to both Watson and Fraunce, the "sweet poets" of l. nine; it is not a reference to Sidney as the *Variorum* editors have suggested.

◄§ 175. ———. *Richard Barnfield, Colin's Child.* Florida State
        University Studies 38. Gainesville: Florida State Univer-
        sity, 1963. 203 pp.
Reviews Barnfield's relations with Sidney and Sidney's influence upon Barnfield's writing (pp. 8–48). Mentions correspondences between Sidney's poetry and Barnfield's.
        Rev.: William Blissett, *ES,* 50 (1969), 88.

◄§ 176. ———. "Thomas Watson and Abraham Fraunce."
        PMLA, 76 (1961), 152–53.
[See 174, 202.] Defends his article concerning Barnfield against
Staton. Admits that the original article is speculative but writes
that Watson himself was concerned at being confused with
Fraunce. Reviews the evidence that indicates Fraunce may have
died prior to 1595.

◄§ 177. MOUNTS, CHARLES E. "Spenser and the Earl of Essex."
        RenP (1958–1960), 12–19.
Essex may not have been Spenser's patron. The model for
Sir Calidore, Book VI, *The Faerie Queene,* may be either Essex
or Sidney. Essex, Penelope Devereux's brother, was the second
husband of Frances Walsingham, who was the probable source
for Pastorella. Spenser's identification of Frances Walsingham as
Stella may have annoyed Essex.

◄§ 178. MUIR, KENNETH. *Sir Philip Sidney.* Writers and Their
        Work 120. London: Longmans, Green and Company,
        1960. 40 pp.
Contains an analysis of Sidney's major works and a bibliography
by G. K. Hunter. One of the main values of the *Defence* is its
style. In structure and ornamentation the New *Arcadia* is superior
to the Old. Describes some rhetorical figures used in it. The sonnets involve the conflict between Stella and Astrophel, and the
conflict in each character's mind.
        Rev.: R. W. Zandvoort, *ES,* 42 (1961), 126–27.

◄§ 179. ———. *Sir Philip Sidney.* British Writers and Their
        Work 8. Lincoln: University of Nebraska Press, 1963.
        Pp. 82–124.
[See 178.] The same essay with the bibliography brought up to
date.

⋙ 180. NEWDIGATE, B. H. "Mourners at Sir Philip Sidney's Funeral." *N&Q*, 180 (1941), 398–401.
[See 121, 142.] Reprints the order of mourners in Sidney's funeral procession; identifies many of them.

⋙ 181. ———. *Michael Drayton and His Circle*. Oxford: Basil Blackwell, 1941. xv, 239 pp.
In the biography of Drayton, includes material on Henry Goodere, who was with Sidney at Zutphen. Drayton mentions Sidney in *The Shepheards Garland* (p. 133).

⋙ 182. NICOLSON, HAROLD. "Marginal Comment." *The Spectator*, 173 (1944), 310.
Retells the story of Sidney's death on the occasion of the 1944 landing at Arnhem.

⋙ 183. OAKESHOTT, WALTER. *The Queen and the Poet*. London: Faber and Faber, 1960. 232 pp.
Assumes that Ralegh's poems were written for special occasions and studies them in relation to his life and the history of the period. Mentions Ralegh's poem about Sidney (p. 133). Suggests Sidney as a source for Ralegh's "Our Passions are most like to Floods and Streams" (pp. 152–53). See also Index.

⋙ 184. ONG, WALTER J. *Ramus, Method, and the Decay of Dialogue*. Cambridge, Mass.: Harvard University Press, 1958. 408 pp.
Studies Ramism in a historical context. Mentions Banosius' dedication of the *Life of Peter Ramus* to Sidney (p. 38). Suggests that Sidney influenced the spread of Ramism in England (p. 302).

⋙ 185. PETER, J. D. "The Identity of Mavortio in Tourneur's 'Transformed Metamorphosis.' " *N&Q*, 193 (1948), 408–12.
The source of Mavortio may be Henry VIII, not Essex, Sir Francis Vere, Marlowe, Spenser, or Sidney. Cannot be Sidney because Elizabeth (Eliza) held a higher rank than Sidney, and it would violate decorum for her to be heir to the virtues of a subordinate. The reference must be to a man of royal rank, probably Henry VIII.

✏ 186. PHILLIPS, JAMES E. "George Buchanan and the Sidney Circle." *HLQ*, 12 (1948–49), 23–55.

Daniel Rogers, Edward Bulkeley, Christopher Goodman, and Thomas Randolph were links between the Sidney circle and Buchanan. Buchanan and Sidney were both against the Queen's proposed marriage to Alençon. Sidney wrote to Buchanan regarding it. Sidney was interested in Buchanan as the tutor of James VI. Several members of the Sidney circle expressed approbation of Buchanan's *De Jure Regni*. The philosophy expressed in it is similar to that in *Arcadia*. Buchanan attacked the opinion that Britain was founded by Brut, and some evidence suggests this to be the attitude of the Sidney circle.

✏ 187. POIRIER, MICHEL. *Sir Philip Sidney: Le Chevalier Poète Élizabéthain*. Travaux et Memoires de L'Universite de Lille 26. Lille: Bibliotheque Universitaire de Lille, 1948. 321 pp.

Interprets Sidney as the last of the *chevaliers* and the first of the Puritans. The works represent an intermediary stage between his early eagerness as a diplomat and his later religious feelings. Sidney's nature was not compatible with his milieu. Philisides and Coredon in Old *Arcadia* may represent Sidney and Edward Dyer; their songs, a love rivalry. Judges Sidney's quantitative verse to be inferior to his sonnets. *Arcadia* is too rich for modern taste, but it is a monument to the taste of the Elizabethans. The Old *Arcadia* is set in an indistinct ancient time, but the New *Arcadia* contains elements of the Middle Ages.

Rev.: H. S. Wilson, *JEGP*, 49 (1950), 111–12; J. J. Lawlor, *RES*, n.s., 2 (1951), 71–72; Geoffrey Bullough, *MLR*, 46 (1951), 478–79.

✏ 188. READ, CONYERS. *Lord Burghley and Queen Elizabeth*. New York: Alfred A. Knopf, 1960. 603 pp.

Examines Burghley's political career. Writes that Sidney was proposed as a match for Burghley's daughter Anne (p. 17). Sidney spent time in Burghley's household (p. 125). Mentions Sidney's role in the proposed marriage with Alençon (p. 127). Mentions Sidney and Leicester in connection with the Netherlands (p. 324).

✏ 189. REES, JOAN. "Fulke Greville's Epitaph on Sidney." *RES*, n.s., 19 (1968), 47–51.

In a letter dated September 4, 1615, Greville asked Coke's opinion on an epitaph for Sidney. Even though the epitaph has the theme that the memory of the living gives immortality to the dead, Greville believed that true immortality lay elsewhere. The epitaph was unfinished, but the theme is contained in *Caelica* 81 and 82.

◄§ 190. RICHMOND, VELMA E. BOURGEOIS. "The Development of the Rhetorical Death Lament from the Late Middle Ages to Marlowe." Ph.D. diss., University of North Carolina, 1959. *DA*, 20 (1960), 2807.
Studies the Medieval tradition of death laments. Includes the narrative laments of Sidney, Spenser, and Greene. Many laments are collected in an appendix.

◄§ 191. ROBERTSON, JEAN. "Sir Philip Sidney and Lady Penelope Rich." *RES*, n.s., 15 (1964), 296–97.
Cites another copy of Cifford's account of Sidney's death. This copy, belonging to Dr. B. F. Juel Jensen, differs from the Vitellius MS in that Sidney is said to mention Lady Rich.

◄§ 192. ———. [Correspondence.] *RES*, n.s., 8 (1957), 42.
[See 127.] The drawing attributed to Mathys van den Bergh in John Buxton's *Sir Philip Sidney and the English Renaissance* had formerly been attributed to Isaac Oliver.

◄§ 193. RÓNA, EVA. "Sir Philip Sidney and Hungary." *Annales Universitatis Scientiarum Budapestiensis de Rolando Eötvös Nominatae. Sectio Philologica*, 2 (1960), 46–50.
Relates the few facts concerning Sidney's journey to Hungary in 1573. While the best sources for Sidney's European travel are the letters to Languet, Sidney did not write from Hungary. He may have spent a month in Hungary, and he may have accompanied Charles de l'Ecluse, a botanist. While in Hungary he developed an interest in the Turco-Hungarian wars and asked Languet to send him books on the subject. He probably met Lazarus Schwendi on this trip.

◄§ 194. ROSCOE, THEODORA. "An Elizabethan Friendship." *Contemporary Review*, 188 (1955), 394–99.
Describes the friendship between Sidney and Languet by reference to their letters and contemporary accounts. Suggests that "Thou blind man's mark . . ." and "Leave me, O love . . ." may have been inspired by love for Languet and sorrow at his death.

↩§ 195. Rosenberg, Eleanor. *Leicester, Patron of Letters*. New York: Columbia University Press, 1955. xx, 395 pp.

Examines patronage to determine the extent to which religion, politics, and the writer's desire for preferment influenced it. Describes *Academiae Cantabrigiensis Lachrymae*, verses commemorating Sidney's death, and suggests G. H. to be Gabriel Harvey. Mentions the two volumes of verse from Oxford, *Exequiae Sidnaei* and *Peplus*, as well as *The Phoenix Nest* (pp. 319–21). Rev.: Jean Robertson, *RES*, n.s., 8 (1957), 285–86.

↩§ 196. Seymour-Smith, Martin. "Sir Philip Sidney." In *Poets Through Their Letters*, pp. 51–63. New York: Holt, Rinehart and Winston, 1969.

Analyzes Sidney's character from his letters to show him serious, unselfish, and impetuous. Suggests that *Astrophel and Stella* was written in 1582. Suggests that poverty, not the Queen's anger, drove Sidney from the court.

↩§ 197. Siegel, Paul N. "Spenser and the Calvinist View of Life." *SP*, 41 (1944), 201–22.

Believes that Spenser's world view was determined by his Calvinism. Quotes de Selincourt that Sidney, a Christian gentleman, was Spenser's ideal. The Red Cross Knight is like Sidney in his seriousness. Contrasts Sidney's religious faith to the earl of Oxford's.

↩§ 198. Simonini, R. C., Jr. *Italian Scholarship in Renaissance England*. University of North Carolina Studies in Comparative Literature 3. Chapel Hill: University of North Carolina Press, 1952. 125 pp.

Sees the study of the Italian language as an influence upon the English Renaissance. Sidney, Spenser, Daniel, and Lyly were taught Italian. See also Index.

↩§ 199. "Sir Philip Sidney's Anniversary." *TLS*, December 10, 1954, p. 812.

Reviews the Sidney exhibition at the Bodleian Library. The exhibition stresses influence as well as achievement. The only copy in England of the first edition of *Arcadia* with Windet's imprint is in the Capell Collection.

◄§ 200. STANFORD, ANN. "Anne Bradstreet's Portrait of Sir Philip Sidney." *EALN*, 1 (1967), 11–13.

Anne Bradstreet's elegy for Sidney is modeled after Joshua Sylvester's elegy for William Sidney. She called *Arcadia* Sidney's "shame." She followed Spencer in identifying Stella as Sidney's wife.

◄§ 201. STARETT, VINCENT. *Books Alive*. New York: Random House, 1940. 360 pp.

A brief life of Sidney under the topic of soldiers who were poets (pp. 109–12).

◄§ 202. STATON, WALTER F., JR. "Thomas Watson and Abraham Fraunce." *PMLA*, 76 (1961), 150–52.

[Answers 174; see also 176.] Points out the lack of evidence for assuming Barnfield a member of the Sidney circle. The reference in *The Affectionate Shepherd* is to Watson, not to Fraunce, and Watson was not a member of the circle.

◄§ 203. STONE, LAWRENCE. *The Crisis of the Aristocracy, 1558–1641*. Oxford: Clarendon Press, 1965. xxiv, 841 pp.

The purpose of the book is "to describe the total environment of an elite, material and economical, ideological and cultural, educational and moral; and secondly, to demonstrate, to explain, and to chart the course of a crisis in the affairs of this elite that was to have a profound effect upon the evolution of English political institutions" (p. 7). Believes that the crisis of the aristocracy was their loss of power to the gentry. The Queen insisted that her peers stay at court, where they were forced to look to her for money. Sidney suggested that he be given freedom to take from Catholics and suggested that the Papists retained their riches because they were not in office (pp. 477–80).

Rev.: J. H. Plumb, *Spectator*, April 30, 1965, pp. 570–71.

◄§ 204. STRONG, R. C., AND J. A. VAN DORSTEN. *Leicester's Triumph*. London: Oxford University Press, 1964. 137 pp.

Gives details concerning Sidney's relations with William of Orange (pp. 8–11). See also Index.

Rev.: *TLS*, July 29, 1964, p. 656.

205. THOMAS, DYLAN. "Sir Philip Sidney." In *Quite Early One Morning*, pp. 86–93. New York: New Directions Publishing Corporation, 1954.

Arcadia is bewildering in its richness. Sidney fell in love with Penelope after her marriage, and the sonnets portray a "progress of passion."

206. VAN DORSTEN, J. A. *Poets, Patrons, and Professors: Sir Philip Sidney, Daniel Rogers, and the Leiden Humanists.* Publications of the Sir Thomas Browne Institute, General Series 2. Leiden: University Press, 1962. 272 pp.

Covers the relations between the Leiden poets and the English poets between the foundation of the University of Leiden in 1575 and Sidney's death in 1586. From 1575 through 1580, Daniel Rogers represented English thought in Leiden. Janus Dousa and van Hout, men interested in vernacular poetry, were friends of the Sidney circle. In 1584 Dousa went with a Dutch embassy to London, where his son translated a poem by Henry Constable into Latin. In 1586 Leicester and Sidney were in the Netherlands. Leicester quarreled with the men at Leiden. After Sidney's death, both the Dutch and the English poets wrote commemorative verse. The younger Dousa wrote a poem indicating a familiarity with Sidney's writings. Includes an appendix of forty Latin poems devoted to Sidney.

Rev.: *TLS*, April 19, 1962, p. 266; Michel Poirier, *EA*, 16 (1963), 383.

207. ———. "Sidney and Languet." *HLQ*, 29 (1965–1966), 215–22.

Languet was influential in Sidney's political life. Some of Languet's unpublished letters indicate how much he influenced Sidney during his first visit to the Continent.

208. WARNER, OLIVER. *English Literature: A Portrait Gallery.* London: Chatto and Windus, 1964. 205 pp.

Contains a short biography and a picture of Sidney.

209. WHITNEY, GEOFFREY. *A Choice of Emblemes*, Henry Green, ed. New York: Benjamin Blom, 1967. 434 pp.

[First published, Leiden, 1586.] Whitney, a member of Leicester's party in Leiden, wrote the first English emblem book. He borrowed emblems from Continental writers, adding dedications.

Numbers 38 and 109 are dedicated to Sidney. Gives a biography of Sidney (pp. 223–27).

210. WILKES, G. A. "The Sequence of the Writings of Fulke Greville, Lord Brooke." *SP*, 56 (1959), 489–503.
Places the date of composition of the *Life of Sidney* between 1610 and 1614. Describes the two manuscript copies of it.

211. WOODWARD, D. H. "Thomas Fuller, William Dugard, and the Pseudonymous Life of Sidney (1655)." *PBSA*, 62 (1968), 501–10.
[See 165.] Thomas Fuller probably wrote the life of Sidney prefixed to the *Arcadia* of 1655. The life may have been commissioned by William Dugard, the printer. Fuller may not have used his name for fear of the Puritans who were aroused by Milton's *Eikonoclastes*. There are many correspondences between the 1655 life and the life given in the *Worthies*.

212. YATES, FRANCES A. *The French Academies of the Sixteenth Century.* London: Warburg Institute, 1947.
xii, 376 pp.
Mentions Sidney as a character in Bruno's philosophical dialogues (p. 102). Gives a quotation from Coleridge concerning Bruno's influence on Sidney and Greville (pp. 227–28).

213. ZANDVOORT, R. W. "Sidney in Austria." *WBEP*, 66 (1958), 227–45.
Describes the summer of 1573, which Sidney spent in Austria. During this time, Sidney wrote thirteen letters to Languet, and Languet wrote thirty-eight to Sidney. Sidney also wrote one letter to Leicester and one to Burghley. While in Vienna he studied and took riding lessons from Pugliano. The letters indicate that he took an interest in the political situation on the Continent.

III

Editions

COLLECTIONS

◄§ 214. *The Complete Poems of Sir Philip Sidney*, Alexander B. Grosart, ed. Freeport, N.Y.: Books for Libraries Press, 1970. 3 vols.
[First published, 1877.]

◄§ 215. *The Miscellaneous Works of Sir Philip Sidney, Knt., with a Life of the Author and Illustrative Notes*, William Gray, ed. New York: AMS Press, 1966. 380 pp.
[First published, 1829.] Contains a life of Sidney, as well as the *Defence, Astrophel and Stella*, miscellaneous poems, *The Lady of May, Valour Anatomized in a Fancy, Letter to Queene Elizabeth, A Discourse in Defence of the Earl of Leicester*, and some letters. In the Introduction, defends the language of *Arcadia* but not the poetry (pp. 22–24). Gives the text of the sonnets written by Henry Constable that were prefixed to the first edition of the *Defence* (p. 5).

◄§ 216. *The Poems of Sir Philip Sidney*, William A. Ringler, ed. Oxford English Texts. Oxford: Clarendon Press, 1962. lxvi, 578 pp.
[Standard edition of the poems.] With the poems includes textual notes and an Introduction. Finds that the eclogues of *Arcadia* are grouped by theme: the first group deals with unrequited love; the second group, with passion and reason; the third group, with married love; and the fourth, with the sorrows of lovers and with death (p. xxxviii). These poems are an important example of Elizabethan pastoral poetry (p. xxxviii). *Astrophel and Stella* is in the form of a dramatic conversation, with Astrophel as the central figure (p. xliv). The poems are arranged to mark stages in a courtship, and the eighth song marks the climax (p. xlviii). Concludes that Sidney's contributions to English poetry were in bringing back feminine rhyme and in bringing out a variety and number of verse forms (p. lvi).
Rev.: *TLS*, January 25, 1963, p. 58; Jack Stillinger, *JEGP*, 62 (1963), 372–78; R. W. Zandvoort, *ES*, 44 (1963), 138–41; William C. McAvoy, *Manuscripta*, 7 (1963), 158–74.

ᴈ§ 217. *The Prose Works of Sir Philip Sidney*, A. Feuillerat, ed. London: Cambridge University Press, 1962. 4 vols. [First published as *The Complete Works*, 1912–1926.] Contains New *Arcadia*, Old *Arcadia*, *The Lady of May*, *Defence of Poesie*, *A Discourse to the Queenes Majesty*, *A Discourse on Irish Affairs*, *Defence of the Earl of Leicester* and a translation of Mornay's *A Woorke concerning the trewnesse of the Christian Religion*. This edition omits most of the poetry contained in the original edition.

ᴈ§ 218. *Five Courtier Poets of the English Renaissance*, Robert M. Bender, ed., pp. 285–466. New York: Washington Square Press, Inc., 1967. Contains poems from *Certain Sonnets, Astrophel and Stella, Psalms of David*, and *Arcadia*. Also contains a short life, a bibliography, and critical comments.

ᴈ§ 219. *Silver Poets of the Sixteenth Century: Sir Thomas Wyatt, Henry Howard, Earl of Surrey, Sir Philip Sidney, Sir Walter Raleigh, Sir John Davies*, Gerald William Bullett, ed. Everyman's Library 985. London: Dent, 1947. xix, 428 pp. Describes the poets as a group, relating each poet to Renaissance thought. Contains all of Sidney's poetry except the Psalms and a few experimental poems.

ᴈ§ 220. *Sir Philip Sidney: Selected Poetry and Prose*, Thomas Wallace Craik, ed. London: Methuen, 1965. 249 pp. Contains selections from *Defence, Astrophel and Stella*, and *Arcadia*, with a Preface and Introduction.

ᴈ§ 221. *Sir Philip Sidney: Selected Prose and Poetry*, Robert Kimbrough, ed. New York: Holt, Rinehart and Winston, Inc., 1969. 539 pp. Contains the *Defence of Poesie* and *Astrophel and Stella*. Contains parts of the other works, including a complete Book One from the Old and the New *Arcadia*.

ARCADIA

ᴈ§ 222. Sidney, Sir Philip. *The Countess of Pembrokes Arcadia*. Kent, Ohio: Kent State University Press, 1970. lxxiii, 361 pp. Contains a facsimile of the 1891 facsimile of the 1590 edition of *Arcadia* with an Introduction by Carl Dennis. The *Arcadia* may be called an epic because of its serious nature, but its subject is love (p. vi). Sidney sets up an opposition between the world of the pastoral and heroic life and embodies this opposition in the characters (pp. viii–ix). As in Christian epics, passive endurance is praised as a high virtue (p. xxi). Analyzes the style (pp. lxiv–lxvii).

223. "The *Arcadia*" (excerpts). In *Elizabethan Fiction*, Robert Ashley and Edwin M. Moseley, eds., pp. 159–96. New York: Rinehart and Company, Inc., 1953.
Excerpts are from Books One and Two of the New *Arcadia*.

224. *Selections from Sidney's* Arcadia, Rosemary Syfret, ed. London: Hutchinson, 1966. 264 pp.
Selections are from Feuillerat's 1912 edition of the New *Arcadia*, Books One through Three. Omits the poems and most of the subplots. Writes that Books Four and Five would have been greatly changed had Sidney finished the revision (p. 45).

ASTROPHEL AND STELLA

225. *Astrophel et Stella*, trans. by Charles M. Garnier, ed. Paris: Aubier, 1943. 203 pp.
Includes a biography of Sidney and critical notes. Gives the English text of *Astrophel and Stella* from Feuillerat's 1922 edition with a French translation.

226. *Astrophil and Stella*, Vanna Gentili, ed. Biblioteca italiana di testi inglesi, No. 10. Bari: Adriatica Editrice, 1965. 507 pp.
Includes a biography and criticism of the sonnet sequence with criticism of the other major works. *Astrophel and Stella* was probably written between 1581 and 1583; possibly some of the poems were written earlier. In it Sidney added drama to the Petrarchan tradition. It may be divided into three parts; the first ending with Sonnet 43, the second with Sonnet 85. Lists editions and gives the text in English with Italian textual notes.

227. *Astrophel and Stella*, Kingsley Hart, ed. London: Folio Society, 1959. 168 pp.

228. "A Critical Edition of Sir Philip Sidney's *Astrophel and Stella* with an Introduction," Ann Romayne Howe, ed. Ph.D. diss., Boston University, 1962. *DA*, 23 (1962), 1686.
An edition of the sonnets based on a collation of the three quartos and the first folio. Records all variants.

229. *Astrophel and Stella*. In Ausw. übertr. v. hrsg. v. Maria Gräfin Lanckorońska. Krefeld: Scherpe-Verlag, 1947.
Listed in *Deutsches Bücherverzeichnis*, 26 (1941–1950), 52.

230. *Astrophel and Stella*. In *Elizabethan Sonnets*, Sidney Lee, ed. New York: Cooper Square Publishers, Inc., 1964. 2 vols.
Introduction traces the history of the sonnet. Sidney is said to imitate earlier writers (I, xxxii–xlix.)

231. *Astrophel and Stella*, trans. by Michel Poirier, ed. Collection Bilingue des Classiques Etrangers. Paris: Aubier, 1948. 221 pp.
Contains a French and English text. Indicates the evidence for an autobiographical interpretation of *Astrophel and Stella*. Identifies the Petrarchan elements in the sonnets and indicates ways in which Sidney departed from tradition.

232. *Astrophel and Stella*, Max Putzel, ed. New York: Doubleday, 1967. 208 pp.
In the sonnets Sidney illustrates the conflict between Platonic and physical love. The sonnets have a plot, but it has no definite turning points. The sonnets are autobiographical.

DEFENCE OF POESIE

233. *The Defence of Poesie*, 1595. Menston, England: The Scholar Press, Limited, 1968. Unpaged.
A facsimile of the 1595 edition, *Short Title Catalogue* 22535. Reproduced by permission of the Trustees of the British Museum.

234. *An Apology for Poetry*. In *Criticism: The Major Texts*, Walter Jackson Bate, ed., pp. 82–106. New York: Harcourt, Brace and Co., 1952.
In the Introduction writes that Sidney's combination of Aristotle, Plato, Horace, and Christian theology makes the *Defence* the most comprehensive work on Renaissance literary theory. Gives a precis of the *Defence*. Follows Olney's text.

❧ 235. *An Apology for Poetry.* In *Great Theories in Literary Criticism*, Karl Beckson, ed., pp. 130–62. New York: Farrar, Straus and Company, 1963.
Follows the Olney text.

❧ 236. *The Defence of Poetry: Con Introduzione, Biografica e Note*, trans. by Adele Biagi, ed. Naples: R. Pironti e Figli, 1958. xxxiii, 116 pp.
Contains a biography and explanatory footnotes.

❧ 237. *Apologia della Poesia*, Elena Buonpane, ed. Florence: 1954.

❧ 238. *Deffensa de Poesia, a Spanish Version*, D. O. Chambers, ed. [n.p.] 1968. 40 pp.
Contains an undated, anonymous Spanish translation of the *Defence* found in the Biblioteca National de Madrid. It had been owned by a man named Bustamente; possibly Juan Ruiz de Bustamente.

❧ 239. *The Defence of Poetry.* H. v. Wolfgang Clemen, ed. Heidelberg: Universität Verlag, 1950. 57 pp.
Lists variant readings and identifies allusions.

❧ 240. "A Critical Old-Spelling Edition of Sir Philip Sidney's *Defence of Poesie*," William A. Elwood, ed. Ph.D. diss., University of Chicago, 1966.
Includes an Introduction, annotations, and William Temple's *Analysis Tractationis de Poesi*, as well as the text based on a scribal copy found among the Sidney papers. Indicates that this text was probably copied from Sidney's own manuscript. Writes that Quintilian was probably a direct source for the *Defence*. Sidney may have been refuting Book Ten of the *Republic*.

❧ 241. *An Apology for Poetry.* In *English Critical Texts: Sixteenth to Twentieth Century*, D. J. Enright and Ernst de Chickera, eds., pp. 3–49. London: Oxford University Press, 1962.
Contains an Introduction in which the function of the critic is defined as first to explain the work and then to judge the work. The critic's standards should be implicit in his criticism of an individual work. Contains text notes (pp. 339–50).

✒§ 242. *Defence of Poetry*. In *Literary Criticism: Plato to Dryden*, Allan H. Gilbert, ed., pp. 404–61. New York: American Book Company, 1940.
Contains text with notes.

✒§ 243. *Un Plaidoyer Pour la Poésie*, trans. by Maurice Lebel, ed. Quebec: Les Presses de l'Université Laval, 1965. 181 pp.
Contains with the English text and a French translation, a biography, an outline of the principal parts of the *Defence*, and a brief treatment of Sidney's sources (pp. 9–24).

✒§ 244. *Defence of Poetry*, Dorothy M. Macardle, ed. London: Macmillan and Company, Ltd., 1959. xvi, 72 pp.
Contains with the text a biography and notes to the text.

✒§ 245. *The Apology for Poetry*, Mary R. Mahl, ed. Northridge, Cal.: San Fernando Valley State College, 1969. xxv, 51 pp.
Contains the text of the Norwich manuscript.

✒§ 246. *La Difensa della Poesie*, trans. by Silvio Policardi, ed. Padua: Dott, 1946. ix, 124 pp.
With the text includes a background of Renaissance criticism.

✒§ 247. *An Apology for Poetry*. In *Criticism: The Foundations of Modern Literary Judgments*, M. Schorer, J. Miles, and G. McKenzie, eds., pp. 407–31. New York: Harcourt, Brace and Company, 1948.
Contains a text based on Olney.

✒§ 248. *An Apologie for Poetry*, Evelyn S. Shuckburgh, ed. Cambridge: University Press, 1951. xxxv, 192 pp.
[First published, 1891.]

✒§ 249. *Sir Philip Sidney's* Defense of Poesy, Lewis Soens, ed. Lincoln: University of Nebraska Press, 1970. xliii, 95 pp.
Text is based on Ponsonby. Outlines the arguments for accepting Ponsonby's text as Sidney's final revision (pp. xxvii–xli).

✒§ 250. *An Apology for Poetry: or, The Defence of Poesy*, Geoffrey Shepherd, ed. Nelson's Medieval and Renaissance Library. London. T. Belson, 1965. xviii, 244 pp.
Contains a selected bibliography (pp. xi–xviii), an Introduction (pp. 1–91), a text based on Olney's edition, and extensive notes.

The *Defence* was not a direct answer to Gosson (p. 3). It was probably written between the years 1581 and 1583 (p. 4). It has the form of a laudatory oration (p. 12). Explicates such terms as *imitation, speaking pictures,* and *utile et dulce* (pp. 46–91).
Rev.: Katherine Duncan-Jones, *RES,* n.s., 17 (1965), 309–10; Jan Van Dorsten, *MLR,* 62 (1967), 308–9.

◄§ 251. *A Defence of Poetry,* Jan A. Van Dorsten, ed. London: Oxford University Press, 1966. 112 pp.
Contains a thirteen-page Introduction, the text, and text notes.
Rev.: *ES,* 48 (1967), 90.

THE LADY OF MAY

◄§ 252. "An Edition of Sir Philip Sidney's *The Lady of May,*" Ophelia V. Boddie, ed. M.A. thesis, Cornell University, 1957.
Reviews the possible allegorical interpretations. Sidney may have symbolized the proposed marriage between Elizabeth and Alençon, or the love of Sidney for Stella, or Sidney's disappointment with court life. Analyzes the language of the play.

◄§ 253. "The Helmingham Hall Manuscript of Sidney's *The Lady of May:* A Commentary and Transcription," Robert Kimbrough and Philip Murphy. *RenD,* n.s., 1 (1968), 103–19.
Includes the text of the Helmingham Hall MS of the work discovered by Miss Jean Robertson, with an explanation of variations in the text. The Helmingham Hall MS contains an epilogue that may have been an appeal from Leicester to the Queen. Possibly this epilogue was dropped from the printed text as anticlimatic.

◄§ 254. "A Critical Edition of Sir Philip Sidney's *Lady of May,*" Philip Michael Murphy, ed. Ph.D. diss., University of Wisconsin, 1969. *DA,* 30 (1969–1970), 5432A.
[See 253.] Includes a modernized edition of *The Lady of May* with a previously unpublished epilogue and a survey of the masque form.

LETTERS

≈§ 255. "The Correspondence of Sir Philip Sidney and Hubert Languet, 1573–1576," Charles Samuel Levy, ed. Ph.D. diss., Cornell University, 1962. *DA*, 23 (1963), 3379–80. Contains the letters with annotations.

THE PSALMS OF DAVID

≈§ 256. *The Psalms of Sir Philip Sidney and the Countess of Pembroke*, J. C. A. Rathmell, ed. New York: New York University Press, 1963. xxxviii, 362 pp.

The Psalms—43 by Sidney, 128 by Mary—were first published as a body in 1823. This edition is based upon Mary's final revision of the Psalms, transcribed by Samuel Woodford in 1694–1695. These Psalms have more literary merit than the psalms of Stern hold and Hopkins, possibly because they were not intended for congregational use.

Rev.: William C. McAvoy, *Manuscripta*, 8 (1964), 146–79.

IV

Arcadia

◄§ 257. ALPERS, PAUL J. *The Poetry of the* Faerie Queene. Princeton, N.J.: Princeton University Press, 1967. 417 pp.
Studies *The Faerie Queene* under such topics as narration, rhetoric, and allegory. Mentions Sidney's use of patterns of speech in *Astrophel and Stella* (pp. 72–73). Sidney's view of poetry as moral teaching supports the judgment that Spenser's poetry is an address to the reader (pp. 280–81). Contrasts pastoral as it appears in *The Faerie Queene* with that of *Arcadia*: Spenser wanted to teach; Sidney wanted the reader to judge (pp. 283–84).
Rev.: A. C. Hamilton, *ELH*, 34 (1967), 618–33; William Nelson, *RQ*, 21 (1968), 486–89.

◄§ 258. ANDERSON, D. M. "The Dido Incident in Sidney's *Arcadia*." *N&Q*, n.s., 3 (1956), 417–19.
The Dido incident is different in tone and may be from *Amadis de Gaule* or from *Morte d'Arthur*.

◄§ 259. ———. "The Trial of the Princes in the *Arcadia*, Book V." *RES*, n.s., 8 (1957), 409–12.
The trial scene does not illustrate a conflict between parental authority and romantic love as Rowe suggested; instead, it illustrates that private injustice is less important than public good. Mornay, whose works Sidney was translating, reached a similar conclusion. The scene is complicated because it is an unrevised part of the Old Arcadia, while the characters of the princes are revised in New *Arcadia*.

◄§ 260. ANDREWS, MICHAEL C. "Sidney's *Arcadia* on the English Stage: A Study of the Dramatic Adaptations of *The Countess of Pembroke's Arcadia*." Ph.D. diss., Duke University, 1966. *DA*, 27 (1967), 3860A–61A.
Studies nine plays that have *Arcadia* as a source: *Mucedorus, Trial of Chivalry, Jack Drum's Entertainment, Cupid's Revenge, Isle of Gulls, Andromana, Argalus and Parthenia, Arcadia,* and *Philoclea.*

261. ———. "The Sources of *Andromana*." *RES*, n.s., 19 (1968), 295–300.

While Sidney's *Arcadia* is a source for the play *Andromana*, a more important source is *Cupid's Revenge*. The characters' names and the Iberian setting indicate familiarity with *Arcadia*, but most of the details of the action and the tragic conclusion are from *Cupid's Revenge*.

262. ARMSTRONG, WILLIAM A. "*King Lear* and Sidney's *Arcadia*." *TLS*, October 24, 1949, p. 665.

The argument between Cecropia and Pamela in Book III may be a source for *King Lear*. Cecropia's "epicurean atheism" is similar to Edmund's opportunism. Shakespeare's "As flies to wanton boys" may derive from Cecropia's analogy of flies to men. Pamela's speech in reply resembles Edgar's "Clearest gods, who make them honours of men's impossibilities" (IV,vi,73–74).

263. ATKINSON, DOROTHY F. "The Pastorella Episode in *The Faerie Queene*." *PMLA*, 59 (1944), 361–72.

The source for the Pastorella cantos of *The Faerie Queene* may be parts two, four, and five of *Mirrour of Knighthood*, rather than *Arcadia*. Many of the details thought to be from *Arcadia* have stronger parallels in the *Mirrour*

264. BABB, LAWRENCE. *The Elizabethan Malady· A Study of Melancholia in English Literature from 1580 to 1642*. East Lansing: Michigan State College Press, 1951. ix, 206 pp.

Describes the melancholy lover (p. 155). Love may be either ignoble or good; both views are expressed in *Arcadia*. The Arcadian lovers exhibit conventional traits of melancholy (p. 158).

Rev.: William Van O'Connor, *BJA*, 11 (1952–1953), 177–78; Murray W. Bundy, *SQ*, 3 (1952), 275–78; *TLS*, January 11, 1952, p. 22; John W. Draper, *MLR*, 47 (1952), 6571–72.

265. BARKER, WILLIAM. "Three Essays on the Rhetorical Tradition." Ph.D. diss., Brandeis, 1968. *DA*, 29 (1969), 2700A.

Elizabethans viewed rhetoric as an ambivalent force originating from God but capable of being used for evil. The judgment scene in *Arcadia* illustrates this ambivalence. Providence, not rhetoric, resolves the conflict.

267. BAUGHAN, DENVER E. "Sidney's *Defence of the Earl of Leicester* and the Revised *Arcadia.*" *JEGP*, 51 (1952), 35–41.

Sidney's *Defence of Leicester* stimulated some revisions in New *Arcadia* and helps to date the revision. As the *Defence* stresses the genealogy of the Dudley family, so do many revisions in *Arcadia* stress genealogy. The ratio of nobles to rustics is higher in the New than the Old *Arcadia*.

267. BEACH, DONALD MARCUS. "Studies in the Art of Elizabethan Prose Narrative." Ph.D. diss., Cornell University, 1959. DA, 20 (1959), 2274–75.

Arcadia is sentimental fiction, separation fiction, and adventure fiction.

268. BEATY, FREDERICK L. "Lodge's *Forbonius and Prisceria* and Sidney's *Arcadia.*" *ES*, 49 (1968), 39–45.

Lodge may have seen a manuscript of *Arcadia* and used its plot in *Forbonius*. The styles are similar.

269. BECKETT, ROBERT D. "The Narrative Structure of the Old *Arcadia* and the New *Arcadia* of Sir Philip Sidney: An Analytic Comparison." Ph.D. diss., Colorado University, 1967. DA, 28 (1968), 3630A–31A.

Analyzes the relationship between the storyteller and the reader, also between the plot, the themes, and the characters of Old and New *Arcadia*. The revised *Arcadia* is the more serious, but it may have been left incomplete because Sidney was unsatisfied.

270. BORINSKI, LUDWIG. "Mittelalter und Neuzeit in der Stilgeschichte des 16. Jahrhunderts." *SJ*, 97 (1961), 109–33.

Arcadia developed out of the chivalric romance of the Middle Ages, but it emphasizes the psychology of the characters more than did the chivalric romance.

271. BRUCKL, O. "Sir Philip Sidney's *Arcadia* as a Source for John Webster's *The Duchess of Malfi.*" *ESA*, 8 (1965), 31–55.

Webster borrowed devices, images, and mood from *Arcadia*. Lucus had identified thirty-six instances of borrowings. In some of these, whole sentences are taken. The borrowings fall into three groups: "The Marqueterie pattern, the twofold or manifold imagery . . . and isolated minor borrowings."

272. BRUSER, FREDELLE. "Concepts of Chastity in Literature, Chiefly Non-Dramatic, of the English Renaissance." Ph.D. diss., Radcliffe College, 1948. HRDP, 1947–1948, p. 23; DDAAU, 15 (1947–1948), 116.

Examines chastity as a literary tradition. Pamela's defense of chastity is based on the relationship between the laws of human nature and of universal nature (pp. 79–85). Compares *Arcadia* with *The Faerie Queene* to show that chastity is not as important in *Arcadia* as it is in *The Faerie Queene* (pp. 194–215). The revised conclusion in New *Arcadia* emphasized honor more than chastity.

273. BULLOUGH, GEOFFREY. *Narrative and Dramatic Sources of Shakespeare*. London: Routledge, 1957. 6 vols.

Suggests that *Arcadia* is an analogue of *Two Gentlemen of Verona* (Vol. 1, 253), and of *Pericles* (Vol. 6, 482).

274. BUSH, DOUGLAS. [Correspondence.] "Marvell and Sidney." *RES*, n.s., 3 (1952), 375.

[See 275, 384.] Martin's article identifying *Arcadia* as a source for Marvell's "The Definition of Love" was preceded by the same identification in *English Literature in the Earlier Seventeenth Century* (pp. 172–73).

275. ———. *English Literature in the Earlier Seventeenth Century*, 1600–1660. New York: Oxford University Press, 1962. 680 pp.

[Revised edition; first edition published, 1945.] Indicates Sidney's influence on such poets as William Drummond and George Herbert. Philoclea's lament may be a source for Marvell's "The Definition of Love" (pp. 172–73).

276. BUXTON, JOHN. " 'A Draught of Sir Philip Sidney's Arcadia.' " In *Historical Essays 1600–1750*, H. E. Bell and R. L. Ollard, eds., pp. 60–77. New York: Barnes and Noble, Inc., 1963.

Prints the unpublished manuscript of a poem, "A Draught of Sir Philip Sidney's Arcadia," by an unknown author around 1645. This poem is the only satiric poem based on *Arcadia*. Mentions a manuscript index to *Arcadia* possibly in the same hand, in which *Arcadia* is considered a heroic poem.

277. ———. *Elizabethan Taste.* London: Macmillan and Company, 1963. xiv, 370 pp.

Evaluates the Elizabethans' response to their own art. Contains a chapter on *Arcadia* and one on *Astrophel and Stella.* The revised *Arcadia* is both a heroic poem and a romance; the two categories are not exclusive (p. 254). Its prose was the first English prose to rival Latin (p. 263 ff.). *Astrophel and Stella* formed the taste of Shakespeare's generation (p. 294). Rev.: Wallace T. MacCaffrey, *AHR,* 70 (1965), 433–34; R. W. Zandvoort, *ES,* 46 (1965), 259–62; *TLS,* August 30, 1963, p. 656.

278. C. "The *Arcadia* Unveiled." *N&Q,* n.s., 3 (1863), 501–3.

Philoclea was modeled after Miss Walsingham, and Kalander's garden after Francis Walsingham's. The story of Zelmane may be the story of Sidney's love for Anne Cecil. Plexirtus may be Lord Burghley. Amphialus may represent Scotland, and Artaxia, Erona, and Helen may represent Elizabeth.

279. CARTER, WILLIAM HOYT, JR. "*Ut Pictura Poesis:* A Study of the Parallel between Painting and Poetry from Classical Times through the Seventeenth Century." Ph.D. diss., Harvard University, 1951. *HRDP,* 1950–1951, p. 11; *DDAAU,* 18 (1950–1951), 225.

The classical period developed a pictorial literature. That literature again became important in Renaissance Italy and later in France and England (pp. 159–64). Descriptions, such as the one of Kalander's garden, were influenced by the literary tradition of the Greek romance and by the work of Italian painters.

280. CASPARI, FRITZ. *Humanism and the Social Order in Tudor England.* Chicago: University of Chicago Press, 1954. ix, 293 pp.

Illustrates the development of humanism. Sidney had a humanistic education, and his writing is the expression of humanistic philosophy. The central themes of *Arcadia* involve friendship and love of virtuous women. Euarchus represents Sidney's ideal of a hereditary monarchy, for while Sidney is sympathetic to the Helots, he is not in favor of revolt against a lawful ruler. In favoring limited government Sidney followed the Aristotelian concept of balance (pp. 157–75).

281. CAZAMIAN, LOUIS F. *The Development of English Humor.* Durham, N.C.: Duke University Press, 1952. viii, 421 pp.
Traces the development of English humor up to the 17th century. *Arcadia* exemplifies "restrained humor." "Sidney's wit is that of delicate hints and light innuendoes" (pp. 138–39).

282. CHALLIS, LORNA. "The Use of Oratory in Sidney's *Arcadia.*" *SP*, 62 (1965), 561–76.
Describes Sidney's use of aural appeal and psychological realism in his set speeches. Cicero and Aristotle may be sources for this technique. Psychological realism, illustrated in the contrast between Philanax' argument and Euarchus', anticipated later developments in fiction.

283. CHANG, H. C. *Allegory and Courtesy in Spenser: A Chinese View.* Edinburgh: Edinburgh University Press, 1955. x, 227 pp.
Contains a chapter comparing *The Faerie Queene* to *Arcadia* (pp. 114–51): both books teach conduct, but *Arcadia* teaches through example, and *The Faerie Queen* through allegory. *Arcadia* helps interpret the Pastorella episode. Compares Timias to Amphialus and Erona to Mirabella. For Sidney the code of chivalry was an ideal; for Spenser it was a symbol of moral virtue.

284. CHARNEY, MAURICE. "Hawthorne and Sidney's *Arcadia.*" *N&Q*, n.s., 7 (1960), 264–65.
Hawthorne did not, as James T. Fields asserted, read *Arcadia* for forty years. Sidney was not one of Hawthorne's favorite authors.

285. COULMAN, D. "Spotted to be Known." *JWCI*, 20 (1957), 179–80.
The device borne by Philisides is mentioned in Abraham Fraunce's *Insignium, Armorum, Emblematum, Hieroglyphicorum et Symbolorum* and is specified as belonging to Sidney. Includes a translation of verses with which Fraunce explained the device.

286. CRAIG, HARDIN. "The Composition of *King Lear.*" *RenP* (1961), 57–61.
Believes that the folio text of *King Lear* is the prompter's copy and that the 1608 quarto was published from the original, uncorrected, manuscript. Supports by counting lines relating to the main

plot and to the subplot. The subplot from *Arcadia* may have provided the impetus to turn the history of King Lear into a tragedy.

287. ———. "Motivation in Shakespeare's Choice of Materials." *ShS*, 4 (1951), 26–34.
Shakespeare did not try to invent new plots; instead, he combined existing material into new patterns. For Shakespeare, as for Sidney, the poet and the historian drew on the same body of knowledge. In *King Lear* Shakespeare combined the Lear story with the incident of the Paphlagonian King and the tragic tone from *Arcadia*. The result is a universal pattern of the effects following filial ingratitude.

288. CROMPTON, N. J. R. "Sidney and Symbolic Heraldry." *The Coat of Arms* (London), 8 (1965), 244–48.
In the 15th and 16th centuries in Italy the impress, with its associated motto, nearly supplanted the badge. The impress signified the spiritual or psychological state of its bearer, not his family. Sidney uses the impress in the jewel of Hercules and the distaff. He uses armor symbolically in the fight between Argulus and Amphialus. Sidney used black to indicate both disguise and a particular state of mind.

289. CUTTS, JOHN P. "Dametas' Song in Sidney's *Arcadia*." *Renaissance News*, 11 (1958), 183–88.
A musical setting for Dametas' song exists in Thomas Ravenscroft's *Pammelia*, and a slightly different version is in Melvill's *Book of Roundels*. Speculates that this part of *Arcadia* may have been given on the stage. Dametas' song is an epitome of his character. Includes both versions of the song.

290. D., A. "Possible Echoes from Sidney's *Arcadia* in Shakespeare, Milton, and Others." *N&Q*, 194 (1949), 554–55.
[See 317.] Suggests nine parallel passages in *Arcadia* and in *Antony and Cleopatra, King Lear, Midsummer Night's Dream, Julius Caesar, Paradise Lost, Samson Agonistes, Lycidas*, also in Drummond of Hawthornden's writings on Donne, and in Fuller's description of Shakespeare and Jonson.

291. DANBY, J. F. *Poets on Fortune's Hill: Studies in Sidney, Shakespeare, Beaumont and Fletcher.* London: Faber, 1952. 212 pp.

[Essay on Sidney first printed as "The Poets on Fortune's Hill: Literature and Society, 1480–1610." *Cambridge Journal,* 2 (1949), 195–211. A revised edition of the book was issued as *Elizabethan and Jacobean Poets: Studies in Sidney, Shakespeare, Beaumont and Fletcher.* London: Faber, 1965. 212 pp.] In Chapter II, "Sidney's *Arcadia:* The Great House Romance," calls *Arcadia* a study of fortune and virtue. The four main characters indicate that for Sidney the primary virtues were patience and magnanimity.

Rev.: *TLS,* November 14, 1952, p. 744.

292. DAVIDSON, CLIFFORD. "Nature and Judgment in the Old *Arcadia.*" *PLL,* 6 (1970), 348–65.

Arcadia is not a return to a prelapsarian world of ideal nature; instead, it is about a world in which passion overcomes reason. When Pyrocles falls in love with Philoclea's picture, his reason is subjugated to sense. Love in Arcadia is a search not for the Platonic ideal, but rather for sensual gratification. The lovers define nature in terms of inclination and are bound to fortune instead of being freed for contemplative life. The judgment scene combines both views of nature through the working of Providence. Sidney was not willing to banish the reality of disruptive passion from *Arcadia.*

293. DAVIS, WALTER R. "Actaeon in *Arcadia.*" *SEL,* 2 (1962), 95–110.

Interprets the cave scene in *Arcadia* by reference to the myth of Actaeon and Diana, and its standard Elizabethan interpretations as an allegory of self-knowledge, curiosity, and lust. Gynecia represents Actaeon and Pyrocles appears to represent Diana, but both Gynecia and Pyrocles are pursued by desire.

294. ———. "A Map of *Arcadia,* Sidney's Romance in its Tradition." In *Sidney's* Arcadia, pp. 1–178. New Haven, Conn.: Yale University Press, 1965.

Proposes that the 1593 *Arcadia* is a pastoral romance, not an epic in prose. Fits it into the pastoral tradition and interprets it in relation to Platonism. The cave is considered the center of the book and a symbol for the ambiguous nature of love. Love brings the hero into the contemplative life, but it inhibits the action necessary for a philosopher king, such as Euarchus. In the eclogues Strephon and Claius are analogues for the two heroes and serve to generalize the plot. The final judgment shows the attainment of natural justice. Musidorus' account of the action is the one the audience is to accept.

Rev.: Jean Robertson, *RES*, n.s., 16 (1966), 430–32; A. C. Hamilton, *MLQ*, 27 (1966), 332–50; Katherine Duncan-Jones, *MLR*, 62 (1967), 699–700.

◆§ 295. ————. *Idea and Act in Elizabethan Fiction*. Princeton, N.J.: Princeton University Press, 1969. viii, 301 pp.

Elizabethan fiction differs from later fiction: the former is fiction about abstract ideas, the other about psychological states. Sidney's *Defence* suggests that an idea embodied in a concrete poetic image has the power to lead men to either shun or perform certain actions. Writers may test certain values by creating characters whose actions explore through experience the worth of an idea. In *Arcadia* Sidney tested ideas about love, finally rejecting many Platonic ideas (pp. 55–69). Other pastoral writers, as well as the courtly writers, used fiction to test ideas. Robert Greene and the "realists" used fiction to reject idealogical patterns.

◆§ 296. ————. "Masking in Arden: The Histrionics of Lodge's *Rosalynde*." *SEL*, 5 (1965), 151–63.

[Incorporated in 295.] Although Lodge borrowed the theme of the ideal and the actual from the pastoral, his use of disguise to embody the theme was new. In a pastoral such as *Arcadia*, the disguised hero tests himself in an ideal world of love and contemplation. In *Rosalynde*, as in *Arcadia*, the disguise indicates the true nature of the character. Through disguise, each finds a "real" self.

◆§ 297. ————. "Thematic Unity in the New *Arcadia*." *SP*, 57 (1960), 123–43.

[See 294, 370.] In New *Arcadia* the plot of Old *Arcadia* is made more complicated and its theme is amplified. In Book I, the addition of three episodes—the story of Argalus and Parthenia, of Helen and Amphialus, and of Phalantus' tourney—helps to define *Arcadia* and to mark three stages of love. In Book II, the incidental episodes function as "mirrors" that show the result of passion to be civil strife. In Book III, Sidney adds the captivity episode and clarifies the relation between the private and public worlds. Explicates many characters' names.

✒️ 298. DELASANTA, RODNEY. *The Epic Voice.* The Hague: Mouton, 1967. 140 pp.
[Ph.D. diss., Brown University, 1962. DA, 23 (1962), 2524.]
Traces the *in medias res* tradition from Homer to Milton. The New *Arcadia* is an epic; the earlier one, a romance. In the New *Arcadia* Sidney used more retrospective narration, less narration from the narrator. Sidney used episodes as *exempla* of his amatory and martial themes.

✒️ 299. DENT, R. W. *John Webster's Borrowing.* Berkeley: University of California Press, 1960. 323 pp.
Studies Webster's literary sources and finds that *Arcadia* is the most frequent source. Lists specific sources for each play (pp. 69–315).

✒️ 300. DIPPLE, ELIZABETH. "The 'Fore Conceit' of Sidney's Eclogues." In *Literary Monographs I*, Eric Rothstein and Thomas K. Dunseath, eds., pp. 3–47, 301–3. Madison: University of Wisconsin Press, 1967.
Explains the "fore conceit" (structure and function) of the eclogues in *Arcadia*. Sidney's term is related to Plato's Idea. On the first level of meaning, the eclogues show the shepherds reacting to the same environment as the royal family. The first eclogue is an examination of the possibilities of love. The second eclogue condemns excessive passion. The third deals with the golden world and possible harmony in a fallen world. The fourth deals with the disharmony caused by Basilius' failure. Believes that the eclogues serve as a parallel and as a contrast to the prose of *Arcadia* but that they may be examined outside their context.

✒️ 301. ———. "Harmony and Pastoral in the Old *Arcadia*." *ELH*, 35 (1968), 309–28.
The movement in the Old *Arcadia* is from harmony to disharmony. *Arcadia* is not a true pastoral because it admits the possibility of a realistic landscape as described by Polybius. The eclogues project the values of the pure pastoral, but the plot of *Arcadia* projects the values of the real world. In both, harmony operates as an image of divine perfection. The princes are heroes from the romantic, Neo-Platonic tradition but are transformed by the realism of *Arcadia*. Finds that each book ends in a climactic moment illustrating the fall into disharmony: in Book I, the lion and the bear; in Book II, the mutiny; in Book III, the cave scene; and in Book

IV, the supposed death of Basilius. Book V ends with harmony restored, but also with the sense of a real continuum operating.

◄§ 302. ————. "Sidney's Changing Concept of *Arcadia*: The Redemption of a Landscape." Ph.D. diss., Johns Hopkins University, 1962. *Index*, 23 (1962–1963), p. 122.
Finds that the two *Arcadias* are different in methods and aims. Sidney changed both intellectual and moral content when writing the New *Arcadia*.

◄§ 303. ————. " 'Unjust Justice' in the Old *Arcadia*." *SEL*, 10 (1970), 83–101.
Studies Books IV and V of Old *Arcadia* in relation to plot and narrator to show the uncertainty of morality. The narrator adopts different voices to show the ambivalence in his theme. Because Philanax allows emotion to overcome his reason, he does not give Euarchus a true picture of events and Euarchus can not judge fairly. Absolute justice in the human situation is impossible; the princes are both guilty and not guilty.

◄§ 304. DUHAMEL, P. ALBERT. "Sidney's *Arcadia* and Elizabethan Rhetoric." *SP*, 45 (1948), 134–50.
[See 362.] Compares Sidney's rhetoric with Lyly's to explain Renaissance writing techniques. Analyzes part of the *Arcadia* to show that Sidney's use of "topics" is in the tradition of Thomas Wilson. Lyly followed the tradition of Erasmus and Cox. Sidney's figures are less ornamental and his arguments more persuasive than Lyly's. Suggests that Elizabethan prose be analyzed by the method taught Elizabethan scholars.

◄§ 305. DUNCAN-JONES, E. E. "Henry Oxinden and Sidney's *Arcadia*." *N&Q*, 198 (1953), 322–23.
Henry Oxinden, in Letter 113 of the *Oxinden Letters*, 1607–1642, quotes word for word, without acknowledgement, some passages from *Arcadia*.

◄§ 306. DUNCAN-JONES, KATHERINE. "Nashe and Sidney: The Tournament in 'The Unfortunate Traveller.' " *MLR*, 63 (1968), 3–6.
Sidney influenced Nashe's writing; the account of Surrey's tournament is borrowed from Phalantus' tournament and from the cowards' combat. Possibly Nashe intended his black knight to parody Musidorus.

307. ———. "Sidney's Urania." *RES*, n.s., 17 (1966), 123–32.

Urania may be a personification of celestial contemplation, but she is marred by an imperfect reconciliation of levels of presentation. The elevating effect of Urania's love upon the shepherds is a contrast with the denigrating effects of love upon the two princes. While it is possible that Urania is the countess of Pembroke, such an identification raises a number of problems. The game of barleybreak may have symbolic meaning in *Arcadia*.

308. DUNN, UNDINE. "The Arcadian Ethic." Ph.D. diss., Indiana University, 1968. *DA*, 29 (1968), 565A.

Analyzes the Old *Arcadia* to show that the narrator's ethic differs from Sidney's. Sidney did not believe in superstitions as his narrator does; Sidney insisted upon active virtue.

309. DURHAM, CHARLES W. III. "Character and Characterization in Elizabethan Prose Fiction." Ph. D. diss., Ohio University, 1969. *DA*, 31 (1970), 1224A.

Studies the characterization in the fiction of Lyly, Sidney, Greene, Lodge, Nashe, and Deloney to show a development toward the use of middle-class and lower-class characters. The fiction, however, remains romantic; the characterization did not become realistic.

310. EAGLE, RODERICK L. "The *Arcadia* (1593) Title-Page Border." *The Library*, 4 (1949), 68–71.

[See 457.] While the 1590 *Arcadia* bears the Sidney coat of arms, the 1593 edition has a crest bearing an animal that resembles both a porcupine and a boar. The medallion of the pig and the plant may be intended to show that dull readers will not like the book. The two principal figures on the title page may represent Musidorus as a shepherd and Pyrocles as Zelmane. The same title-page border was used on other books.

311. ———. "The *Arcadia* (1593)—Spenser (1611) Title-Page." *Baconiana*, 29 (1945), 97–100.

Reproduces the title page of the 1611 edition of Spenser, the block for which had been used for the 1593 *Arcadia*. Explains the significance of the figures of the pig, the marjoram, and the motto: the book is not for the general public.

◄§ 312. ECCLES, MARK. "A Survey of Elizabethan Reading." *HLQ*, 5 (1942), 180–82.

The *Short Title Catalogue* lists *Arcadia* seventeen times. It was one of the twenty-five favorite works of the Elizabethan period.

◄§ 313. ELTON, WILLIAM R. *King Lear and the Gods*. San Marino, Cal.: Huntington Library, 1966. 369 pp.

Studies *King Lear* in relation to Christian optimism and finds that *Lear* is closer to pagan tragedy and skepticism. Both *King Lear* and *Arcadia* may have been influenced by Calvanistic theology (pp. 36–37). In *Arcadia* Sidney expresses four attitudes toward providence. Pamela, in her argument with Cecropia, expresses the view that natural reason can lead a pagan to divine truth. Cecropia's argument is atheistic. Basilius' view is superstitious. Pyrocles and later King Lear express a fourth view—that man has a sense of a hidden divine power but that man's reason is corrupted.
Rev.: Paul N. Siegel, *MLR*, 64 (1969), 137.

◄§ 314. EVANS, ROBERT O. "Spenser's Role in the Controversy over Quantitative Verse." *NM*, 57 (1956), 246–56.

While it is possible to write English quantitative verse, Sidney's experiments are hard to scan and confused. Quantitative verse may have been a game with the Sidney circle, not a real poetic issue. Sidney and Spenser may not have used the same rules for quantitative verse.

◄§ 315. FADER, DANIEL NELSON. "Aphthonius and Elizabethan Prose Romance." Ph.D. diss., Stanford University, 1963. *DA*, 24 (1964), 3335.

Examines structuring elements drawn from precepts of Latin composition found in *Arcadia*, *Euphues*, and *Rosalynde*. Many passages in these works were based on exercises in Aphthonius' *Progymnasmata*.

◄§ 316. FLUCHÈRE, HENRI. *Shakespeare*, trans. by Guy Hamilton. Foreword by T. S. Eliot. London: Longman's Green and Company, 1953. 272 pp.

Explicates Shakespeare's plays in relation to his age and its dramatic traditions. The writing of Lyly, Spenser, and Sidney influenced the use of pastoral themes on the stage. Sidney and Spenser, however, were unable to go beyond the pastoral conventions (p. 168).

Rev.: *TLS*, July 3, 1953, p. 428; Michel Poirier, *EA*, 7 (1954), 115–16.

‹§ 317. FOGEL, EPHIM G. "Milton and Sir Philip Sidney's *Arcadia*." *N&Q*, 196 (1951), 115–17.
[See 290.] Agrees with A. D. that the opening lines of *Samson Agonistes* were taken from *Arcadia*. Writes that Milton's comment on *Arcadia* may be taken for polemic, not judgment.

‹§ 318. FORD, PHILIP J. "*Paradise Lost* and the Five-Act Epic." Ph.D. diss., Columbia University, 1967. *DA*, 28 (1967), 2207A.
Relates Old *Arcadia*, d'Urfé's *Astrée*, and Chamberlayne's *Pharonnida* to 15th-century aesthetic theory. All three works are didactic, preserve verisimilitude, and borrow from the romance tradition. *Paradise Lost* may have been intended as a five-act epic.

‹§ 319. FORKER, CHARLES R. "Robert Baron's Use of Webster, Shakespeare, and other Elizabethans." *Anglia*, 83 (1965), 176–98.
Indicates that Baron borrowed from *Arcadia*. Baron also borrowed from Webster, who had borrowed from *Arcadia*.

‹§ 320. "Frank Hogan's Library." *TLS*, June 14, 1946, p. 288.
The library contained a 1590 *Arcadia* and a 1595 *Apologie for Poetrie*.

‹§ 321. FRAUNCE, ABRAHAM. *The Arcadian Rhetorike*, Ethel Seaton, ed. Oxford: Blackwell, 1950. lv, 136 pp.
[Text is from 1588 edition.] Fraunce drew primarily on the Old *Arcadia* but knew the New *Arcadia* as well (p. xxxvii).

‹§ 322. FREEMAN, ROSEMARY. *English Emblem Books*. London: Chatto and Windus, 1948. xiv, 256 pp.
Relates the taste for emblem books to the taste for allegory in the period between 1586 and 1686. Quotes Sidney's account of Phalantus' tournament as an example of a burlesque of what had been a ritual (pp. 35–36).
Rev.: Mario Praz, *ES*, 30 (1949), 51–54; H. P. G., *QQ*, 56 (1949), 309–10.

◄§ 323. FRYE, NORTHROP. *Anatomy of Criticism: Four Essays.*
Princeton, N.J.: Princeton University Press, 1957. 383 pp.
Mentions *Arcadia,* among other pastorals, as an example of
archetypal symbolism (p. 100).
Rev.: David Daiches, *MP,* 56 (1958–1959), 69–72; G. L. Anderson, *SCN,* 16 (1958), 17–18.

◄§ 324. ————. "Varieties of Literary Utopias." *Daedalus,* 94
(1965), 323–47.
The Utopian myth, in contrast with the myth of the social contract, is a myth of the goal of a society. In a Utopia, people behave
ritualistically; their behavior is rational only when explained by a
member of the society. These rituals are a rational equivalent of
the habits of the writer's society. In an Arcadian version of Utopia,
man is influenced by a nature in which the satisfaction of desires
is paramount.

◄§ 325. GALM, JOHN ARNOLD. "Sidney's Arcadian Poems." Ph.D.
diss., Yale University, 1963. *Index,* 23 (1963), 124.
Examines the poems in a context of the prose. Writes that the
1593 folio contains the best arrangement of the poems. The poems
of each book relate to the action of that book. The theme is the
conflict of reason and passion.

◄§ 326. GEROULD, GORDON HALL. *The Patterns of English and
American Fiction: A History.* New York: Russell and Russell, 1966. 526 pp.
Arcadia is important because of its merit and influence. The
style is appropriate to its content, if not to the usual representation
of life given in a novel. It is a romance, not a novel, but Sidney is
a forerunner of the novelists (pp. 22–27).

◄§ 327. GILBERT, ALLAN H. *Machiavelli's* Prince *and its Forerunners:* The Prince *as a Typical Book de Regimine Principum.* Durham, N.C.: Duke University Press, 1938. xii,
266 pp.
Indicates the extent to which Machiavelli followed tradition.
Illustrates the concept of the good ruler with quotes from *Arcadia.*
Sidney seemed to believe that severity is sometimes necessary in a
ruler.

✍§ 328. ———. "A Poem Wrongly Attributed to Sidney." *MLN*, 57 (1942), 364.

In Feuillerat's *Complete Works of Sidney* the nine-line poem appearing in Volume II, p. 342, is a stanza from Spenser's *Faerie Queene*.

✍§ 329. GODSHALK, W. L. "Gabriel Harvey and Sidney's *Arcadia*." *MLR*, 59 (1964), 497–99.

Gabriel Harvey is not the author of the marginalia in the Harvard copy of the 1613 *Arcadia*. The handwriting is not his. Dates the marginalia by a ten-page insert published after 1616.

✍§ 330. ———. "Sidney and Shakespeare: Some Central Concepts." Ph.D. diss., Harvard University, 1963. *Index*, 23 (1963), 129.

Does not trace influence; compares Sidney's use of such themes as the role of the hero, the king, and the shepherd with Shakespeare's.

✍§ 331. ———. "Sidney's Revision of the *Arcadia*, Books III–V." *PQ*, 43 (1964), 171–84.

Reassesses the evidence that Sanford revised Books III–V of the 1593 edition of the *Arcadia* and concludes that the state of the text indicates that he did not. Contemporary evidence indicates that Sidney had not finished revising. Sanford leaves unrevised passages for which revision would be obvious. The revisions are consistent with Sidney's method.

✍§ 332. GOHN, ERNEST S. "Primitivistic Motifs in Sidney's *Arcadia*." *PMASAL*, 45 (1960), 363–71.

Agrees with Lois Whitney [*SP*, 24 (1927)] that the major emphasis in *Arcadia* is on political philosophy and the necessity for virtuous action, but suggests that a minor theme is one of primitive simplicity. Suggests that the failure to reconcile the two themes flaws the book. Using the age of chivalry as the setting indicates "chronological primitivism." The natives of Arcadia live in a state of cultural primitivism. One of these natives, Dorcus, condemns civilization.

✍§ 333. GOLDMAN, MARCUS S. "Sidney and Harington as Opponents of Superstition." *JEGP*, 54 (1955), 526–48.

Indicates that Sidney was antagonistic toward superstition. Refutes the evidence that Sidney was interested in astrology.

Sidney visited Dr. Dee to please friends. Sonnet 26 was not intended literally. The oracles in *Arcadia* are designed to show either that such utterances are fraudulent or that they are inexorable decrees of fate. Supports this stand by reference to the speeches of Musidorus and Philanx.

*§ 334. GREAVES, MARGARET. *The Blazon of Honour: A Study in Renaissance Magnanimity*. New York: Barnes and Noble, 1964. 142 pp.

Traces the use of the word "magnanimity" through Medieval and Renaissance literature. Writes that Sidney personified that ideal and that his characters Musidorus and Pyrocles exhibit it (pp. 62–74). Traditionally this ideal includes courtesy, chivalry, and generosity; Sidney added to these qualities love of learning and desire for public service.

Rev.: O. B. Hardison, Jr., *Renaissance News*, 18 (1965), 152–53.

*§ 335. HALLAM, GEORGE WALTER, JR. "Functional Paradox in Sidney's Revised *Arcadia*." Ph.D. diss., University of Florida, 1959. *DA*, 20 (1959), 1014.

Theme, structure, plot, and style of the revised *Arcadia* give it unity. It should be interpreted in the framework of Ramistic logic.

*§ 336. HALLIDAY, F. E. *A Shakespeare Companion, 1550–1950*. New York: Funk and Wagnalls, 1952. xiv, 742 pp.

Along with the subplot of *King Lear*, Shakespeare borrowed some of the names used in *Cymbeline*, *The Winter's Tale*, and *Pericles* from *Arcadia*.

*§ 337. HAMILTON, A. C. "Et in Arcadia Ego." [Review article.] *MLQ*, 27 (1966), 332–50.

[See 294, 366, 542.] Writes that Davis encounters problems in interpretation because of his 1593 text. Questions Davis' Christian reading of the text and his argument that the eclogues divide the book into themes. Criticizes Lanham's discussion of Gynecia. Kalstone's study is more accomplished that either of the others, possibly because Kalstone had a greater body of criticism to use, but his method is too limiting for a thorough examination of the sonnets.

❧ 338. HANFORD, JAMES HOLLY, AND SARA RUTH WATSON. "Personal Allegory in the *Arcadia:* Philisides and Lelius." *MP,* 32 (1934), 1–10.

Arcadia's allegory is similar to *The Faerie Queene*'s in that it is inconsistent. The earliest allegorical identifications—those in Aubrey's *Brief Lives*—were Lady Northumberland with Pamela, Frances Walsingham with Helen, Philip Sidney with Amphialus and with Philisides, Penelope Devereux with Philoclea, Lady Cox with Miso, Lady Lucy with Mopsa, Lord Rich with Pyrocles, and the earl of Northumberland with Musidorus. Writes that the tournament held in honor of the Queen of Iberia may be based on a tournament held November 17, 1581, in which Sir Henry Lee and Sidney ran in competition against one another. Sir Henry Lee may be the prototype for Lelius. Elizabeth may be the model for Andromana.

❧ 339. HANSSEN, SELBY. "An Analysis of Sir Philip Sidney's Metrical Experiments in the *Arcadia.*" Ph.D. diss., Yale University, 1942. *DDAAU,* 9 (1942), 109.

Studies Sidney's attempts to write quantitative verse. Lists common Latin meters and traces Renaissance attempts to use them. Analyzes "O my thoughts' sweet food, my, my only owner," "If mine eyes can speak to do hearty errand," "O sweet woods, the delight of solitariness," "Reason, tell me thy mind, if here be reason," "My muse, what ails this ardour," and "Fair rocks, goodly rivers, sweet woods, when shall I see peace? Peace." Does not find much poetic merit in the verse.

❧ 340. HELTZEL, VIRGIL B. "The Arcadian Hero." *PQ,* 41 (1962), 173–80.

Pyrocles and Musidorus, like Sidney himself, exemplify the ideal prince and hero. This hero inspires admiration by his truthfulness and courtesy. The chief attribute of the hero is probably greatness of mind, but beauty of body and noble birth are also attributes. The hero is motivated by a love of virtue and virtuous action.

❧ 341. HENDRICKSON, G. L. "Elizabethan Quantitative Hexameters." *PQ,* 28 (1949), 237–60.

Quantitative verse was pronounced by actual English accents. Illustrates with verses from Sidney and Harvey. The 19th-century opinion of Sidney's quantitative verse is incorrect.

◄§ 342. HENINGER, S. K., JR. "The Renaissance Perversion of Pastoral." *JHI*, 22 (1961), 254–61.

Writes that the Renaissance perverted the classical genre of the pastoral. In its pure form, the pastoral is optimistic and simple, as it is in Spenser's Pastorella episode. The Renaissance changed both purpose (using it as either satire or allegory) and method (no longer a dialogue form). Both satire and moral allegory are foreign to the pure pastoral. Sidney's *Arcadia* is a perversion of the pastoral form. Pastoral was not a great Renaissance genre.

◄§ 343. HIGHET, GILBERT. *The Classical Tradition: Greek and Roman Influences on Western Literature.* London: Oxford University Press, 1949. xxxviii, 763 pp.

Arcadia is both pastoral and romance (pp. 169–77).

◄§ 344. HOGAN, PATRICK G., JR. "Sidney and Titian: Painting in the *Arcadia* and the *Defence.*" *South Central Bulletin*, 27, No. 4 (1967), 9–15.

Studies the influence of iconographic materials upon *Arcadia*, *Astrophel and Stella*, and the *Defence*. Finds similarities between Titian's work and Sidney's. The description of Basilius as Danäe's governess (Book II) was based on a painting, possibly one by Titian. Likewise the song in Book II that mentions Leda may be based on a painting. Either Titian's or Tintoretto's painting of Tarquin and Lucretia may be the source of the reference to Lucretia in the *Defence*. The picture of Diana and Actaeon in Book I of *Arcadia* may refer to a painting by Titian.

◄§ 345. ———. "Sir Philip Sidney's *Arcadia* and Edmund Spenser's *Faerie Queene*: An Analysis of the Personal, Philosophic, and Iconographic Relationships." Ph.D. diss., Vanderbilt University, 1965. *DA*, 26 (1965), 1021–22.

Traces the relationship between the two men. Evaluates the evidence for a friendship and indicates the use each made of Renaissance traditions. Indicates the influence of pictorial works on each.

◄§ 346. HOLZINGER, WALTER. "*Der Abentheurliche Simplicissimus* and Sir Philip Sidney's *Arcadia*." *CollG*, 2 (1969), 184–94.

Arcadia influenced Grimmelshausen's *Simplicissimus*. The description of the battle of Wittstock, instead of being autobiographical, is taken from Martin Opitz' translation of *Arcadia*.

ᴥᵹ 347. HUDSON, HOYT HOPEWELL. *The Epigram in the English Renaissance.* Princeton, N.J.: Princeton University Press, 1947. viii, 178 pp.

Defines the epigram and examines the epigrams of Renaissance writers. Mentions several of Daniel Rogers' poems that might be useful in a biography of Sidney (p. 137). Sidney's poem, "Virtue, beauty, and speech . . . ," is a *carmen correlativum.*
Rev.: Leicester Bradner, *MLN*, 63 (1948), 577–78; V. B. Heltzel, *PQ*, 27 (1948), 285–88.

ᴥᵹ 348. HUGHES, MERRIT Y. "New Evidence on the Charge that Milton Forged the Pamela Prayer in the *Eikon Basilike*." *RES*, n.s., 3 (1952), 130–40.

Reviews the evidence against Milton on the occasion of Madan's *A New Bibliography of the* Eikon Basilike *of King Charles I with a Note on the Authorship.* Agrees with Madan that King Charles probably annexed the prayer.

ᴥᵹ 349. HUNTER, G. K. "The Marking of *Sententiae* in Elizabethan Printed Plays, Poems, and Romances." Transactions of the Bibliographical Society. *The Library*, 5th series, 6 (1951), 171–88.

Between 1500 and 1600 many books, including *Arcadia*, were printed with *sententiae* marked by such typographical devices as gnomic pointing. The 1655 edition of *Arcadia* seems to have been a pedagogical text, for nearly all the *sententiae* are marked. Lists the gnomic pointing in a number of editions of *Arcadia*. Of the texts of the Old *Arcadia*, only the Clifford MS has gnomic pointing, possibly done by the owner.

ᴥᵹ 350. ISLER, ALAN D. "The Allegory of the Hero and Sidney's Two *Arcadias*." *SP*, 65 (1968), 171–91.

The meaning of the hero is central to *Arcadia*. His main attributes are courage and wisdom, polarities around which related values assemble: wisdom draws the values of reason, soul, and contemplation; courage draws the values of the body, action, and passion. Pyrocles represents courage; Musidorus represents wisdom. All the names taken by either prince relate to his value. Pyrocles kills the lion, an animal noted for its courage; Musidorus kills the bear, noted for its stupidity. In the trial episode Pyrocles is accused of rape; Musidorus, of treason. If either of the princes is pre-eminent, it is Musidorus.

◄§ 351. ———. "Heroic Poetry and Sidney's Two *Arcadias*."
   PMLA, 83 (1968), 368–79.
Both *Arcadias* belong to the genre of heroic poetry. Neither
should be measured by 20th-century standards of the pastoral or
the epic, nor by Italian Renaissance standards of proper structure.
For the Elizabethans a heroic poem had a serious, moral purpose
and was in the form of a fictional narrative. The *Defence* indicates
that Sidney believed poetry to be a better teaching device than
history because the poet tells what ought to be.

◄§ 352. ———. "Moral Philosophy and the Family in Sidney's
   Arcadia." *HLQ*, 31 (1968), 359–71.
Examines *Arcadia* in terms of *recta ratio* and Elizabethan ideas
of correspondence. Basilius' failure to use reason causes a failure
in proper degree, which results in a disordered kingdom. His fall
begins when he attempts to know the future. Reason corresponded
for the Elizabethans with the father or the governor. After Basilius'
fall, other members of his family fall also. The episode of the
Paphlagonian King functions as a subplot mirroring the main
action. Many of the themes of *Arcadia* relate to the concept that
reason should rule passion.

◄§ 353. ———. "The Moral Philosophy of Sidney's Two *Arcadias*: A Study of Some Principal Themes." Ph.D. diss.,
   Columbia University, 1966. *Index*, 26 (1966), 143;
   DA, 30 (1969), 1567A.
Both *Arcadias* are heroic literature, based on the allegory of
the hero. Both deal with the relation between the body politic
and the natural body. *Arcadia* is built on the polarities of courage
and wisdom, of passion and reason, of the allegorical significance
of Achilles and Ulysses. Each prince represents the pole that his
name implies (pp. 132–45). Musidorus represents wisdom, and
Pyrocles courage (p. 145). The main plot deals with Basilius and
the theme of the correspondence of the body politic with the
natural body (pp. 162–76).

◄§ 354. ———. "Sidney, Shakespeare, and the 'Slain–Not
   Slain.'" *UTQ*, 37 (1968), 175–85.
While Sidney may have felt it the duty of men to rebel against
a tyrant, in the commons' revolt of *Arcadia* he expresses contempt
for the rebels. While the humor of this scene has been criticized
by Zandvoort and Praz, Sidney had to preserve decorum. The
nobles could not fight in equal battle with the rebels. Compares

the scene to Jack Cade's rebellion in 2 *Henry VI*; in both, rebellion is given the tone of a saturnalia. But Sidney mocks the victim; Shakespeare does not. Suggests that Kenneth Burke's phrase the "slain–not slain" applies here. The mob is cartoonlike; the reader is not supposed to take them as real characters.

◄§ 355. JAKOBSON, ROMAN. "The Grammatical Texture of a Sonnet from Sir Philip Sidney's *Arcadia*." In *Studies in Language and Literature in Honour of M. Schlaugh*, Mieczyslaw Brahmer, Stanislaw Helsztynshi, and Julian Krzyzanowski, eds., pp. 165–73. Warsaw: Scientific Publishers, 1966.

Analyzes "Loved I am, and yet complaine of love" in relation to its syntactical elements, shifts in pronouns, variations of the root word "love" (*lev*), and the structural pattern.

◄§ 356. JEWKES, W. T. "The Literature of Travel and the Mode of Romance in the Renaissance." *BNYPL*, 67 (1963), 219–36.

Travel narratives have many of the characteristics of romance and should be considered literature. Both present an idealized concept of the self, deal in shipwrecks, and use the journey motif. In Hakluyt, as in Sidney, experience is idealized. The captains from travel literature resemble the heroes from *Arcadia*. Both genres include noble savages.

◄§ 357. JUEL-JENSEN, BENT. "Sidney's *Arcadia*, 'London, 1599': A Distinguished 'Ghost.' " *BC*, 16 (1967), 80.

The *Arcadia* listed by Ramage as published in 1599 by Matthew Lownes is actually a 1613 *Arcadia* lacking the title page. Alexander Pope substituted the title page that bears the imaginary date of 1599.

◄§ 358. ————. "Sir Philip Sidney's *Arcadia*, 1638: An Unrecorded Issue." *The Library*, 22 (1967), 67–69.

Lists variations in a preliminary text for the 1638 edition. The known 1638 edition is a reprint of the 1633 edition. The newly found preliminary text consists of the first four leaves and differs from the 1638 text in both type and ornament.

◄§ 359. ————. "Some Uncollected Authors XXXIV: Sir Philip Sidney, 1554–1586." *BC*, 11 (1962), 468–79.

Gives a check list of editions of *Arcadia* up to 1739, the location of copies, and textual comments on the editions.

✌§ 360. KALSTONE, DAVID. "The Transformation of *Arcadia*: Sannazaro and Sir Philip Sidney." *CL*, 15 (1963), 234–49.
Traces the motif of the exiled lover from Petrarch to Sannazaro to Sidney. Petrarch often uses a pastoral landscape to remind the lover of his absent love. Sannazaro idealized the Arcadian landscape. In a double sestina based upon Petrarch's "enclosed valley," he combines complaint and joy when the lover is rewarded as a poet because he is unhappy as a lover. Sidney's eclogues borrow their dramatic structure from Sannazaro. The poem "Ye goatherd gods . . ." begins with the "enclosed valley," and the elements of the landscape become metaphors for the inner world. But Sidney emphasizes the pain, not the joy, of the pastoral. His poem is a criticism of the Arcadian world.

✌§ 361. KAULA, DAVID. "The Low Style." *SEL*, 6 (1966), 43–57.
Nashe's style parodies the "complex harmonies" of *Arcadia* and *Faerie Queene*. Nashe's world view is one of chance and violence, consequently he uses the low style.

✌§ 362. KING, WALTER N. "John Lyly and Elizabethan Rhetoric." *SP*, 52 (1955), 149–61.
[See 304.] Analyzes Lyly's use of logic in its context to find that he adapted rhetoric to narrative. Sidney's logic taken out of context is superior to Lyly's, as Duhamel writes, but Lyly's purpose was narrative, not argumentative. He wanted to adapt rhetoric to narrative. In the debate Duhamel analyzes, Lyly's purpose is to show Euphues as a false wit.

✌§ 363. KNOLL, ROBERT E. "Spenser and the Voyage of the Imagination." *WHR*, 13 (1959), 249–55.
The lines in *Muiopotmos* that describe the rape of Europa were inspired by Titian, as well as by Ovid. Sidney may have brought a reproduction of Titian's painting to England, where Spenser may have seen it. Titian's painting of Actaeon and Diana is similar to the description of them in *Arcadia*.

✌§ 364. LAGUARDIA, ERIC. "Figural Imitation in English Renaissance Poetry." In *Proceedings of the 4th Conference of the Institute of Comparative Literature Association, Fribourg, 1964*, Francois Yost, ed., pp. 844–54. The Hague: Mouton, 1966.
Distinguishes between Medieval figural imitation, with its dependence upon divine order, and Renaissance imitation, which

gives more value to temporal experience. The "Garden of Adonis" illustrates the conjunction of ideal and real nature. Mira in *Arcadia* joins both human love and cosmic harmony. Marvell's "The Coronet" unites experience with the ideal in art.

365. ———. *Nature Redeemed: The Imitation of Order in Three Renaissance Poems.* Studies in English Literature 31. The Hague: Mouton Press, 1966. 180 pp.

Studies Books III and IV of *The Faerie Queene, Comus,* and *All's Well that Ends Well* to illustrate the problem of dealing with divine order without losing earthly order. The episode between Pamela and Cecropia in *Arcadia* shows the conflict between two types of love, natural and spiritual. Pamela tries to reconcile the two (pp. 40–46).

366. LANHAM, RICHARD A. "The Old *Arcadia.*" In *Sidney's* Arcadia, pp. 181–405. New Haven, Conn.: Yale University Press, 1965.

[Ph.D. diss., Yale University, 1963. *Index,* 23 (1963), 124.] In Old *Arcadia* the Duke's retreat provides motivation for the plot and illustrates the dangers of retirement. Major themes are the conflict between love and reason and between political life and private passion. Analyzes the formal speeches in terms of classical rhetoric and concludes that some speeches are parodies. The narrator's role is similar to that of the Greek chorus: to evaluate the action.

Rev.: Jean Robertson, *RES,* n.s., 16 (1966), 430–32; A. C. Hamilton, *MLQ,* 27 (1966), 332–50 [See 337].

367. LEVIN, HARRY. *The Myth of the Golden Age in the Renaissance.* Bloomington: Indiana University Press, 1969. 231 pp.

Surveys uses of the golden-age myth. Chapter I describes the growth of the myth in Greek and Roman literature. Chapter II notes that passionate love became associated with the myth later than its origins. Chapter III deals with the effect of Renaissance exploration upon the myth. Chapter IV relates fictional uses of the myth to social criticism. The plot of *Arcadia* indicates that even in the golden age, perfection is impossible (p. 98). The final chapters deal with playwrights' use of the myth and the historical time at which the golden age was believed to occur.

൴§ 368. Lewis, C. S. "Sidney and Spenser." In *English Literature in the Sixteenth Century Excluding Drama*, pp. 318–93. Oxford: Clarendon Press, 1954.

Compares Sidney's verse with that of Sackville and Wyatt to illustrate the change from "drab" to "golden" poetry (pp. 325–27). Sonnet cycles, such as *Astrophel and Stella*, are lyrical meditations, not narratives (pp. 327–28). For the literary historian the 1593 text of *Arcadia* is the most important; it was the one read by Sidney's contemporaries (p. 333). Defends its style; its decorations are functional (p. 337). It is the expression of an ideal (p. 340). The *Defence* shows man surpassing nature (p. 345).

Rev.: R. W. Zandvoort, *ES*, 37 (1956), 271–74; Yvor Winters, *HudR*, 8 (1955–56), 281–87; *TLS*, September 17, 1954, p. 592.

൴§ 369. Lewis, Piers Ingersoll. "Literary and Political Attitudes in Sidney's *Arcadia*." Ph.D. diss., Harvard University, 1964. *Index*, 24 (1964), 130.

Sidney illustrates in Pyrocles and Musidorus a fortunate fall from the world in which reason should govern passion and in which a man must choose between contemplative and active life (p. 1). Both lovers are improved by their fall (p. 1). In *Arcadia's* golden world Sidney can maintain both heroic and pastoral values (p. 42). The conflict of values appears only in love, not in politics (p. 129). In *Arcadia* public good depends upon private love (p. 141).

൴§ 370. Lindheim, Nancy Rothwax. "Sidney's *Arcadia*, Book II; Retrospective Narration." *SP*, 64 (1967), 159–86.

[See 297; also Edwin A. Greenlaw. "Sidney's *Arcadia* as an Example of Elizabethan Allegory." *Kittredge Anniversary Papers*, 1913, pp. 327–37.] Greenlaw and Davis oversimplify the retrospective narration of Book II. These narratives give alternate views about moral virtue. Musidorus' stories illustrate public virtue; Pyrocles' stories illustrate public integrity. The movement is from simple to complex. The tales show the princes testing their education.

൴§ 371. ———. "The Structures of Sidney's *Arcadia*." Ph.D. diss., University of California, 1966. *DA*, 27 (1967), 3462A.

Studies three types of structure in *Arcadia*. The rhetorical structure is composed of antithetic *topoi*, such as reason-passion; the tonal structure involves the operation of a three-part scheme;

and the narrative structure provides the relation between episodes and main plot.

◄§ 372. LINDSAY, JEAN STIRLING. "A Survey of the Town-Country and Court-Country Themes in Non-Dramatic Elizabethan Literature." Ph.D. diss., Cornell University, 1943. Cornell University, *Abstracts of Theses Accepted in Partial Satisfaction of the Requirements for the Doctor's Degrees* (1943), 37–40.

Town-country and court-country themes were popular in literature written between 1558 and 1603. Sidney, as well as Wyatt, Spenser, Lyly, Gascoigne, Lodge, and Greene, used these themes even though he, as were most of the other writers, was from the city. Sidney's pastoralism was literary, not personal.

◄§ 373. McALEER, JOHN I. "Thomas Lodge's Verse Interludes." *College Language Association Journal*, 6 (1962), 83–89.

The verse interludes are Lodge's best work. When Lodge followed Lyly's euphuism, Greene's narratives, or Sidney's poetry, he harmed his literary output. In *Forbonius and Prisceria* he tried to blend the style of Lyly and Sidney. The lyric tone of *Rosalynde* also shows Sidney's influence. Shakespeare retained this lyricism in *As You Like It*.

◄§ 374. McCOWN, GARY MASON. "The Epithalamium in the English Renaissance." Ph.D. diss., University of North Carolina, 1968. DA, 30 (1969), 220A.

Renaissance writers, such as Sidney, Davies, Spenser, and Chapman, revived the classical epithalamium. The form was first used in the Neo-Latin verse of Pontano and Erasmus. Sidney's epithalamium in *Arcadia* brought the form to England. Spenser used it to promote Christian and humanistic ideas of marriage. In the Stuart period it was used for courtly compliment. By the 18th century the form was no longer popular.

◄§ 375. McCoy, DOROTHY SCHUCHMAN. *Tradition and Convention: A Study of Periphrasis in English Pastoral Poetry from 1557–1715*. London: Mouton and Company, 1965. 289 pp. [Ph.D. diss., University of Pittsburgh, 1962. DA, 23 (1963), 3888–89.] Pastoral poetry was associated with a low style in the Renaissance in which periphrasis was inappropriate. But Spenser, Sidney, and others used it in pastorals, and its use led to a false pastoral language and setting. In *Arcadia*, style follows content (pp. 54–61). Periphrasis occurs in the shepherds' descriptions of their loves (p. 56). Few examples of it occur in the middle style (p. 57), but it occurs in the high style and in the narrator's comments (pp. 58–59).

ᴈ§ 376. McNEIR, WALDO F. "The Behaviour of Brigadore: *The Faerie Queene* V, 3, 33–34." *N&Q*, n.s., 1 (1954), 103–4.
Suggests that Brigadore's behavior upon being restored to Guyon has its source in Ariosto, Montaigne, and Heliodorus, perhaps even in Sidney. Musidorus calms his horse in Book II of *Arcadia* in the same way that Guyon calms Brigadore.

ᴈ§ 377. ———. "Trial by Combat in Elizabethan Literature." *NS*, 15 (1966), 101–12.
Traces the history of the Medieval trial by combat and examines its effect on Elizabethan literature. The Elizabethans knew Caxton's translation of the *Boke of Fayttes of Armes and of Chyvalrye* and Thomas of Woodstock's *Ordenaunce and Fourme of Fighting within Listes*. Such trials took place during the Medieval period. *Arcadia* includes several such trials and concludes with Euarchus refusing one to Pyrocles. Greene used the device in his translation of *Orlando Furioso*, as did Spenser in *The Faerie Queene* and Shakespeare in the history plays.

ᴈ§ 378. McPHERSON, DAVID C. "A Possible Origin for Mopsa in Sidney's *Arcadia*." *RenQ*, 21 (1968), 420–28.
Accepts Ringler's suggestion that Mopsa may be drawn from Virgil's Mopsus, but suggests that she, unlike Virgil's Mopsus, is neither eloquent nor successful in love. The source for Mopsus' name may be the Dutch word for pug-dog, *mops*. A print by Bruegel supports a combination of the two sources. Sidney's treatment of Mopsa indicates the superiority of the New to the Old *Arcadia*.

ᴈ§ 379. MARENCO, FRANCO. *Arcadia Puritana: L'uso della tradizione nella prima* Arcadia *di Sir Philip Sidney*. Bari: Adriatica Editrice, 1968. 240 pp.
Reinterprets Sidney's Old *Arcadia* in relation to contemporary religious thought. Each of the first four books deals with a separate virtue: prudence, temperance, justice, and fortitude. The fifth book illustrates the triumph of Providence over pagan fortune.

≈§ 380. ———. "Double Plot in Sidney's Old *Arcadia*."
MLR, 64 (1969), 248–63.

Critical emphasis upon political ideas and genres has tended to overlook the subplot of Dametas and his family. The princes move from virtue to vice, and this progressive anarchy mirrors the rebellion in Arcadia.

≈§ 381. ———. "Per una nuova interpretazione dell *Arcadia* di Sidney." *EM*, 17 (1966), 10–48.

Interprets *Arcadia* in relation to Protestant Neo-Platonism, not in relation to genres. It is an allegory of human life based on Calvinistic thought. Relates it to the writings of Greville and Davies.

≈§ 382. ———. "Sidney e l'*Arcadia* nella critica letteraria." *FeL*, 12 (1966), 337–76.

Reviews the scholarship on *Arcadia* from the time of its publication to the present. Suggests that such genres as pastoral and romance are inadequate to describe it. *Arcadia* has the form of a drama and may be called a moral allegory.

≈§ 383. MARSH, T. N. "Elizabethan Wit in Metaphor and Conceit: Sidney, Shakespeare, Donne." *EM*, 13 (1962), 25–29.

Both Donne and Shakespeare use images appearing in *Arcadia*. Donne's and Shakespeare's inversion of conventional compliments are like Sidney's poem about Mopsa. Donne and Shakespeare both wrote descriptions similar to the shipwreck in Book I of *Arcadia*.

≈§ 384. MARTIN, L. C. "Marvell, Massinger and Sidney." *RES*, n.s., 2 (1951), 374–75.

[See 274, 275.] The *Arcadia* of 1590 may be the source for stanza seven of Marvell's "The Definition of Love." Philoclea's soliloquy in Book II, chapter 5, contains similar themes of love, hope, despair, and impossibility.

≈§ 385. MILL, ADAIR. "Quantitative Verse and the Development of Sixteenth Century English Prosody." *Ingiliz Filolojisi Dergisi* (Studies by Members of the English Department, University of Istanbul), 2 (1951), 29–54.

Quantitative verse influenced the development of English verse by promoting freedom of rhythm and an interplay of stress and quantity. Sidney's quantitative verse tends to ignore the actual length of syllables and depends instead on position. Although Sidney's quantitative verse is not outstanding, Sidney did not, as Harvey did, confuse stress with quantity. Campion's system was the most realistic.

᷍§ 386. MITCHELL, ALISON, AND KATHARINE FOSTER. "Sir William Alexander's Supplement to Book III of Sidney's *Arcadia*." *The Library*, 25 (1969), 234–41.

Four breaks in a triangular tailpiece indicate that Stansby's shop printed the 1627 *Arcadia*. The Supplement was probably printed after August 31, 1616. Since the two Supplements owned by Dr. Juel-Jensen differ in words and punctuation, Alexander may have revised the first text. The amended text was used in the Dublin, 1621, printing.

᷍§ 387. MONTEMAYOR, JORGE DE. *A Critical Edition of Yong's Translation of George of Montemayor's* Diana *and* Gil Polo's Enamoured Diana, Judith M. Kennedy, ed. Oxford: Oxford University Press, 1968. lxxx, 468 pp.

Contains the text of both works and an analysis of the pastoral form. *Diana* was influential in England. Sidney translated two songs from *Diana* in his *Certain Sonnets* (xxxiii). *Diana* was both a model and an inspiration for *Arcadia* (pp. xxiv–xxv). Although both *Arcadia*s are pastorals, in his revision Sidney follows *Diana* most closely adding more narration by the characters, more heroic material, Neo-Platonic ethics, a humorous treatment of love, and additional variety of rhyme (pp. xxv–xxxviii).

᷍§ 388. MOREAU, P. "Un poèm de Sir Philip Sidney traduit par Paul Claudel." *Bulletin de la Société Paul Claudel*, 8 (1961), 4–5.

Contains the text of Claudel's translation of "My true love hath my heart . . .".

᷍§ 389. MORRIS, HARRY. "Richard Barnfield: The Affectionate Shepheard." *Tulane Studies in English*, 10 (1960), 13–38.

Barnfield's pastoral verse has not received the attention it deserves. Barnfield praised Sidney in "The Shepherd's Content." Sidney influenced "The Affectionate Shepherd," but there is no evidence of borrowing in "The Tears" and in "The Content."

✍§ 390. MUIR, KENNETH, AND JOHN F. DANBY. "*Arcadia* and *King Lear*." *N&Q*, 195 (1950), 49–51.

From *Arcadia* Shakespeare may have borrowed the use of the words "unnatural dealings," as well as Plangus' and Basilius' debate on suicide and the description of Philoclea weeping in Book III.

✍§ 391. NEELY, CAROL THOMAS. "Speaking True: Shakespeare's Use of the Elements of Pastoral Romance." Ph.D. diss., Yale University, 1969. *DA*, 30 (1970), 3433A.

Shakespeare adapted the four elements of the pastoral: the characteristic story, the two communities, the landscape, and the lovers. These elements, used in *Arcadia* and *The Faerie Queene*, culminate in *The Winter's Tale*.

✍§ 392. NORTON, DAN S., AND PETER RUSHTON. *Classical Myths in English Literature*. New York: Rinehart, 1952. 444 pp.

Mentions the use of Arcadia as a place name in Greece and in literature (pp. 49–54). Identifies Sidney's use of the myth of Philomela in "The nightingale, as soon as April bringeth," (p. 301).

✍§ 393. O'BRIEN, PAULINE W. "The 'Speaking Picture' in the Works of Sidney." Ph.D. diss., Duke University, 1954. *DDAAU*, 21 (1954), 260.

Descriptions help establish the themes of love and beauty in *Arcadia*. The "speaking picture" is at the heart of the *Defence*. Sidney believed that the painter should convey a conceptual meaning (p. 68). In both *Defence* and *Arcadia*, pictures are a representation of virtues, vices, and passions (p. 92). Much of the material added to the revised *Arcadia* illustrates the theme of beauty or of love.

✍§ 394. OLSON, PAUL A. "*A Midsummer Night's Dream* and the Meaning of Court Marriage." *ELH*, 24 (1957), 95–119.

The occasion for *A Midsummer Night's Dream* is important to an understanding of its meaning and the Renaissance philosophy of love. In the play, iconological referents are used to embody such abstractions as love and reason. Theseus is a symbol of reason, and his marriage to Hippolita symbolizes reason ruling passion. Pyrocles' disguise in *Arcadia* indicates passion ruling reason. The settings and the other lovers in the play illustrate both reasonable and unreasonable love.

✥§ 395. PARKER, ROBERT W. "Narrative Structure and Thematic Development in Sidney's Original *Arcadia.*" Ph.D. diss., Columbia University, 1965. *DA,* 28 (1967), 1406A.

Reconciles the comic plot of *Arcadia* with its moral themes. *Arcadia* is syllogistic, not, as *Aethiopica,* episodic.

✥§ 396. PATCHELL, MARY. *The Palmerin Romances in Elizabethan Prose Fiction.* New York: Columbia University Press, 1947. xiii, 157 pp.

Palmerin and *Amadis* were the type for the Spanish romance. *Amadis* influenced Sidney and may have been a source for *Arcadia* (pp. 115–27). The motifs of falling in love with a picture and of faithful friends occurs in both. Sidney's characterization is better than that used in the Spanish romances.

✥§ 397. PERKINSON, RICHARD H. "The Epic in Five Acts." *SP,* 43 (1946), 465–81.

The Old *Arcadia, Gondibert,* and *Pharonnida* follow a structure developed in the Middle Ages and derived from Senecan drama. In Old *Arcadia* the division into five books follows the five-act division of a Senecan play; the eclogues in *Arcadia* function as chorus. That Sidney revised *Arcadia* suggests he found dramatic structure limiting.

✥§ 398. PETTET, E. C. *Shakespeare and the Romantic Tradition.* London: Staples, 1949. 208 pp.

Romance literature came to Elizabethan England through Medieval romance, the Italian romantic epic, Petrarchan poetry, and early Spanish and Italian novels. Sidney and Spenser were influenced by romantic writings, and they then influenced other Elizabethan writers. *Arcadia* is a typical romance, concerned with lovemaking and adventure and with the convention of poetic justice. Sidney and Spenser may have used this form because it was one of the few nondidactic forms available (pp. 23–32). See also Index.

Rev.: *TLS,* April 28, 1950, p. 258; Kenneth Muir, *MLR,* 45 (1950), 529–31.

✥§ 399. POIRIER, MICHEL. "Quelques Sources des Poemes de Sidney." *EA,* 11 (1958), 150–54.

Ovid's *Metamorphoses* may be the direct or indirect source of allusions to Daphné and Hyacinthe in *Arcadia;* the "Seven wonders of England" and the poem addressed to a glove were both borrowed from Petrarch; and either Ronsard or Petrarch may be the source for the image of tears swelling a brook.

◄§ 400. ———. "Sidney's Influence on A Midsummer Night's Dream." SP, 44 (1947), 483–89.

Suggests some previously unnoticed verbal parallels between Sidney's works and Shakespeare's plays. The "induction" scene in The Taming of the Shrew contains a description similar to the one of the paintings in Kalander's garden. Daphné is similar to Atalanta. Hippolyta's account of the hunt is similar to one in Arcadia. Theseus' speech, "lunatic, lover and poet," may be taken from the account of poetic imagination in the Defence.

◄§ 401. POTEZ, HENRI. "Le Premier Roman Anglais Traduit en Français." RHL, 11 (1904), 42–55.

Answers Jusserand (Le Roman au Temps de Shakespeare. Paris, 1887.) Pandosto, translated by L. Regnault in 1615, not Arcadia, translated by Baudoin in 1624, was the first novel translated into French. Regnault's translation is a free one.

◄§ 402. PRAZ, MARIO. "The Duchess of Malfi."

TLS, June 18, 1954, p. 393.

While the supposed execution in Arcadia is the source for the execution in The Duchess of Malfi, as Lucas suggests in his edition of the Works, the source for the dead man's hand is Herodotus.

◄§ 403. PYLE, FITZROY. "King Lear and Sidney's Arcadia."

TLS, November 11, 1949, p. 733.

[See 262.] Denies that the image "As flies to wanton boys" comes from Arcadia, as Armstrong suggested. The image was an Elizabethan commonplace.

◄§ 404. ———. "Twelfth Night, King Lear and Arcadia."

MLR, 43 (1948), 449–55.

Arcadia is a source for Twelfth Night, as well as King Lear. The tone, the comic duel, and the gulling of Malvolio come from Arcadia. In Lear, the subplot and possibly the disguises, as well as the theme connecting the king's welfare with the country's welfare, are from Arcadia.

405. QUAINTANCE, RICHARD E., JR. "The French Source of Robert Greene's 'What Thing is Love.'"
N&Q, 208 (1963), 295–96.

Points out that Greene's poem is a translation in part of "Description d'Amour" by Mellin de Saint Gelais. Mentions that Doron's eclogue is more mock pastoral than mock blazon. The poem about Mopsa is an example of mock blazon. Sidney redistributed the conventional comparisons, while Greene replaced them with more rustic ones.

406. RANSOM, JOHN CROWE. *The New Criticism*. Norfolk, Conn.: New Directions, 1941. xiii, 339 pp.

Quotes Sidney's "Ye goatherd gods . . ." with Empson's explication. Agrees with Empson's use of the term "diffuse" to explain the effect of the metrical pattern, but writes that the poem is a miniature tragedy and that it is a conventional expression of sorrow (pp. 103–14).

Rev.: L. Bogan, *Nation*, 153 (1941), 37.

407. REES, JOAN. "Fulke Greville and the Revisions of *Arcadia*." *RES*, n.s., 17 (1966), 54–57.

Greville's directions for revision of Books IV and V of *Arcadia* may refer to a third version, a revised Old *Arcadia*. Little evidence exists for concluding the *Arcadia* of 1593 with the revised last two books from the Old *Arcadia*. The revisions were probably Sidney's, however.

408. RIBNER, IRVING. *Jacobean Tragedy: The Quest for Moral Order*. London: Methuen and Company, 1962. 179 pp.

Suggests that Ford's *Broken Heart* is reminiscent of *Arcadia* (p. 156).

409. ———. "Machiavelli and Sidney: The *Arcadia* of 1590." *SP*, 47 (1950), 152–72.

Even though Machiavelli was a model for some of the villains in *Arcadia*, Sidney's theories of government agree with Machiavelli's. Basilius is similar to Machiavelli's rulers. Sidney's theories on subjugation, illustrated in the war between the Helots and Lacedœmonians and explained in *Discourse on Irish Affairs*, echo Machiavelli. Also, Sidney's suggestions for reforming a corrupt state parallel Machiavelli's. Probably Sidney did not borrow directly from Machiavelli.

⋐§ 410. ———. "Machiavelli and Sir Philip Sidney." Ph.D. diss.,
University of North Carolina, 1950. *University of North
Carolina Record* No. 478, *Research in Progress*
(1950), 113–15.
Compares *The Prince* and the *Discourses* with *Arcadia* to show
that Sidney held the same views of politics that Machiavelli held,
but that Sidney used his villians to refute the popular concept of
Machiavelli's thought. Both were concerned with practical problems of government, but Sidney made personal morality his
criterion, while Machiavelli made success his. The legend of
Machiavelli differed from his writings.

⋐§ 411. ———. "A Note on Sidney's *Arcadia* and *A Midsummer
Night's Dream.*" *Shakespeare Association Bulletin*,
23 (1948), 207–8.
The love tangle in *Midsummer Night's Dream* may have its
source in the Arcadian tangle composed of Zelmane, Philoclea,
Basilius, and Gynecia.

⋐§ 412. ———. *Patterns in Shakespearian Tragedy.* New York:
Barnes and Noble, Inc., 1960. 205 pp.
Traces the development of Shakespeare's tragedies in relation
to ethical values. Discusses the influence of *Arcadia* upon the subplot in *King Lear* (pp. 130–31).
Rev.: Philip Edwards, *MLR*, 56 (1961), 582; R. Davril, *EA*,
14 (1961), 146–47.

⋐§ 413. ———. "Sidney's *Arcadia* and the Machiavelli Legend."
Italica, 27 (1950), 225–35.
The Elizabethan legend of Machiavelli and his actual writings
differed. While Sidney gave his villains characteristics similar to
the legend, his political thought was similar to Machiavelli's.
Sidney's villains fail because they do not follow the writings of
Machiavelli. Machiavellian villains include the King of Phrygia,
the King of Pontus, Plexirtus, and Amphialus. Amphialus fails
when he ceases to follow Machiavelli's principles.

⋐§ 414. ———. "Sidney's *Arcadia* and the Structure of *King
Lear.*" *SN*, 24 (1952), 63–68.
The subplot of the King of Paphlagonia in *Arcadia* and that of
Gloucester in *Lear* are analogues to each main plot. The political
theme of *Arcadia*—that of the relation between the king and his

kingdom—is also an important theme in *Lear*. In both works the subplot gives a cosmic application to the main plot.

◄§ 415. ————. "Sir Philip Sidney on Civil Insurrection."
      JHI, 13 (1952), 257–65.
Replies to Briggs [*SP*, 28 (1931)]. Sidney believed in the Tudor doctrine of absolute monarchy, not in a limited monarchy. Suggests that the Helots were trying to regain liberty, not to overthrow a tyrant. Even though Philisides says that the king's power is from the people, not from God, he does not recommend rebellion. Sidney believed that God would punish tyrants.

◄§ 416. RINGLER, WILLIAM. "Master Drant's Rules."
      PQ, 29 (1950), 70–74.
Gathers together three of Sidney's own statements concerning quantitative verse and rhyme: Lalus' and Dicus' discussion in the Old *Arcadia*, the part of the *Defence* dealing with quantitative verse, and the unpublished note in a St. John's College, Cambridge, copy of Old *Arcadia* that gives Sidney's version of the rules of quantity.

◄§ 417. ROBERTSON, JEAN. "Sidney and Bandello." *The Library*,
      21 (1966), 326–28.
Sidney did not use Bandello's stories to any great extent in *Arcadia* even though Sidney owned a copy of the Boaistuau-Belleforest translation of Bandello, now in the Hugh Walpole Collection, King's School, Canterbury.

◄§ 418. ROSE, MARK. *Heroic Love: Studies in Sidney and Spenser*.
      Cambridge, Mass.: Harvard University Press, 1968.
      vii, 156 pp.
Sidney and Spenser reconciled passion with reason through the institution of marriage, reconciling the Christian and Italian traditions of love. Old *Arcadia* is an attack on passion, but the New *Arcadia* is more complex (p. 38). The Urania episode illustrates the central problem of reconciling passion and reason (p. 45). The central philosophy of the book involves the conflict between Stoicism and Epicurianism (pp. 57–62). Both Sidney and Spenser tend to see love as heroic and not antithetical to virtue.

≈§ 419. ———. "Sidney's Womanish Man."
RES, n.s., 15 (1964), 353–63.

[See 125, 291.] Refutes Boas' interpretation of transvestism as part of the Elizabethan tradition and Danby's interpretation of transvestism as a superior blend of masculine and feminine virtue. Suggests that it is a criticism of men who allow passion to overcome reason. Analyzes the images of Amazons, eagles and doves, and of Hercules.

≈§ 420. ROSENMEYER, THOMAS G. The Green Cabinet: Theocritus and the European Pastoral Lyric. Berkeley: University of California Press, 1969. 351 pp.

Describes the origin of pastoral poetry and many of its qualities, such as simplicity and freedom. In Arcadia, Sidney combined an Epicurean pleasure with a Stoic mistrust of pleasure (p. 73). Sidney helped develop the melancholy of the pastoral (pp. 226–27).

≈§ 421. ROTA, FELICIA. L'Arcadia di Sidney e il teatro, con un testo inedito. Biblioteca di studi inglesi 6. Bari: Adriatica, 1966. 390 pp.

Indicates the relationship between Arcadia and a number of plays based upon it. Ile of Gulls, Cupid's Revenge, Argalus and Parthenia, Aroadia (by James Shirley), Andromana, Loves Changelings Changed, and Arcadia Lovers.

Rev.: Katherine Duncan-Jones, RES, n.s., 18 (1967), 491.

≈§ 422. ROWE, KENNETH T. "Romantic Love and Parental Authority in Sidney's Arcadia." UMCMP, 4, Ann Arbor, 1947. 59 pp.

Parental authority and romantic love are in unresolved conflict in Arcadia. Only in Arcadia is parental authority idealized; in the events Sidney writes about outside of Arcadia, parental authority is either vicious or ineffectual. While Euarchus does not have a direct source, his ethical system comes from Aristotle and Cicero. The source for conjugal love is classical; the source for romantic love is Christian and Medieval. Destiny resolves the actual conflict in Arcadia. The theoretical conflict is left unresolved except that both sides represent a form of virtue.

423. SANNAZARO, JACOPO. Arcadia *and* Piscatorial Eclogues, trans. by Ralph Nash. Detroit: Wayne State University Press, 1966. 219 pp.

Contains the text of both books with an Introduction. Mentions that the most interesting development in the 16th-century pastoral was its combination with the heroic to show different value systems. Sidney, Spenser, and Shakespeare combined the two (p. 18).

424. SAVAGE, JAMES E. "Beaumont and Fletcher's *Philaster* and Sidney's *Arcadia.*" *ELH*, 14 (1947), 194–206.

Arcadia is the source for *Philaster*, not *Diana* as T. P. Harrison suggested. *Arcadia* is the source for five characters in *Philaster* and for seven characters in *Cupid's Revenge*. The plot of *Cupid's Revenge* is taken from the Plangus and Erona episode in *Arcadia*.

425. ———. "Notes on *A Midsummer Night's Dream.*" *University of Mississippi Studies in English*, 2 (1961), 65–78.

[See 401.] The marriage between Thomas Berkeley and Elizabeth Carey may have been the occasion for *A Midsummer Night's Dream*. Supports Poirier's belief that the description of the hunt derives from Kalander's hunt. Also suggests that the term "Spartan" is a tribute to *Arcadia* and that the bear bayed by Hercules may have been influenced by the bear in *Arcadia*.

426. SCHLAUCH, MARGARET. *Antecedents of the English Novel, 1400–1600: From Chaucer to Deloney*. London: Oxford University Press, 1963. viii, 264 pp.

The realistic novel began before 1600. Sidney experimented with colloquial speech in his presentation of Dametas and his family, but *Arcadia* is not similar to a modern novel (pp. 174–84).

427. SCRIBNER, BROTHER SIMON. *Figures of Word-Repetition in the First Book of Sir Philip Sidney's Arcadia*. Washington: Catholic University of America, 1948. xxix, 112 pp.

[Ph.D. diss., Catholic University of America, 1948.] Surveys the types and uses of word repetition in Book I of the 1590 *Arcadia*. Divides into twelve types on the basis of position and syntactical elements, and explains use. All repetitions are used to achieve order, enhance the style, and contribute to the sound of the words. In *Arcadia* Sidney used the rules given in *Defence*.

428. SHAKESPEARE, WILLIAM. *King Lear*, Kenneth Muir, ed. London: Methuen and Company, Ltd., 1952. lxiv, 259 pp.
The tale of the Paphlagonian King is reprinted in an appendix (pp. 243–49). Suggests that Shakespeare borrowed characters, phrases, images, and even doctrine from *Arcadia* (pp. xxxvii–xlii).

429. SMITH, HALLETT. "Shakespeare's Romances." *HLQ*, 27 (1964), 279–87.
Reviews the criticism that deals with Shakespeare's change from tragedy to romance. The difference may have been caused by Shakespeare's reading of *Arcadia* and his discovery of the motif of reconciliation, reunion, and discovery while writing *King Lear*. In *Arcadia* Shakespeare found an example of sophisticated romance.

430. STATON, WALTER F., JR. "Characters of Style in Elizabethan Prose." *JEGP*, 57 (1958), 197–207.
Three possible styles of Elizabethan prose are the plain style, marked by ordinary diction, proverbs, humor, and use of logical proof; the middle style, marked by elevated diction and figures of sound and thought; and the lofty style, ornate and passionate. Sidney used the middle style in the *Defence* and the lofty style in *Arcadia*. Also analyzes the prose of Lyly, Greene, and Nashe.

431. STEEVES, HARRISON R. *Before Jane Austen: The Shaping of the English Novel in the Eighteenth Century.* New York: Holt, Rinehart and Winston, 1965. xii, 399 pp.
Instead of being an important development in the novel, *Arcadia* is a return to the conventional romantic tradition (pp. 9–11).

432. STRATTON, CLARENCE. "The Italian Lyrics of Sidney's *Arcadia*." *SR*, 25 (1917), 305–26.
Identifies Italian verse forms, modifications, and the Italian poets who used each. Of the Italian forms, Sidney used the madrigal and ottava rima in *Arcadia*. The best sonnets in *Arcadia* are in the English form.

433. STRONG, ROY C. "The Popular Celebration of the Accession Day of Queen Elizabeth I." *JWCI*, 21 (1958), 86–103.
The source of the tournament held on the wedding anniversary of Queen Andromana was Elizabeth's Accession Day Feast. Drayton and Spenser also used this motif. Traces the development of the celebration, which continued after Elizabeth's death.

◆§ 434. TALBERT, ERNEST WILLIAM. *The Problem of Order: Elizabethan Political Commonplaces and an Example of Shakespeare's Art.* Chapel Hill: University of North Carolina Press, 1962. ix, 244 pp.

Sidney's argument against Elizabeth's marriage and his doctrines in *Arcadia* illustrate beliefs common to many writings in the 16th century. In *Arcadia* the king is not an absolute ruler, and Sidney criticizes absolutism in his letter to Elizabeth. Philisides' beast poem also criticizes it. *Arcadia* also deals with the concept of justice (pp. 91–117).

Rev.: Alvin Kernan, *Yale Review*, 52 (1963), 458.

◆§ 435. TAYLER, EDWARD WILLIAM. *Nature and Art in Renaissance Literature.* New York and London: Columbia University Press, 1964. ix, 225 pp.

Relates the terms "nature" and "art" to Renaissance theory and shows them in a historical perspective. Suggests that the pastoral is a vehicle for dealing with the distinction between nature and art. These terms are the basis for pastoral literature. A pastoral may be either decorative or symbolic. In *Arcadia* the pastoral setting represents Eden, and when Basilius returns to it, he becomes a truant from the moral realm (pp. 122ff.).

◆§ 436. TAYLOR, A. B. "A Note on Ovid in *Arcadia.*" *N&Q,* 16 (1969), 455.

In the analogy between Philoclea and Arethusa, Sidney has confused Ovid's description of Daphne with that of Arethusa.

◆§ 437. TEETS, BRUCE E. "Two Faces of Style in Renaissance Prose Fiction." In *Sweet Smoke of Rhetoric,* Natalie Grimes Lawrence and J. A. Reynolds, eds., pp. 69–81. Coral Gables, Fla.: University of Miami Press, 1964.

Examines the *estilo culto* writing of Sidney and Lyly, as well as the colloquial style of Greene, Nashe, and Deloney. The *estilo culto* was characterized by artificial expression. Finds that Lyly's style is based on complicated figures of sound that produce the effect of poetic meter and rhyme. Finds that Sidney's style consists of descriptions, such figures as metaphors and similes, and details. The colloquial style derived from the Medieval prose tradition. Concludes that neither group produced prose masterpieces.

◄§ 438. THOMPSON, JOHN. *The Founding of English Meter.* New York: Columbia University Press, 1961. 181 pp.

Traces the development of English meter from Wyatt to Sidney, showing that a tension exists between meter and language. Explains classical meters as Sidney understood them. With Sidney the relation between language and verse took its modern form: he understood that he could establish a meter and still maintain normal phrasing. Sidney used an extremely precise meter, with few extra syllables. In *The Lady of May* Sidney imitated Gascoigne.

Rev.: Robert Lowell, *HudR*, 15 (1962–1963), 317–18.

◄§ 439. ———. "Sir Philip and the Forsaken Iamb." *KR*, 20 (1958), 90–115.

Uses Sidney's poetry to show that meter creates tension, with prose language patterns causing a feeling of imitation. This imitation is the justification of meter; it is not justified by its contribution to meaning as Stein wrote [*KR* (Summer, 1956)]. The meter of *Arcadia* is highly regular. The meter in *Astrophel and Stella* creates tension with prose patterns because the normal accent of the words is different from the metrical pattern. Lists types of poems in *Arcadia*.

◄§ 440. TILLYARD, E. M. W. *The English Epic and Its Background.* New York: Oxford University Press, 1954. x, 548 pp.

Traces the epic from classical literature through Pope and Gibbon. Includes the 1590 *Arcadia* as an epic fragment. *Arcadia* was revised in light of Italian theories of the epic. Sidney used a variety of styles to give it the range of the epic. Does not find the style as bad as Hazlitt's attack indicates. The New *Arcadia* stresses ethics and religion, while Old *Arcadia* stresses politics.

◄§ 441. ———. *The Epic Strain in the English Novel.* Fair Lawn, N.J.: Essential Books Company, 1958. 207 pp.

[A continuation of *The English Epic.*] Describes an author or novel in each chapter. Suggests that Sidney's *Arcadia* influenced Fielding (p. 53).

Rev.: Mark Schorer, *MLN*, 74 (1959), 643–44.

◄§ 442. ———. "Milton and Sidney's *Arcadia.*" *TLS*, March 6, 1953, p. 153.

Suggests that lines 836–39, Book XI, of *Paradise Lost* resemble the description of the shipwreck in *Arcadia*.

◆§ 443. ———. *Shakespeare's History Plays.* London: Chatto
and Windus, 1944. viii, 336 pp.

Discusses Shakespeare's history plays in relation to Elizabethan
ideas of order and of history. Suggests that Elizabethans regarded
Arcadia as an epic (p. 91). Sidney, in his writings, tends to depict
the England of his time (p. 263).

◆§ 444. TOWNSEND, FREDA L. "Sidney and Ariosto."
PMLA, 61 (1946), 97–108.

Sidney followed Ariosto in abandoning classical simplicity for a
new combination of epic, romance, and pastoral. While Sidney
followed Ariosto in his use of the interrupted narrative to create
suspense, and in his use of the episodic material, Sidney did not
borrow directly. Does not agree with Dobell [*Quarterly Review,*
211 (1909)] and Zandvoort [See 836.] that unity is sacrificed to
diversity in New *Arcadia.*

◆§ 445. TRIENENS, ROGER J. "The Green-Eyed Monster: A Study
of Sexual Jealousy in the Literature of the English Renaissance." Ph.D. diss., Northwestern University, 1951. Northwestern University, Graduate School, *Summaries of Doctoral Dissertations Submitted to the Graduate School of
Northwestern University in Partial Fulfillment of the Requirements for the Degree of Doctor of Philosophy,*
19 (1951), 45–49.

Surveys classical literature, Medieval literature and Elizabethan
literature for treatments of jealousy. Considers its causes and the
symbols used to convey it in literature. Includes a treatment of
Gynecia.

◆§ 446. TRUESDALE, CALVIN WILLIAM. "English Pastoral Verse
from Spenser to Marvell: A Critical Revaluation." Ph.D.
diss., University of Washington, 1956. DA, 17 (1957), 1087.

Assesses the variety possible within the rigid convention of the
pastoral. Examines the pastoral as a vehicle for flattery and for
criticism of society. *Arcadia* is partially a vehicle for political
satire (p. 74). Sidney used many traditional themes. Strephon and
Claius are a combination of the theme of the "sad shepherd" and
the Petrarchan tradition (pp. 138–41). In "Ye goatherd gods . . ."
Sidney uses tradition as an objective correlative while examining
the subjective effects of love (pp. 165–72). "Ring out your
bells . . ." is also conventional (pp. 235–40).

⋘§ 447. TUFTE, VIRGINIA. "England's First Epithalamium and the 'Vesper Adest' Tradition." *EM*, 20 (1969), 39–51.

Although Sidney is usually credited with writing the first English epithalamium, Henrie Wotton included one in his book *A Courtlie Controversie of Cupid's Cautels*, published in 1578. His poem is an adaptation of Catullus' Carmen 62 and is a "Vesper adest," or singing match on the subject of the choice between marriage and virginity. Wotton probably knew Jaques Yver's French translation of the poem, not the original.

⋘§ 448. ———. *The Poetry of Marriage: The Epithalamium in Europe and Its Development in England*. University of Southern California, Studies in Comparative Literature 2. Los Angeles: Tinnon-Brown, Inc., 1970. 341 pp.

Traces the pre-Renaissance use of the form and its development in the Renaissance. The consistent themes of the genre are union and order. The classical writers developed the idea of human union, the Medieval period preferred a mystic union, and the Renaissance combined the two by relating human marriage to the cosmos. Sidney was not the first English writer of an epithalamium; he was preceded by John Lydgate, William Dunbar, and Henrie Wotton (pp. 141–42). Sidney's epithalamium in *Arcadia* is didactic; it is structured of eleven appeals and a recapitulative conclusion (pp. 152–55).

⋘§ 449. TURNER, MYRON. "The Heroic Ideal in Sidney's Revised *Arcadia*." *SEL*, 10 (1970), 63–82.

In *Arcadia* Sidney tries to fuse Christian virtues with the traditional virtues of the hero. Euarchus, the ideal prince, tries to establish heavenly order on earth. Musidorus and Pyrocles harmonize Aristotelian ethics with Christian virtue. In battle the two princes are treated ironically in order to show the need for internal balance.

⋘§ 450. ———. "Majesty in Adversity: The Moral Structure of Sidney's *Arcadia*." Ph.D. diss., University of Washington, 1965. *DA*, 26 (1965), 1636.

Studies the theme of *Arcadia*: in Musidorus and Pyrocles, Sidney joins Christian humility or imperfection with majesty. Such a union joins nature with grace.

✒§ 451. UHLIG, CLAUS. "Der weinende Hirsch: As You Like It, II, i, 21–66, und der historische Kontext." SJH (1968), 141–68.

Traces the humanistic tendency to moralize hunting scenes. Jaques' view of hunting is similar to that of Philisides. Philisides may even be a source for Jaques.

✒§ 452. UNDERDOWN, MARY EBBA INGHOLT. "Sir Philip Sidney's Arcadian Eclogues: A Study of his Quantitative Verse." Ph.D. diss., Yale University, 1964. DA, 25 (1964), 1222.

Sidney believed that native "rimed" verse and classic "measured" verse could both be used effectively. Analyzes Sidney's quantitative verse in relation to its classical elements.

✒§ 453. VAN DORSTEN, JAN A. "Gruterus and Sidney's Arcadia." RES, n.s., 16 (1965), 174–77.

Contains five tributes to Sidney. Melissus' ten-line epigram was written before Sidney's death. Gruterus' epigram suggests that he had read parts of Arcadia, probably earlier than the first printed edition. This is the first indication that Sidney's work was known to the men at Leiden before their commemorative verse was written.

✒§ 454. VICKERS, BRIAN. "In Search of Arcadia." Cambridge Review, 89 (1966), 62–64.

[See 294, 366.] The reason for the lack of interest in Arcadia is the notion that the style is difficult. In fact, the style is varied to fit the occasion, and Sidney is a very good rhetorician. Reviews Davis and Lanham.

✒§ 455. WAITH, EUGENE M. The Pattern of Tragicomedy in Beaumont and Fletcher. New Haven, Conn.: Yale University Press, 1952. xiv, 214 pp.

Re-evaluates the plays of Beaumont and Fletcher in relation to the genre. Suggests that Sidney's rhetoric is an instrument for showing the emotion of the hero caught in a dilemma for which no solution is apparent.

✒§ 456. WALKER, D. P. "Ways of Dealing with Atheists: A Background to Pamela's Refutation of Cecropia." BHR, 17 (1955), 252–77.

Pamela's attempt to refute Cecropia indicates that Sidney believed a pagan could arrive at Christian truth through reason.

Cecropia is an atheist because she desires profit and pleasure from the world. Pamela, shown to be a Christian in her prayer, tries to convert her by the use of natural reason, as Mornay had suggested. Her argument is based on design with emphasis upon chance; she appeals to the emotions by mentioning God's vengeance.

◆§ 457. WALTERS, PERCY. "The Hidden Meaning of the Title Page of *Arcadia.*" *Baconiana,* 29 (1945), 159–60.
[See 310.] Answers Eagle. Uses numerical ciphers to support the hypothesis that Bacon may have written parts of *Arcadia.*

◆§ 458. WATKINS, W. B. C. *Shakespeare and Spenser.* Princeton, N.J.: Princeton University Press, 1950. ix, 339 pp.
Contains eight essays, all developing themes of transience, love, and union of physical and spiritual. Both Shakespeare and Spenser owe a debt to *Arcadia* (p. 43).

◆§ 459. WATSON, GEORGE. "Ramus, Miss Tuve, and the New Petromachia." *MP,* 55 (1958), 259–62.
[Response to A. J. Smith, *RES,* n.s., 7 (1956).] Ramus did influence 16th-century literature. Sidney was interested in Ramus' theories. Finds no evidence linking Ramus to the metaphysical poets, however.

◆§ 460. WEINER, ANDREW DAVID. " 'Erected Wit' and 'Infected Will': A Study of Sir Philip Sidney's Old *Arcadia.*" Ph.D. diss., Princeton University, 1969. *DA,* 31 (1970), 736A.
The Old *Arcadia* should not be considered a heroic poem. It illustrates the progressive stages of evil in the individual and in the state. None of the characters in it is a model of virtue. It might be considered a pastoral in the comic mode.

◆§ 461. WHITTEMORE, NENA LOUISE T. "Unity and Variety in Sir Philip Sidney's New *Arcadia* (1590)." Ph.D. diss., The City University of New York, 1968.
DA, 29 (1968), 1521A–22A.
Contrasts the unity of the Old *Arcadia* reflecting the belief in an ordered universe, with the variety of the New *Arcadia* reflecting a world view of abundance. New *Arcadia* combines an epic framework with the variety of the romance. Each book of New *Arcadia* moves from love lament to entertainment to a conclusion of

heroic action. This structure mirrors the theme of conflict between the inward and the outward man.

◄§ 462. WILES, A. G. D. "The Date of Publication and Composition of Sir William Alexander's Supplement to Sidney's *Arcadia*." *PBSA*, 50 (1956), 387–92.

William Alexander wrote his Supplement to the third book of the revised *Arcadia* between 1613 and 1616, and it was published in 1621. Earlier dates of publication seem unlikely, and manuscript evidence in Feuillerat's edition indicates 1621 as the probable date.

◄§ 463. ———. "James Johnstoun and the *Arcadian* Style." *RenP* (1957), 72–81.

James Johnstoun imitated Sidney's style and content in his continuation of Book III of *Arcadia*. Analyzes a passage from each. Johnstoun is successful with Sidney's parallel sentences and repetitions but not with his metaphors, personifications, and similes. Concludes that Johnstoun was successful with only the external elements of Sidney's style.

◄§ 464. ———. "Parallel Analyses of the Two Versions of Sidney's *Arcadia*." *SP*, 39 (1942), 167–206.

Concludes that the revised *Arcadia* is superior to the original. It is more dramatic because of its epic structure. The addition of Cecropia adds suspense, the subplots add variety, and the careful motivation adds verisimilitude. Contains a synopsis of both versions, showing changes.

◄§ 465. ———. "Sir William Alexander's Continuation of the Revised Version of Sir Philip Sidney's *Arcadia*." *SSL*, 3 (1965), 221–29.

Most critics believe Alexander's continuation lacks Sidney's style, but in plot and character Alexander successfully imitates Sidney. The identification of Philisides with the "knight of the sheep" can be supported from the text.

◄§ 466. WILKINS, ERNEST HATCH. "Arcadia in America." *PAPS*, 101 (1957), 4–30.

Traces the name "Arcadia" in America. Sidney's *Arcadia* was the source for Arcadia, Virginia. Lope de Vega and Sannazaro were other sources. Gives classical sources.

467. WILLIAMS, GEORGE WALTON. "The Printer of the 1st Folio of Sidney's *Arcadia.*" *The Library*, 12 (1957), 274–75.
Windet, not Creede, probably printed the 1593 *Arcadia.* The title-page border probably belonged to Ponsonby. Field used it in his 1598 *Arcadia.* Windet, who printed the 1590 quarto for Ponsonby, probably printed the 1593 folio.

468. WILSON, F. P. *Elizabethan and Jacobean.* Oxford: Clarendon Press, 1945. vi, 144 pp.
Suggests differences in the literature of Elizabethan and of Jacobean England. Defends *Arcadia and The Faerie Queene* against the charge that they contain more rhetoric than matter (pp. 51–52). See also Index.
Rev.: Paul Victor, *ES*, 29 (1948), 156–57.

469. WRIGHT, THOMAS EDWARD. "The English Renaissance Prose Anatomy." Ph.D. diss., University of Washington, 1963. *DA*, 24 (1964), 4181.
Describes the genre and its customary rhetorical devices, such as the traveler's tale. Chapter 6 contains an analysis of More's *Utopia* and the New *Arcadia*, both revised by use of "anatomy forms."

470. YATES, FRANCES A. "Elizabethan Chivalry: The Romance of the Accession Day Tilts." *JWCI*, 20 (1957), 4–25.
Suggests a connection between religious reformation and the Elizabethan interest in chivalry and suggests that the Accession Day tilts helped shape imaginative literature. The Iberian joust in *Arcadia* may reflect the pageantry of the Accession Day tilt; Philisides' contest with Lelius may reflect Sir Philip Sidney's joust with Sir Henry Lee in 1581. Von Wedel's eyewitness account indicates that the pageantry described in *Arcadia* may be realistic. Sir Henry Lee may be the author of "Tale of Hemetes," which, prior to *Arcadia*, combined Greek romance with chivalric romance.

471. ZANDVOORT, R. W. "Fair Portia's Counterfeit." *RLMC*, n.s., 2 (1951), 351–56.
Considers Sidney's and Shakespeare's descriptions of paintings and allusions to paintings in relation to the tradition of artistic realism. The Renaissance inherited from antiquity the convention of "deceptive realism" used in describing pictures.

V

Astrophel and Stella

⊷§ 472. ADAMS, ROBERT M. *Strains of Discord: Studies in Literary Openness.* Ithaca, N.Y.: Cornell University Press, 1958. xi, 220 pp.

Includes an interpretation of Sonnet 1, *Astrophel and Stella,* in relation to its structure. The poem consists of two approaches to writing: the first culminates in the violent metaphors of lines 11–13 and is contrasted with the second approach of line 14 (pp. 4–6).

Rev.: Marius Bewley, *HudR,* 12 (1959–1960), 130–34; Hermann Peschmann, *English,* 12 (1959–1960), 237; Donald Sutherland, *KR,* 21 (1959), 305–8.

⊷§ 473. AHRENDS, GUNTER. "Liebe, Schönheit und Tugend als Strukturelemente in Sidneys *Astrophel and Stella* und in Spensers *Amoretti.*" Ph.D. diss., Bonn, 1966. 231 pp.

Explicates structural metaphors of love, beauty, and virtue.

⊷§ 474. ALDEN, RAYMOND MACDONALD. "The Lyrical Conceit of the Elizabethans." *SP,* 14 (1917), 129–52.

Studies the Petrarchan conceit as used by Sidney and Shakespeare. Divides it into verbal, imaginative, and logical conceits and lists poems by Sidney under each classification. Concludes that Sidney is better at the witty conceit than is Shakespeare. The conceit is more likely to control the structure of Sidney's sonnets than it is Shakespeare's.

⊷§ 475. ALLEN, DON CAMERON. *The Star-Crossed Renaissance: The Quarrel About Astrology and Its Influence in England.* Durham, N.C.: Duke University Press, 1941. xi, 280 pp.

The Sonnet 26 of *Astrophel and Stella* is the prototype for the English astrological sonnet (p. 158). Shakespeare's Sonnet 14 may be an answer to Sidney's Sonnet 28 (p. 165).

Rev.: Una Ellis-Fermor, *MLR,* 37 (1942), 497–98.

⊷§ 476. BENJAMIN, EDWIN B. "Fame, Poetry, and the Order of History in the Literature of the English Renaissance." *SRen,* 6 (1959), 64–84.

Deals with personal fame and national fame. Begins with the treatment of fame in Chaucer's *The House of Fame.* During the

Elizabethan age the poet was concerned with three areas: celebration of the fame of a mistress, indication of a moral order through fame, and education of young men through fame. This last is the "Sidneian-Spenserian tradition." Fame motivates Pyrocles and Musidorus.

477. BLUDAU, DIETHILD. "Sonettstruktur Bei Samuel Daniel." *SJW*, 94 (1958), 63–89.
Sidney's sonnets influenced Daniel's development of a smooth line in his sonnets and his use of conventions. Daniel thought of the sonnet as an instrument for a certain view of life; Sidney, however, thought of it as an instrument of dialogue.

478. BLUM, IRVING D. "The Paradox of Money Imagery in English Renaissance Poetry." *SRen*, 8 (1961), 144–54.
In Renaissance poetic tradition, money was used to praise good or attack evil. Spenser pictured Avarice loaded with gold, but he also described his mistress' hair as "finest gold." In Sonnet 24 Sidney combined both traditions when he scorned "rich fools," yet used money as a symbol for Stella. Other poets used the tradition.

479. BOND, WILLIAM H. "Sidney and Cupid's Dart." *MLN*, 63 (1948), 258.
Sidney's Sonnet 5, which contains an image of cupid's dart, may be a reference to the pheon on Sidney's coat of arms. This reference adds support to the theory that the sonnets are autobiographical.

480. BOOTH, STEPHEN. *An Essay on Shakespeare's Sonnets.* New Haven, Conn.: Yale University Press, 1969. xv, 218 pp.
Describes Shakespeare's sonnets in relation to a reader's response. In "Not at first sight, nor with a dribbed shot," Sidney combined the Italian and English sonnet forms to integrate the couplet with the preceding lines of the poem (pp. 34–35).

481. BRADBROOK, MURIEL C. *Shakespeare and Elizabethan Poetry: A Study of His Earlier Work in Relation to the Poetry of the Time.* New York: Oxford University Press, 1952. viii, 279 pp.
Sidney, Spenser, Ralegh, and Lyly wrote poetry concerned with the arts of courtship and of living. Sidney tried to adapt Petrarchan conceits into arguments (pp. 22–23). See also Index.
Rev.: M. A. Shaaber, *SQ*, 4 (1953), 343–44.

◄§ 482. BROADBENT, J. B. *Poetic Love*. London: Chatto and Windus, Ltd., 1964. vii, 310 pp.

Traces love poetry from the Medieval period through the eighteenth century. Love poetry during this period was an attempt to unite such dualities as body and soul, or sacred and profane love. Sidney began the revolt against Petrarch, Ronsard, Ovid, and Plato that Donne continued. He denied that the body was inferior to the soul, but he was unable to suggest any real theory of love. Sidney used the colloquial style but, unlike Donne, only as a stylistic device (pp. 129–42).

Rev.: Rev. John Carey, *EIC*, 15 (1965), 334–37.

◄§ 483. BRODWIN, LEONORA L. "The Structure of Sidney's *Astrophel and Stella*." *MP*, 67 (1969), 25–40.

[See 216, 539, 616.] Reviews Young's, Kalstone's, and Ringler's descriptions of the structure of the sonnets and suggests alternate divisions based on action and imagery. The first part, concluding with Sonnet 35, describes Astrophel's motivation. The second part, concluding with Sonnet 87, contains the greatest action. The final part shows Astrophel's unhappy state. Descriptions of Stella's eyes are an important image for determining structure. These descriptions change from images of distance, to images of the dazzling sun, to images of darkness and loss. One theme is the choice between a life that gratifies human desire and a life of contemplation.

◄§ 484. BULLITT, JOHN M. "The Use of Rhyme Link in the Sonnets of Sidney, Drayton, and Spenser." *JEGP*, 49 (1950), 14–32.

Attacks through irony the use of rhyme link. Uses Bray's method of rhyme link to analyze Sidney's, Drayton's, and Spenser's sonnets. Finds that only in Sidney's Sonnets 96 through 107 can he have tried to make a conscious link through repetition of rhyme words. Writes that even here the link may be chance.

◄§ 485. BURHANS, CLINTON S., JR. "Sidney's 'With How Sad Steps, O Moon.'" *Expl*, 18 (1960), Item 26.

The last line of the sonnet should be read ironically and may be paraphrased, "And do they make such ungratefulness all the more ironic by calling it virtue."

486. Buxton, John. "On the Date of SYR P.S. *His Astrophel and Stella* . . . Printed for Matthew Lownes."
BLR, 6 (1960), 614–16.
Reviews the printing history of *Astrophel and Stella*. Newman published two quartos in 1591. An undated quarto was published by Matthew Lownes, possibly in 1597 or 1598; it was not printed in 1591, as has been suggested.

487. ———. *A Tradition of Poetry*. London: Macmillan Press, 1967. 190 pp.
Contains essays on eight poets. Writes in the essay on Michael Drayton that Sidney's poetry influenced Drayton's (pp. 63, 70). Drayton was a page of Sir Henry Goodere, Sidney's cousin. Drayton fought at Zutphen (pp. 60–61).
Rev.: Martin Dodsworthy, *Listener*, 78 (1967), 824.

488. Cairncross, Andrew S. "The Rival Poet."
TLS, December 1, 1950, p. 767.
[See 561; also 508, 512, 517.] Answers Murray by suggesting that Chapman is referring to Harvey.

489. Castley, J. P. S. J. "*Astrophel and Stella*—High Sidnacan Love, or Courtly Compliment?" *Melbourne Critical Review*, No. 5 (1962), 54–65.
Interpretations of the sonnets in light of their possible biographical significance exaggerate their seriousness. The tone of Sonnet 20 is playful. The poems do not develop a story, and Astrophel is not a dramatically or poetically significant character. The sonnets are unified by Astrophel's self-awareness, but this characteristic is static.

490. Cawley, Robert R. *Unpathed Waters: Studies in the Influence of the Voyagers on Elizabethan Literature*. Princeton, N.J.: Princeton University Press, 1940. viii, 285 pp.
Sidney's comparison of his mistress' kiss to a "newfound paradise" [AS 81] has its source in the Medieval tradition (p. 30). See also Index.
Rev.: E. G. R. Taylor, *RES*, n.s., 17 (1941), 475–79; George B. Parks, *JEGP*, 40 (1941), 582–84; Hardin Craig, *AHR*, 46 (1940–1941), 893–94.

ᵉᵍ 491. CHAMBERS, D. D. C. "Sidney's Rhetoric." *Cambridge
Review*, 89 (1966), 67–69.
[See 539.] Reviews Kalstone's book *Sidney's Poetry*. Suggests that
Kalstone fails to see the relation between action and rhetoric.

ᵉᵍ 492. COLIE, ROSALIE L. *Paradoxia Epidemica: The Renaissance Tradition of Paradox*. Princeton, N.J.: Princeton University Press, 1966. xvii, 553 pp.
Sidney is one of Petrarch's imitators. But he is original in the
use of language as a theme in *Astrophel and Stella*. Throughout
the sequence Sidney exploits paradox (pp. 89–95).
Rev.: Leonard Nathanson, *Shakespeare Studies*, 3 (1967), 265–
69; Sister Miriam Joseph, *ELN*, 5 (1967–1968), 142–47; Margaret
Greaves, *RQ*, 20 (1967), 271–72.

ᵉᵍ 493. COMBELLACK, C. R. B. "Sidney's 'With How Sad Steps,
O Moon.'" *Expl*, 20 (1961), Item 25.
Takes "ungratefulness" to mean "unpleasantness."

ᵉᵍ 494. COOPER, SHEROD M., JR. *The Sonnets of Astrophel and
Stella: A Stylistic Study*. The Hague: Mouton Press, 1968.
183 pp.
[Ph.D. diss., University of Pennsylvania, 1963. *DA*, 24 (1963),
1612–13.] In Sidney's theory of poetry, the poet adopts various
stylistic devices in order to make his art a more convincing imitation of nature (p. 26). These devices aid in unifying *Astrophel and
Stella* (pp. 27–32). Sidney's rhyme scheme reinforces the logic of
his poems (pp. 64–74). His style is marked by rhetorical devices
(pp. 94–117) and imagery (pp. 118–38). Sidney incorporated English and Continental traditions of poetry (p. 158).

ᵉᵍ 495. COTTER, JAMES FINN. "The 'Baiser' Group in Sidney's
Astrophil and Stella." *TSLL*, 12 (1970–1971), 381–403.
In the poems between the second and third songs, Sidney's real
subject is invention in poetry, while his apparent subject is the
kiss. While all these poems deal the *baiser* convention, it is
transformed by Sidney's inventions. Sidney is writing about a stolen
kiss, but he is also writing about the poet inventing.

◄§ 496. ———. "A Glasse of Reason: The Art of Poetry in Sidney's *Astrophil and Stella*." Ph.D. diss., Fordham University, 1964. *DA*, 24 (1964), 5382.

Suggests that the purpose of Sidney's sonnet cycle was to put into practice his theory of poetry. Compares theory to practice. Studies *Astrophel and Stella* in terms of classical rhetoric.

◄§ 497. ———. "Sidney's *Astrophel and Stella*, Sonnet 40." *Expl*, 27 (1969), Item 51.

Sonnet 40 combines love, astrology, and rhetoric as Dante does in the *Convivio*. Sonnets 31 through 40 have sleep as their subject, but their theme is the poetic process.

◄§ 498. ———. "Sidney's *Astrophel and Stella*, Sonnet 75." *Expl*, 27 (1969), Item 70.

The topic of Sonnet 75, King Edward IV, was one that might be handled ironically. Suggests readings for some phrases.

◄§ 499. ———. "The Songs in *Astrophil and Stella*. *SP*, 67 (1970), 178–200.

In *Astrophel and Stella* Sidney demonstrated his poetic theory that reason governs poetry. The songs do not intrude into the sonnets but serve both to tell the narrative and to recapitulate. Songs five through nine, beginning with the fifth song, all belong to different genres and have different verse forms. Each shows the author capable of exercising art. The sequence as a whole serves to metamorphose passion and reason.

◄§ 500. COWAN, STANLEY A. "Sidney's *Astrophel and Stella*, IX, 12–14." *Expl*, 20 (1962), Item 76.

[See 574.] Suggests an alternate reading. "Touch" may be a transition word between two image patterns—the first, the stone, "touchstone," and the other, "touchbox." The last line may be paraphrased, "Of touch [stone] they are that without touch [contact] doth touch [inflame]."

◄§ 501. CUTTS, JOHN P. "Falstaff's 'Heavenlie Jewel.' Incidental Music for *The Merry Wives of Windsor*." *SQ*, 11 (1960), 89–92.

Falstaff's line is the first line of one of Sidney's poems, "Have I caught my heavenlie jewel?" In the folio, "thee" is inserted between "caught" and "my." Reprints the song and the music as found in British Museum Additional MS 15117, f. 19.

502. D., A. "Shakespeare's Sonnets." *N&Q*, 196 (1951), 5–6.
Sidney's Sonnet 64 is similar to Shakespeare's Sonnet 29. Both contain a catalogue of degradation; both refer to the other men's talents; both contain similar material.

503. DAHL, CURTIS. "Sidney's *Astrophel and Stella*, LXXXIV." *Expl*, 6 (1948), Item 46.
The road referred to in the sonnet may be White Chapel Road. Sidney may have learned the legal terminology of lines 9–11 while helping his father in Wales.

504. DAVIE, DONALD. *Articulate Energy: An Enquiry into the Syntax of English Poetry*. New York: Harcourt, Brace and Company, 1955. 173 pp.
Analyzes several critical theories to show that each is inadequate to describe actual syntax in poetry. By Fenollosa's theory, Sidney's "Come sleep . . ." is a bad poem. Fenollosa describes poetry as a sequence of forces passing from agent to object. As Sidney used copulative, not active, verbs and dealt with abstractions, if Fenollosa's theory is correct, then "Come sleep . . ." is an inferior poem.
Rev.: *TLS*, November 4, 1955, p. 658.

505. ———. *Purity of Diction in English Verse*. London: Chatto and Windus, 1952. viii, 211 pp.
Poetic diction varies in relation to the genre of a poem, the culture from which a poem springs, and the necessity for a consistent tone in a poem. Sidney's poetry is an example of composition when poems are taken to be artificial objects (pp. 125–26). See also Index.
Rev.: *TLS*, February 6, 1953, p. 90; *QQ*, 61 (1954), 136–37.

506. DE MOURGUES, ODETTE. *Metaphysical, Baroque and Précieux Poetry*. Oxford: Clarendon Press, 1953. 184 pp.
Attempts to clarify the terminology of the period. Analyzes Sidney's Sonnet 5 in terms of logic and determines that Sidney's arguments are not serious (pp. 12–20). Sonnet 49 is an example of précieux rhetoric (p. 123). Sidney is a précieux, not a metaphysical, poet (p. 131).

507. DICKSON, ARTHUR. "Sidney's *Astrophel and Stella*, Sonnet 1." *Expl*, 3 (1944), Item 3.
Examines the structure of Sonnet 1. In lines 5–8 the poet hunts for fitting words, then he tries to find effective inventions and examines the poems of other writers. Lines 9–11 describe the

effects of the three methods. In lines 12–13 he expresses his desire
to write in his use of the metaphor of motherhood.

◄§ 508. DISHER, M. WILSON. "The Trend of Shakespeare's
Thoughts." *TLS*, October 20, 1950, p. 668;
October 27, 1950, p. 684; and November 3, 1950, p. 700.
[See 488, 512, 517, 561; also, L. Chambrun, *TLS*, February 2,
1951, p. 69.] Shakespeare accepted the concept of virtue expounded
in *Arcadia*. Both Spenser and Shakespeare followed Sidney's man-
date to "look in thy heart and write." The young man of the sonnets may be William Herbert.

◄§ 509. DONOW, HERBERT S. *A Concordance to the Sonnet Sequences of Daniel, Drayton, Shakespeare, Sidney, and
Spenser*. Carbondale: Southern Illinois Press, 1969. xi,
772 pp.
A computer listing of all the words except conjunctions and
articles in selected poems from each author. Lists 2,591 words
Sidney used and gives frequency of usage.

◄§ 510. DOUGHTIE, EDWARD. "Sidney, Tessier, Batchelar and *A
Musicall Banquet*: Two Notes." *Renaissance News*,
18 (1965), 123–26.
Writes that Daniell Batchelar, a composer represented in *A
Musicall Banquet*, was Sidney's page. The Tessier who wrote the
setting for the eighth song from *Astrophel and Stella* was named
Guillaume, not Charles. Adds to the evidence for French influence
on English songs.

◄§ 511. DUDLEY, FRED A. "Sidney's *Astrophel and Stella*, IX,
12–14." *Expl*, 20 (1962), Item 76.
[See 574.] "Touch" may mean "touch powder" and hint at an
explosive. It may also have an erotic meaning.

◄§ 512. DURRELL, LAWRENCE. "The Rival Poet."
TLS, January 5, 1951, p. 7.
[See 508; also 488, 517, 561.] Marlowe is as likely to be the rival
poet as Chapman.

◄§ 513. EMERSON, OLIVER FARRAR. "Shakespeare's Sonneteering."
SP, 20 (1923), 111–36.
Traces the sonnet in England. Surrey's form of the sonnet was
more popular than Wyatt's among the earliest sonneteers. Sidney
used it in *Arcadia*, then used the Italian form in *Astrophel and*

Stella. Even in these he used alternating rhyme in the sestet. The publication of *Astrophel and Stella* gave the greatest impulse to sonnet writing: it was published in 1591 and between 1592 and 1602, twenty sonnet cycles were printed. Shakespeare's earliest sonnets—those in *Love's Labour's Lost, Romeo and Juliet,* and *All's Well that Ends Well*—may have been influenced by Sidney. Sidney and Shakespeare were the first poets to compose Alexandrine sonnets. Shakespeare used Surrey's form more frequently because of its popularity.

514. ENDICOTT, ANNABEL. "Pip, Philip and Astrophel: Dickens' Debt to Sidney?" *Dickensian,* 63 (1966), 158–62.
Sidney was the inspiration of Dickens' concept of a gentleman as given in *Great Expectations.* Philip and Estella have parallels with Philip and Stella. Both Philips love married women of higher rank; both have friends who try to dissuade them. The words "great expectations" occur in Sonnet 21. Dickens may have been exploring the idea of the Petrarchan convention; certainly Estella resembles the Petrarchan mistress.

515. ESSIG, ERHARDT H. "Sidney's 'With How Sad Steps, O Moon.'" *Expl,* 20 (1961), Item 25.
Recalls Lamb's reading of the last line.

516. FALLS, CYRIL. "Penelope Rich and the Poets: Philip Sidney to John Ford." EDH, 28 (1956), 123–37.
Interprets the sonnets as biographical. Probably Sidney was not important to Lady Rich. Henry Constable and John Ford also wrote poetry about her.

517. FEASEY, LYNETTE. "The Rival Poet."
TLS, December 8, 1950, p. 785.
[See 488; also, 508, 512, 561.] Agrees with Cairncross. Harvey is Chapman's object of attack in the dedication to *The Shadow of Night.* Marlowe may be the rival poet of Shakespeare's sonnets.

518. FINN, SISTER DOROTHY MERCEDES. "Love and Marriage in Renaissance Literature." Ph.D. diss., Columbia University, 1955. DA, 15 (1955), 2188–89.
The Renaissance inherited both Medieval and classical ideas concerning love. The sonnet writers imitated the sensual poetry of the classics, but the Medieval tradition influenced Renaissance attitudes toward marriage.

⚡§ 519. FOGEL, EPHIM G. "The Mythical Sorrows of Astrophil." In *Studies in Language and Literature in Honour of M. Schlaugh*, Mieczyslaw Brahmer, Stanislaw Helsztynshi, and Julian Krzyzanowski, eds., pp. 133–52. Warsaw: Scientific Publishers, 1966.

A biographical approach to *Astrophel and Stella* leads to misinterpretation of some sonnets, particularly Sonnet 2 and Sonnet 33. Sonnet 2 may be interpreted as illustrating Sidney's regret that he did not marry Penelope, but the sonnet follows the Petrarchan tradition and may be read as one stage of love. Supports Grosart's suggestion that Sonnet 33 should be read as a reference to Astrophel's absence, with the light and dark imagery symbolizing presence and absence.

⚡§ 520. ——. "The Personal References in the Fiction and Poetry of Sir Philip Sidney." Ph.D. diss., Ohio State University, 1958. DA, 19 (1958), 809.

Re-examines the supposed personal references in *Arcadia* and *Astrophel and Stella* to separate the improbable from the probable and to place the probable in a context of literary tradition. Concludes that personal references help explain Sidney's life and that they give a sense of reality to the sonnet sequence.

⚡§ 521. FORSTER, LEONARD. *The Icy Fire: Five Studies in European Petrarchism*. Cambridge: University Press, 1969. xvi, 204 pp.

The Petrarchan mode became international and influenced the development of poetic diction in many countries. Sidney and Spenser used Petrarch, the school of Serafino, and the Pléiade as models (p. 50). Sidney wrote the first epithalamium in English (p. 105). See also Index.

⚡§ 522. FOWLER, ALASTAIR. *Triumphal Forms: Structural Patterns in Elizabethan Poetry*. Cambridge: University Press, 1970. 234 pp.

Studies numerical organization in Elizabethan literature. Sidney used both triumphal and temporal patterns in the sonnets. Indicates the allegorical meaning of some of Sidney's numbers. The sonnet cycle contains 108 sonnets—the number of Penelope's suitors—and the number indicates that Stella is faithful. The first 63 sonnets are unbroken by songs; 63 is the climacteric age and indicates crisis. The fifth, sixth, and seventh songs are structural centers (pp. 175–80).

◄§ 523. GENTILI, VANNA. "La Tragicomedy dell'*Astrophel and Stella.*" *AUL,* 1 (1963–1964), 57–92.

Astrophel and Stella is unified and should be classed as a tragicomedy. It has three parts: the first, an anatomy of love; the second part, through the first three songs, an attempted seduction; the third part, the defeat. The third part climaxes with Sonnets 84 and 85.

◄§ 524. GOLDMAN, LLOYD NATHANIEL. "Attitudes toward the Mistress in Five Elizabethan Sonnet Sequences." Ph.D. diss., University of Illinois, 1964. *DA,* 15 (1965), 6590–91.

Examines the sonnets of Sidney, Drayton, Shakespeare, Daniel, and Spenser as works of art and in relation to their literary background. Determines the attitude of each poet to his mistress by his conceits. Concludes that Sidney, Shakespeare, and Drayton are interested in the attitudes of the persona; and that Daniel and Spenser are interested in illustrating the persona.

◄§ 525. GOTTFRIED, RUDOLF. "Autobiography and Art: An Elizabethan Borderland." In *Literary Criticism and Historical Understanding: Selected Papers from the English Institute,* Phillip Damon, ed., pp. 109–34. New York: Columbia University Press, 1967.

A knowledge of biographic material may be valuable in understanding a work of art. Works with an autobiographic element are in a borderland between reality and art. In Thomas Whythorne's *Autobiography* and in Gascoigne's *Adventures of Master F. J.,* the authors imply that they unite autobiography and convention. Petrarch began the use of specific detail which Sidney followed when he described the Devereux coat of arms in a sonnet. Daniel followed him in this practice. Spenser moved back and forth between reality and art in his sonnets. *Colin Clouts Come Home Againe* is the best autobiographical poem of the period; in it, reality and art are mingled.

◄§ 526. GRIGSON, GEOFFREY. *Poets in Their Pride.* London: Phoenix House, 1962. 151 pp.

Sketches the lives of ten poets and gives a few poems from each. Describes the romance between Sidney and Penelope Rich. *Astrophel and Stella* probably was begun after her marriage.

Rev.: *TLS,* December 7, 1962, p. 956.

ᵍᵍ§ 527. GROOM, BERNARD. *The Diction of Poetry from Spenser to Bridges*. Toronto: University of Toronto Press, 1955. viii, 284 pp.

Argues that Spenser had the greatest influence on the diction of English poetry from the Renaissance to Bridges. Discusses Sidney's use of the expletive "doth" (p. 49), and his struggle for simple diction (p. 56).

ᵍᵍ§ 528. GRUNDY, JOAN. "Shakespeare's Sonnets and the Elizabethan Sonneteers." *ShS*, 15 (1962), 41–49.

Examines Shakespeare's attitude toward the poetic techniques of earlier sonnet sequences. "Loving in truth . . ." is an example of the poem as a "speaking picture." Although Shakespeare adopted this mode, he did not write a love complaint. Only Sidney and Shakespeare question the values of the Petrarchan convention. Both men raise the question of excessive praise; Shakespeare manages to turn the excessive praise of the earlier sonneteers into truth by adding critical and philosophic depth.

ᵍᵍ§ 529. GUSS, DONALD L. *John Donne, Petrarchist: Italianate Conceits and Love Theory in* The Songs and Sonnets. Detroit: Wayne State University Press, 1966. 230 pp.

Places Donne's poetry within the Petrarchan tradition. Petrarchan poetry as Sidney and Spenser practiced it aimed to surpass, not imitate, models (p. 22). "Loving in truth . . ." is conventional (p. 192).

Rev.: P. Grant, *JEGP*, 66 (1967), 580–82; Joseph S. M. J. Chang, *MLJ*, 51 (1967), 504–5.

ᵍᵍ§ 530. HAMILTON, A. C. "Sidney's *Astrophel and Stella* as a Sonnet Sequence." *ELH*, 36 (1969), 59–87.

After analyzing the arguments for a three-part structure, decides that the sequence is structured around the stages of love. Sonnets 1 through 6 define the poet's method and the nature of his love. Sonnets 7 through 12 treat the lover and his mistress. Sonnets 13 through 35 place Astrophel in society. Sonnets 36 through 70 give the experience of writing and loving. Sonnets 71 and 72 show Astrophel unable to separate Petrarchan love from desire. The remaining sonnets show the consequences of triumphant desire. The last two sonnets indicate a return to active life.

◄§ 531. HARFST, B. P. "*Astrophel and Stella:* Precept and Example." *PLL,* 5 (1969), 397–414.
Points out structural similarities between *Astrophel and Stella* and the *Defence.* Astrophel tries to prove Stella beneficial just as Sidney tries to show that poetry is. The sonnets have the same structure as the *Defence:* exordium, Sonnets 1–2; narratio, Sonnets 3–28; propositio, Sonnets 29–35; partitio, Sonnets 29–40; confirmatio, Sonnets 41–72; reprehensio, Sonnets 73–85; digressio, Sonnets 86–106; peroratio, Sonnets 107–8.

◄§ 532. HENDERSON, KATHERINE USHER. "A Study of the Dramatic Mode in the English Renaissance Love Lyric: Sidney's *Astrophil and Stella* and Donne's *Songs and Sonnets.*" Ph.D. diss., Columbia University, 1969.
DA, 30 (1969–1970), 4313A–14A.
Traces the dramatic lyric and its departure from the Petrarchan tradition. Most of the sonnets in *Astrophel and Stella* are dramatic and unified. Of Donne's poetry, the genre poems are the most dramatic. The dramatic tradition continued into the 17th century.

◄§ 533. HERBERT, GEORGE. *Selected Poems from George Herbert with a Few Representative Poems by his Contemporaries,* Douglas Brown, ed. London: Hutchinson and Company, 1960. 159 pp.
Sidney's love poems and Psalms affected Herbert's poetry (p. 24).

◄§ 534. HOBSBAUM, PHILIP. "Elizabethan Poetry." *PoetryR,* 56 (1965), 80–97.
Elizabethan poetry is unpopular because it is assumed to be in the tradition of Surrey, Sidney, and Spenser, but the best poetry of the period is realistic and follows English Medieval patterns. This poetry, written by Chapman, Marston, Ralegh, and Greville, is neglected. Sidney is overrated; *Astrophel and Stella* is chilly, and *Arcadia* is dull.

◄§ 535. HOWE, ANN ROMAYNE. "*Astrophel and Stella:* Why and How." *SP,* 61 (1964), 150–69.
The sonnets are a Christian romance showing a lover caught between passion and reason. All but seven of the first twenty-five sonnets were composed at an earlier date than the rest. Questions the location of the songs. Includes an appendix of rhetorical devices.

536. Hudson, Hoyt H. "The Transition in Poetry."
HLQ, 5 (1942), 188–90.
The transition between Elizabethan and Jacobean poetry was
reached before Elizabeth's death. *Astrophel and Stella* and *Colin
Clouts Come Home Againe* are among the last of the Elizabethan
poems. The new poetry was rational, skeptical, and cynical.

537. Hunter, G. K. "The Dramatic Technique of Shakespeare's Sonnets." *EIC*, 3 (1953), 152–64.
Contrasts Shakespeare's sonnets with Sidney's and concludes
that Sidney's are more analytic.

538. Juel-Jensen, Bent. "Some Uncollected Authors XXXIV:
Sir Philip Sidney, 1554–1586." *BC*, 12 (1963), 196–201.
[Continues 359.] Contains a list of editions of *Astrophel and
Stella*, the first edition of the *Psalms of David, Defence*, a letter to
Robert Sidney, miscellaneous works, and some spurious works.

539. Kalstone, David. *Sidney's Poetry: Contexts and Interpretations.* Cambridge, Mass.: Harvard University Press,
1965. viii, 195 pp.
[Ph.D. diss., Harvard University, 1961. *Index*, 21 (1961), 121.]
Analyzes individual poems to show Sidney's use of the pastoral
tradition in *Arcadia* and the Petrarchan tradition in the sonnets.
Both traditions are in contrast to the heroic tradition that Pyrocles
and Musidorus abandon on reaching Arcadia. Sidney may have
held an ambiguous attitude toward love and the pastoral tradition.
Contrasts Petrarch's image of Laura with Sidney's of Stella: Petrarch in *Rime* 248 admires Laura from a distance, but Sidney
considers desire, as well as ideal love, in Sonnet 71.
Rev.: Katherine Duncan-Jones, *RES*, n.s., 17 (1966), 457;
Patricia Thomson, *MLR*, 61 (1966), 486–87; Robert L. Montgomery, Jr., *JEGP*, 65 (1966), 167–68; A. C. Hamilton,
MLQ, 27 (1966), 323–31.

540. ————. "Sir Philip Sidney and 'Poore Petrarchs Long
Deceased Woes.'" *JEGP*, 63 (1964), 21–32.
Explicates Sonnets 1 and 71 to show that Sidney's poems de-
velop a conflict between the Petrarchan convention and real desire.
Writes that the first thirteen lines of Sonnet 1 are conventional
rhetoric; the last line is colloquial.

◆§ 541. KINSMAN, ROBERT S. "Sidney's *Astrophel and Stella*, Sonnet XII, 1–2." *Expl*, 8 (1950), Item 56.

Believes that "day-nets" in Quarto 2 is a better reading than "dimnesse," because it refers to Stella's eyes and is paralleled in Sonnet 11 by Stella's cheeks, described as "pitfall."

◆§ 542. KREMER, CHARLES F., JR. "Studies in Verse Form in Non-Dramatic English Poetry from Wyatt to Sidney." Ph.D. diss., Northwestern University, 1942. Northwestern University, Graduate School, *Summaries of Doctoral Dissertations Submitted to the Graduate School of Northwestern University in Partial Fulfillment of the Requirements for the Degree of Doctor of Philosophy*, 10 (1942), 30–32.

Studies verse form from 1526 to 1586. The poets of this period borrowed from French and Italian verse, but they also followed native English verse, as well as inventing new forms. Wyatt and Sidney show a greater foreign influence than any other poets.

◆§ 543. KRIEGER, MURRAY. "The Continuing Need for Criticism." *Concerning Poetry*, 1 (1968), 7–21.

Defends criticism of individual poems on the grounds that the poem is an object and may be criticized as such. Illustrates with Wyatt's "Divers doth use . . ." and *Astrophel and Stella*, Sonnet 35. Notes Sidney's repetition of the word "praise" and his attempt to go beyond words into an ideal world. Contrasts Sidney's use of language with Wyatt's.

◆§ 544. LEVER, JULIUS WALTER. *The Elizabethan Love Sonnet*. London: Methuen and Company, 1956. x, 282 pp.

The poetry in *Arcadia* was the first major poetry after Surrey's, and it was in the tradition of Wyatt and Surrey. In *Astrophel and Stella* Italian conventions become an aid to communication. Compares Sidney's Sonnet 71 to Petrarch's *Rime* 210 to illustrate Sidney's modification of the conventions: Laura is a revelation, but Stella is only a heroine, for Sidney was interested in society, not metaphysics. Gives sources for many of Sidney's sonnets. Suggests internal conflicts caused by romance to be the theme of the sonnets (pp. 51–91).

Rev.: J. B. Leishman, *MLR*, 52 (1957), 251–55; Jean Robertson, *RES*, n.s., 8 (1957), 429–32; Robert Ellrodt, *EA*, 14 (1957), 235–37.

◄§ 545. LEWIS, C. S. *Studies in Medieval and Renaissance Liter-ature*, collected by Walter Hooper. Cambridge: University Press, 1966. x, 196 pp.

A collection of essays. All the good poetry comes from the last 20 years of the 16th century; Sidney and Spenser were the earliest of the good poets (p. 127). See also Index.

Rev.: *TLS*, July 14, 1966, p. 616.

◄§ 546. LYLES, ALBERT M. "A Note on Sidney's Use of Chaucer." *N&Q*, 198 (1953), 99–100.

Suggests a parallel passage in Sonnet 39 of *Astrophel and Stella* and lines 242–64 of *The Book of the Duchess*; in both are promises to pay a tribute to sleep.

◄§ 547. MAHONEY, JOHN F. "The Philosophical Coherence and Literary Motive of *Astrophel and Stella*." *DSPS*, 5 (1964), 24–37.

Astrophel and Stella is a poetic application of the Neo-Platonic theory of love given in Castiglione's *The Courtier*. It shows the course of "an erring courtier's love" if the two sonnets "Thou blind man's mark . . ." and "Leave me, O love . . ." are included in the sequence. Renunciation is a common theme in sonnet cycles. Points out parallels between *The Courtier* and Sidney's sonnets and summarizes the Neo-Platonic elements common to both.

◄§ 548. MAHOOD, M. M. *Poetry and Humanism*. New Haven, Conn.: Yale University Press, 1950. 335 pp.

Explores the post-Renaissance religious faith of such poets as Marlowe, Donne, Milton, and Vaughan, as expressed in their poetry. Herbert's poetry owes a debt to Sidney's (p. 41). Compares Sidney to Donne (p. 90).

◄§ 549. MARENCO, FRANCO. "*Astrophel and Stella*." *FeL*, 13 (1967), 72–91, 162–91.

Compares Sidney with Caravaggio. Sidney restored the accent of truth to the tradition, also the moral tone; from these restorations derive the novelty and value of his sonnets. Sidney moved in the direction that Shakespeare was to take. Describes *Astrophel and Stella* in terms of its protagonists. Sidney avoided the clichés of the tradition.

550. MAZZARO, JEROME. *Transformations in the Renaissance English Lyric.* Ithaca, N.Y.: Cornell University Press, 1970. 214 pp.

In the early English Renaissance both music and poetry had the function of restoring harmony. Later lyric poetry became more social than religious. Sidney's lyrics were imitative but also original; his persona controls the sonnet sequence, while Laura controls Petrarch's (pp. 101–7).

551. MILES, JOSEPHINE. *Eras and Modes in English Poetry.* Berkeley: University of California Press, 1957. 233 pp.

Studies sentence structure from 1330 to the 20th century. Most poets tend to prefer certain patterns. Gives the proportion of nouns, verbs, and adjectives in Sidney's poetry (p. 220). Writes that Sidney preferred clausal sentences to either balanced or phrasal sentences. No index, but contains other references to Sidney.

Rev.: *TLS*, September 12, 1958, p. 512; Derek Stanford, *English*, 12 (1958–1959), 24–25; Roy Harvey Pierce, *HudR*, 10 (1957–1958), 447–57.

552. MÖNCH, WALTER. *Das Sonett: Gestalt und Geschichte.* Heidelberg: F. H. Kerle Verlag, 1955. 341 pp.

Studies the sonnet in various countries, including England. Includes a study of basic rhyme schemes, structure, and themes. Indicates the role of Spenser, Sidney, and Shakespeare in the development of the sonnet (pp. 135–39).

553. MONTGOMERY, ROBERT L., JR. "Donne's 'Ecstasy,' Philosophy, And The Renaissance Lyric." *Kerygma*, 4 (1964), 3–14.

Sidney, Shakespeare, and Donne fused philosophy with experience in their poetry. These lyrics differ from earlier English poetry because within them, the poet analyzes his emotions and relates his experience to doctrinal teaching. In *Astrophel and Stella* Sidney related his experience to teachings about the soul. Shakespeare integrated philosophy with poetry in his sonnets. In "The Ecstasy" Donne used the structure of a lover explaining his experience of love to expound a reaction against the whole Petrarchan doctrine of love.

◄§ 554. ———. "Reason, Passion, and Introspection in *Astrophel and Stella*." *UTS*, 36 (1957), 127–40.

The themes of passion versus reason and of introspection provide a way to look at some of the sonnets. Sonnet 10 explores the theme that reason should deal with intellectual pursuits, not with passion; Sonnet 18 illustrates that passion leads to a loss of self. Sonnets 41, 42, and 43 deal with an attempt to accept Platonic love. With Sonnet 66 Astrophel abandons introspection for the role of the seducer. Sonnets 107 and 108 show that Astrophel cannot escape. Concludes that the central interest of the sonnets is the psychological state of Astrophel.

◄§ 555. ———. *Symmetry and Sense: The Poetry of Sir Philip Sidney*. Austin: University of Texas Press, 1961. vii, 134 pp. [Ph.D. diss., Harvard University, 1956. *Index*, 16 (1956), 140.]

Concludes that Sidney's plain and ornate styles are a result of differences in purpose, not the growth of poetic power. In *Arcadia* Sidney sacrificed other possible goals to experimentation with verbal ornament. Suggests that the musical quality of this verse is caused by repetitious structures and tempo. Examines Sidney's use of imagery, structure, and personification in relation to the Elizabethan view of imitation. *Astrophel and Stella* is a study of the paradox of reason and passion, but the paradox is left unresolved.

Rev.: Thomas O. Sloan, *QJS*, 48 (1962), 210–11; *TLS*, October 13, 1961, p. 684.

◄§ 556. MOORE SMITH, G. C. "*Astrophel and Stella*." *TLS*, September 18, 1930, p. 735.

[See 612.] Replies to Mona Wilson that "glass" in Sonnet 105 refers to the poet's eyes, which see less well than does the imagination.

◄§ 557. MORRIS, CHRISTOPHER. *The Tudors*. New York: Macmillan, 1956. 202 pp.

Studies the influence of the Tudors on history. Ralegh, Spenser, and Sidney believed that poetry could be used to educate the gentry. *Astrophel and Stella* is an early personal examination of passion (p. 20). Sidney and Spenser sided with the Puritans in belief (p. 176).

◄§ 558. Muir, Kenneth. "*Astrophel and Stella*, XXXI." *N&Q*,
n.s., 7 (1960), 51–52.

The last line of the sonnet may be an attack upon the persona.
It might be paraphrased, "Are the men in the moon persons who
call virtue ungratefulness?"

◄§ 559. Murphy, Karl M. "Studies in *Astrophel and Stella*."
Ph.D. diss., Harvard University, 1949. *DDAAU*, 16 (1949),
148.

Gathers and judges material dealing with the sonnets. Of the
texts, the countess of Pembroke's edition is the best. The sonnets
follow the Italian and French octave with a contrapuntal sestet.
Supports a biographical approach to the sonnets. Traces their influence.

◄§ 560. Murphy, William M. "Thomas Watson's *Hecatompathia* [1582] and the Elizabethan Sonnet Sequence."
JEGP, 56 (1957), 418–28.

Hecatompathia was the first published lyrical sequence in English, but *Astrophel and Stella* was the first widely imitated. Sidney
was able to transcend Petrarchisms, while Watson and his followers were not.

◄§ 561. Murray, Howard. "The Trend of Shakespeare's
Thought." *TLS*, January 5, 1951, p. 7.

[See 488, 508, 512, 517.] Shakespeare probably did not know
Sidney and probably did not see a manuscript of Sidney's work.
Disher's list of similarities in Sidney's Sonnet 84 and Shakespeare's
Sonnet 50 are coincidental.

◄§ 562. Nelson, T. G. A. "*Astrophel and Stella*: A Note on Sonnet LXXV." *AUMLA*, 27 (1967), 79–80.

Does not agree with Ringler's interpretation of the sonnet. Believes that most Elizabethans would have been indulgent toward
Edward's frailties. If Ringler is correct, then Harington must have
misread the sonnet, for he uses it in his defense of the House of
York.

◄§ 563. Ogden, James. "Hazlitt, Lamb and *Astrophel and
Stella*." *Trivium*, 2 (1967), 141–42.

Hazlitt may have criticized the sonnets because he did not understand the biographical background. Lamb, who defended the sonnets, may be the first modern critic to be aware of the biographical application.

564. PARSONS, ROGER LOREN. "Renaissance and Baroque: Multiple Unity and Unified Unity in the Treatment of Verse, Ornament, and Structure." Ph.D. diss., University of Wisconsin, 1959. *DA*, 19 (1959), 2958.

The 17th-century poetry reveals "unified unity," and 16th-century poetry reveals "multiple unity." Contrasts Sidney's and Spenser's images with Donne's.

565. PATTISON, BRUCE. *Music and Poetry of the English Renaissance.* London: Methuen, 1948. ix, 220 pp.

Poetry and music were mutually influential during the 16th century. Sidney and Spenser may have tried to justify quantitative verse by setting it to music (pp. 62–64). They taught other poets how to be free (p. 145).

Rev.: Frank Kermode, *RES*, 25 (1949), 265–69.

566. PELLEGRINI, ANGELO MARIO. "Bruno and the Elizabethans." Ph.D. diss., University of Washington, 1942. University of Washington, *Abstracts of Theses, Faculty Bibliography and Research in Progress*, 7 (1943), 211–16.

Bruno was not very influential in England because his philosophy was one for which the Elizabethans were not ready. There is no evidence that Spenser, Sidney, Greville, and Ralegh were influenced by Bruno.

567. ——. "Bruno, Sidney, and Spenser." *SP*, 40 (1943), 128–44.

Contrary to Frances Yates's *A Study of Love's Labour's Lost*, Bruno had no influence on Sidney. Sidney would not have been interested in Bruno's philosophy. The only evidence that the two were friends is in the dedication of the *Spaccio*. This dedication is not an attack. Tradition accounts for the later sonnets that Miss Yates believed to be influenced by Bruno.

568. PETER, JOHN. *Complaint and Satire in Early English Literature.* Oxford: Clarendon Press, 1956. 323 pp.

Examines satire in the Renaissance by comparing it with the complaint. Only the sonnets of Sidney and Shakespeare may be excepted from the "cloyingly sweet" poetry produced by the sonneteers (p. 297). Either Sidney or Ralegh may be the prototype for Tourneur's Mavortio, but probably Henry VIII was intended (pp. 305–8).

Rev.: *TLS*, January 11, 1957, p. 24; J. W. M. Smart, *MLR*, 53 (1958), 423–24; Leicester Bradner,

MLN, 73 (1958), 57–58;
Sears Jayne, *MP*, 55 (1957–1958), 200–202.

❦ 569. PETERSON, DOUGLAS L. *The English Lyric from Wyatt to Donne: A History of the Plain and Eloquent Styles.* Princeton, N.J.: Princeton University Press, 1967. 391 pp. [Ph.D. diss., Stanford University, 1957. *DA*, 17 (1957), 2598–99, as "The Development of the English Lyric in the Sixteenth Century: A Study of Styles and Structure."] Traces changes in the English lyric by examining plain and eloquent styles. The plain style became identified with truth; the eloquent style, with worldliness and the court. In the last part of the 16th century, poets turned more toward the plain style. Sidney repeatedly, even though writing in the Petrarchan convention, advocates a plain style (p. 186). Sidney was not a serious Platonist; Astrophel tries but fails to be a Platonic lover (pp. 194–96). Even though Sidney wrote in the eloquent tradition, he also wrote contemplative poems in the style of Donne and Greville (p. 201).
Rev.: Hallett Smith, *MLQ*, 29 (1968), 105–6; Winifred Maynard, *RES*, n.s., 19 (1968), 427–30.

❦ 570. PETTET, E. C. "Sidney and the Cult of Romantic Love." *English*, 6 (Summer, 1947), 232–40.
Compares Sidney's poems with the traditions of the cult of romantic love. Sidney followed convention in believing that love is the supreme human experience. But in *Astrophel and Stella* Sidney recognized that romantic love has a bad side and that physical desire exists.

❦ 571. PETTIT, HENRY. "Sidney's *Astrophel and Stella*." *Expl*, 1 (1943), Item 26.
Explicates lines 12–14 of Sonnet 1: the poet cannot write because poetry is an unfamiliar task and the use of meter is uncongenial.

❦ 572. POTTER, JAMES LAIN. "The Development of Sonnet-Patterns in the Sixteenth Century." Ph.D. diss., Harvard University, 1954. *HRDP*, 1953–1954, p. 14; *DDAAU*, 21 (1953–1954), 261.
Sidney's sonnets have the value of great precision. The sonnets in Old *Arcadia* are English in form and are experimental. They were probably written before the sonnets of *Astrophel and Stella*, which are in the Italian form. The typical pattern for Sidney's

Italian sonnets is one of distinct quatrains with a break after the octave.

◆§ 573. PRINCE, F. T. "The Sonnet from Wyatt to Shakespeare."
In *Elizabethan Poetry*, pp. 11–29. Stratford-upon-Avon
Studies 2. New York: St. Martin's Press, 1960.

Petrarch's sonnets were only one type of Italian sonnet, but the type most influential with English sonneteers. Their problem was fitting the English language to the form. The "pausing line" of Skelton and Chaucer was the closest English meter to the Italian hendecasyllable. Wyatt tried to use it. Sidney started the sonneteering of the 1590's. His sonnets were in the Petrarchan form, but his followers preferred the English form. Sidney used a form that allowed the couplet to become an epigram. His sonnets have a reality that only Shakespeare's equal. The men who followed him did not adhere rigidly to the sonnet form.

◆§ 574. PUTZEL, MAX. "Sidney's *Astrophel and Stella*, IX."
Expl, 19 (1961), Item 25.

[See 500.] The metaphor comparing Stella's eyes to a window for the soul begins a series of meanings for the word "touch." This word can mean basanite, or the lowest of the senses, or the touchstone.

◆§ 575. RASPA, ANTHONY. "Distinctions in Poetry." *Cambridge Review*, 89 (1966), 64–66.

The distinction made between the poetry of Sidney and that of Donne is not altogether accurate. While the two poets differed in technique, they held some philosophical views in common.

◆§ 576. REES, D. G. "Italian and Italianate Poetry." In *Elizabethan Poetry*, pp. 53–70. Stratford-upon-Avon Studies 2. New York: St. Martin's Press, 1960.

Surveys the literary scene of 15th-century Italy. It had a tradition going back to the 13th century. Because English poetry lacked such a tradition, the Italian influence upon Wyatt and Surrey was very important. Not until the time of Sidney and Watson, however, did Italian influence really become felt in England. Sidney owed a debt to Petrarch even though he appears to deny imitation. Discusses the Italianisms of Daniel, Spenser, Donne, and Shakespeare.

≈§ 577. REICHERT, JOHN FREDERICK. "Formal Logic and English Renaissance Poetry." Ph.D. diss., Stanford University, 1963. DA, 24 (1963), 1174.
Uses the logical structures of poems by Sidney, Daniel, Spenser, Shakespeare, Herbert, and Donne to contrast their styles. Most of Sidney's poems are structured around two opposed points of view. Some of the sonnets end with a paradox, some with an unresolved conflict.

≈§ 578. RICHMOND, H. M. The School of Love: The Evolution of the Stuart Love Lyric. Princeton, N.J.: Princeton University Press, 1964. 338 pp.
Studies the evolution of themes and styles in love poetry. Compares Petrarch's Rime 94 with Sidney's Sonnet 54 to find that Sidney's is more argumentative (pp. 45–46). The plain style of "drab" poetry is more forceful than the style of "golden" poetry (pp. 254–55).
Rev.: Roger B. Rollin, SCN, 23 (1965), 25–27; Kenneth R. R. Gros Louis, Comparative Literature Studies, 2 (1965), 278–80; Hallett Smith, CL, 17 (1965), 365–66.

≈§ 579. ROBERTSON, JEAN. "Macbeth on Sleep: 'Sore Labour's Bath' and Sidney's Astrophil and Stella, XXXIX." N&Q, 14 (1967), 139–41.
"Baiting place of wit" may mean a stopping place for rest and also be a metaphor for the earth as hospitium, rather than as domus. Shakespeare may have seen the 1591 quarto where the word appears as "bath," not "bait."

≈§ 580. ——. "Sir Philip Sidney and His Poetry." In Elizabethan Poetry, pp. 111–29. Stratford-upon-Avon Studies, 2. New York: St. Martin's Press, 1960.
Examines Sidney's life in relation to his writing and gives an analysis of his poetry. Philisides probably represents Sidney. Sonnet 30 identifies Sidney with Astrophel. The sonnet sequence is part fiction and part autobiography.

≈§ 581. RUDENSTINE, NEIL L. Sidney's Poetic Development. Cambridge, Mass.: Harvard University Press, 1967. 313 pp.
[Ph.D. diss., Harvard University, 1964. Listed in DDAAU, 24 (1964), 130, as "Sir Philip Sidney: The Styles of Love."] Indicates the continuity of Sidney's poetic development and his attempt to find an expression for the theme of love. Sidney was drawn to

the life of retirement, as well as a life of service. In Old *Arcadia* the two are at variance (p. 38). The *Defence* also is part of this continuing conflict (pp. 46–47). Sidney's style did not change between *Arcadia* and *Astrophel and Stella*; instead, in both he was governed by decorum and convention (pp. 150–52). Sidney's sonnets combine conversational speech and poetic speech to achieve "Energia" (p. 166).

Rev.: Joan Grundy, *MLR*, 64 (1969), 631–32; *TLS*, December 14, 1967, p. 1206; Robert L. Montgomery, *JEGP*, 67 (1968), 695–97; Jean Robertson, *RES*, n.s., 19 (1968), 307–10.

582. ———. "Sidney and Energia." In *Elizabethan Poetry: Modern Essays in Criticism*, Paul J. Alpers, ed., pp. 210–33. New York: Oxford University Press, 1967.
[Abridged from 581.] Both *Arcadia* and *Astrophel and Stella* are characterized by "Energia," a word Sidney used in the *Defence* as a synonym for "forciblenes." In *Arcadia*, Energia arises from the use of "high rhetoric"; in *Astrophel and Stella*, from the interplay between the accents of speech and metrics. In both, Sidney tried to fit words to content.

583. RYKEN, LELAND. "The Drama of Choice in Sidney's *Astrophel and Stella.*" *JEGP*, 69 (1969), 648–54.
Modifies the concept of Astrophel as a man in conflict between reason and passion. Many sonnets, beginning with Sonnet 2, emphasize his choice of one attitude over another. Astrophel moves from freedom to bondage because of his choices.

584. SANDERS, GERALD. "Sidney's *Astrophel and Stella.*" *Expl*, 1 (1943), Item 26.
Explicates lines 8–14 of Sonnet 1. These lines include a progression of metaphors, each growing out of the one preceding.

585. SAUNDERS, J. W. "The Stigma of Print: A Note on the Social Bases of Tudor Poetry." *EIC*, 1 (1951), 139–64.
Printing was not important for such poets as Sidney, Wyatt, and Greville because their poetry reached its audience in manuscript form. While Spenser and Shakespeare earned money by publishing their poetry, Sidney's poetry existed in manuscript for fourteen years. Because of the stigma attached to printing one's poetry, the poets used false names or offered the plea that friends insisted upon publication. Most court poetry was private. Sidney's poetry was written for Dyer and Greville. Even the professional

poets tried to preserve gentility, but for them, publication was a means to patronage. The court poets were the best poets.

⋙ 586. SCHAAR, CLAES. *Elizabethan Sonnet Themes and the Dating of Shakespeare's Sonnets. LSE* 32. Lund: C. W. K. Gleerup, 1962. 199 pp.

Attempts to date Shakespeare's sonnets by noting parallels with the sonnets of other writers, including Sidney, and with Shakespeare's plays. No Index.

Rev.: F. T. Prince, *SN*, 35 (1963), 307–10.

⋙ 587. SCHIRMER, WALTER F. "Das Sonett in der englishchen Literatur." *Anglia*, o.f. 49, n.f. 37 (1926), 1–31.

Traces the development of the sonnet from Wyatt through the Victorian period. Notes that Sidney used traditional material, but with the addition of sincerity.

⋙ 588. SCOTT, WILLIAM O. "Structure and Repetition in Elizabethan Verse." Ph.D. diss., Princeton University, 1959. *DA*, 20 (1960), 3752.

Compares Wyatt, Sidney, Spenser, and Donne on the basis of their use of repetition. Repetition is normally used for either emphasis or transition. Sidney used repetition organically "as a process of self-realization."

⋙ 589. SELLS, A. LYTTON. *Animal Poetry in French and English Literature and the Greek Tradition.* Bloomington: Indiana University Press, 1955. xxxiv, 329 pp.

Compares animal poetry in a study of the tradition. Animal poems were written by the learned class in the Renaissance. Sidney's animal poems were among the first (pp. 78–79).

Rev.: Philip A. Wadsworth, *JEGP*, 55 (1956), 277.

⋙ 590. SHIRREFF, A. G. "A Suggested Emendation in Sidney's Sonnets." *N&Q*, 194 (1949), 129.

[See 591.] "Pindar's apes" should not be emended to "Petrarch's apes," as Siegel suggests. Sidney probably knew Horace's second ode of Book IV where there is the line, "Pindarum quisquis studet aemulari."

◆§ 591. SIEGEL, PAUL N. "A Suggested Emendation for One of Sidney's Sonnets." N&Q, 194 (1949), 75–76.
"Pindar's apes" in Sonnet 3 should be emended to "Petrarch's apes." In Sonnet 3 Sidney is linking Petrarchism and euphuism. Sonnets 6 and 15 also seem to criticize Petrarchan imitators.

◆§ 592. ———. "The Petrarchan Sonneteers and Neo-Platonic Love." SP, 42 (1945), 164–82.
Distinguishes between the Neo-Platonic sonnets of Sidney and Spenser and the Petrarchan sonnets of Watson and Barnes. The sonnets of Watson, Barnes, and Griffin are sensual, containing typical Petrarchan conceits. Spenser writes, in the tradition of The Courtier, of love in which reason rules passion and the mistress is seen as a manifestation of God. Sidney writes of a conflict between physical and rational love. Suggests that the sonnets "Leave me, O love . . ." and "Thou blind man's mark . . ." probably were intended to conclude Astrophel and Stella.

◆§ 593. SMITH, BARBARA HERRNSTEIN. Poetic Closure: A Study of How Poems End. Chicago: University of Chicago Press, 1968. xvi, 289 pp.
The reader's previous experience allows him to distinguish the conclusion of a poem. Poetic closure is the point at which the total structure of a poem is understood. A poem is mimetic, and the sense of closure depends upon the setting and a knowledge of forms and conventions. Sidney's Sonnet 4 is a framing poem in which the dialogue indicates the persona's divided mind, which is framed by the conclusion. Sidney's Sonnet 71 concludes with a surprise ending. After a Neo-Platonic statement of the relation of beauty to virtue, the poet returns to reality and in so doing modifies the meaning of the first lines of the sonnet (pp. 213–14).

◆§ 594. SMITH, HALLETT. Elizabethan Poetry: A Study in Conventions, Meaning, and Expression. Cambridge, Mass.: Harvard University Press, 1952. viii, 355 pp.
Analyzes Astrophel and Stella in relation to its dramatic framework, persona, and audience. It was the most important sonnet cycle during the Elizabethan period because of its influence and artistic worth. In it Sidney has two audiences, Stella and the reader. But by focusing upon the dramatic framework, Sidney gives the poetry a realistic tone (pp. 142–57). Sidney's eclogues in Arcadia are similar to The Shepheardes Calender in purpose and method (pp. 51–54).

Rev.: Herbert Goldstone, *MLQ*, 15 (1954), 274–76; *TLS*, June 5, 1953, p. 366; Leicester Bradner, *MLN*, 68 (1953), 425–26.

⋅⋅§ 595. SPENCER, THEODORE. "The Poetry of Sir Philip Sidney." *ELH*, 12 (1945), 251–78.

[Reprinted in *Theodore Spencer: Selected Essays*, Alan C. Purves, ed., pp. 73–99. New Brunswick, N.J.: Rutgers University Press, 1966.] "Art, imitation and exercise" are the keys to Sidney's poetry. In the Psalms Sidney experimented with metrics. In *Arcadia* he tried classical and Italian patterns. He wrote *Astrophel and Stella* in a simple and direct style. Sidney tried to free himself from convention and to substitute for it a logical structure. Sidney's love poetry is better than Spenser's.

⋅⋅§ 596. STACK, RICHARD C. "From Sweetness to Strength: A Study of the Development of Metrical Style in the English Renaissance." Ph.D. diss., Stanford University, 1968. *DA*, 29 (1968), 616A.

A linguistic study of the shift in style between Sidney and Spenser, and Donne. Through a study of the poets' use of suprasegmental patterns of stress, pitch, and juncture, Stack finds that Donne's rough line imitates speech inside the poetic line.

⋅⋅§ 597. STILLINGER, JACK. "The Biographical Problem of *Astrophel and Stella*." *JEGP*, 59 (1960), 617–39.

There is very little evidence to indicate that Sidney was in love with Penelope Rich, and a biographical approach to Sidney's sonnets tends to neglect the poems. The poems may have been courtly compliments.

⋅⋅§ 598. STROUP, THOMAS B. "The 'Speaking Picture' Realized: Sidney's 45th Sonnet." *PQ*, 29 (1950), 440–42.

Following the principles of the *Defence*, Sidney wrote sonnets that imitated life. Sidney wrote that such an imitation moves the audience to virtue more readily than reality could.

⋅⋅§ 599. SWALLOW, ALAN. "Principles of Poetic Composition from Skelton to Sidney." Ph.D. diss., Louisiana State University, 1942. *University Bulletin Louisiana State University*, n.s., 34 (1942), 21–23.

During the Renaissance, poetic methods of composition changed. Skelton was the first English poet to use the new methods. Sidney used the same methods that Wyatt used. Both men tried to objectify the experience of the poem by such devices as a dramatic structure.

◄§ 600. TAYLOR, ARVILLA KERNS. "The Manège of Love and Authority: Studies in Sidney and Shakespeare." Ph.D. diss., University of Texas, 1969. *DA*, 30 (1969), 3025A.

Both Shakespeare and Sidney use the metaphor of the rider and his horse to symbolize the rational mind controlling passion. In *Astrophel and Stella*, Astrophel becomes a horse ridden by Eros. The imagery breaks down in the final part of the sequence as Astrophel fails to achieve his object. Shakespeare uses similar imagery in *Love's Labour's Lost* and in *Much Ado About Nothing* to symbolize awareness of desire. In *Richard II* manège imagery points out the difference between Richard and Bolingbroke.

◄§ 601. THOMPSON, JOHN. "The Iambic Line from Wyatt to Sidney." Ph.D. diss., Columbia University, 1957. *DA*, 18 (1958), 1040.

Applies structural linguistics to the analysis of early 16th-century metrics. In *Arcadia* Sidney managed to perfect the synthesis of metrical pattern with language. In *Astrophel and Stella* he joined colloquial language to a metrical pattern. This system became the standard English verse system because it allowed more precise imitation.

◄§ 602. THOMSON, P. "Petrarch and the Elizabethans." *English*, 10 (1955), 177–80.

Petrarch's poetry has worth, as well as artificiality, and Sidney condemned Petrarch's imitators, not Petrarch. In Petrarchan poetry the barrier between the lovers becomes a third character in the narrative. In *Astrophel and Stella* Stella's marriage is the barrier. Believes that while Sidney disliked the "dictionary method," he learned more from Petrarch than is obvious.

◄§ 603. TUVE, ROSEMOND. *Elizabethan and Metaphysical Imagery: Renaissance Poetic and Twentieth-Century Critics*. Chicago: University of Chicago Press, 1947. xiv, 442 pp.

Recreates the criteria for poetic imagery in the Renaissance. Mentions *Defence* frequently in establishing criteria, such as "sensuous vividness" and "significance" (pp. 79–247). Many of Sidney's poems contain images based on logical patterns. In *Astrophel and Stella*, Sonnet 54 Sidney uses the conventional adjuncts of the lover to characterize the true lover (pp. 312–13).

In Sonnet 34 Sidney structures his poem around a search for final cause (pp. 324–25). See also Index.
Rev.: George R. Potter, *MLQ*, 9 (1948), 359–60; Rosemary Freeman, *RES*, 25 (1949), 331–32; H. M. McLuhan, *HudR*, 1 (1948), 270–73.

๛ 604. U., R. "Sidney's *Astrophel and Stella*, Sonnet 1." *Expl*, 1 (1942), Q8.
Asks if the last six lines are one metaphor or two.

๛ 605. VICKERS, BRIAN. *Classical Rhetoric in English Poetry*. London: Macmillan and Company, 1970. 180 pp.
Gives a history of rhetoric and explains its function. In the Renaissance, rhetoric again became an important study. *Astrophel and Stella* is a rhetorically complex series of poems (pp. 155–56). In Sonnet 44 Sidney used the figures of gradation, place, epistrophe, and anthypophora. Sidney shifts from figures of word patterns to sensory tropes.

๛ 606. VOSS, ANTHONY E. "The Search for Words: The Theme of Language in Four Renaissance Poems." Ph.D. diss., University of Washington, 1967. *DA*, 28 (1968), 3690A–91A.
Renaissance poets believed that poetry required not only matter, but also adequate form. Treats *Astrophel and Stella*, Book VI of *The Faerie Queene, Troilus and Cressida*, and *The Anniversaries*. Sidney forged his own language in the sonnets; he refused to use traditional grammar and philosophy.

๛ 607. WEISS, WOLFGANG. *Der Refrain in der elisabethischen Lyrik*. Studien zur Entwicklungsgeschichte eines Literarischen Formelements. Diss., Ludwig-Maximillians Universität, München, 1965. 111 pp.
In the period between Wyatt and Sidney, the lyric tended toward the use of an iambic line and strict stanzaic forms. Sidney's artistic effect is achieved by the relationships between words, meter, and rhythm. Sidney stands at the beginning of a new epoch in lyric forms. Like Wyatt, Sydney employed one static half-line with a variable one. Sydney exceeds Wyatt in the use of short refrains. Sidney used the counterrefrain with a varying line length to produce an emotional effect. Concludes that Sidney made two innovations in the lyric: the use of refrain for rhythm patterns and the use of an unchanged refrain.

৺§ 608. WEST, BILL COVODE. "Anti-Petrarchism: A Study of the Reaction Against the Courtly Tradition in English Love Poetry from Wyatt to Donne." Ph.D. diss., Northwestern University, 1950. Northwestern University, Graduate School, *Summaries of Doctoral Dissertations Submitted to the Graduate School of Northwestern University in Partial Fulfillment of the Requirements for the Degree of Doctor of Philosophy,* 18 (June–September, 1950), 35–37.

Surveys Petrarchisms and anti-Petrarchisms. Anti-Petrarchism is a tradition even though the English poets did not learn it from the Continental poets. Most Petrarchan poets also wrote anti-Petrarchan poetry. In his major works Sidney criticized Petrarchism.

৺§ 609. WICKES, GEORGE. "A Portrait of Penelope Rich." *RenP* (1957), 9–14.

It was not Penelope Rich's beauty, but the ideal created by Sidney that inspired many poets to write about her. Sidney's description is stylized, not realistic.

৺§ 610. WILLIAMSON, GEORGE. *Seventeenth Century Contexts.* Chicago: University of Chicago Press, 1960. 291 pp.

Relates "The Ecstasy" to Sidney's eighth song in *Astrophel and Stella* and the convention of the lovers' argument. Sidney's poem involves Platonism and a contrast between spiritual and physical love. Concludes that his treatment is inferior to Greville's in *Caelica,* Sonnet 75 (pp. 63–77).

Rev.: Clifford Leech, *MLR,* 56 (1961), 405–6; Karina Williamson, *RES,* n.s., 12 (1961), 295–96.

৺§ 611. WILSON, HAROLD S. "Sidney's *Astrophel and Stella,* Sonnet 78." *Expl,* 2 (1944), Item 17.

Explicates the sonnet as an attack upon Lord Rich, a dragon-like figure with the "many eyes" of Argus. Instead of joy, the monster finds only the pain of jealousy. The horns of the final line refer to the horns both of Satan and of the cuckold.

৺§ 612. WILSON, MONA. "*Astrophel and Stella.*" *TLS,* September 11, 1930, p. 716.

[See 556.] Asks for an interpretation of Sonnet 105. What "glass" was Sidney referring to? The telescope that Pollard suggested was not invented until 1609.

◄§ 613. WINTERS, YVOR. "English Literature in the Sixteenth Century." *HudR*, 8 (1955), 281–87.
[Reprinted in *The Function of Criticism, Problems and Exercises*, pp. 191–200. Denver: Alan Swallow, 1957.] Reviews C. S. Lewis, *English Literature in the Sixteenth Century* [See 362.]; *Sixteenth Century English Poetry*, Norman E. McClure, ed.; *Sixteenth Century English Prose*, Karl J. Holzknecht, ed. The drama and the prose of the Renaissance are overrated. Music and the short poem were the achievements of the Renaissance. Does not like Lewis' classification of "drab" and "golden" poetry. There are good poems in both categories.

◄§ 614. ———. "The Sixteenth Century Lyric in England." *Poetry*, 53 (1939), 258–72, 320–35; 54 (1939), 35–51.
The major tradition of the 16th century is represented by the complex and profound poems of Gascoigne, Ralegh, and some of the poems of Greville, Jonson, Donne, and Shakespeare, not by the poems of Sidney, Spenser, and the songbooks. The early poets were better than the later, Petrarchan, poets. Wyatt is superior to Sidney. Sidney and Spenser, however, contributed elaborate techniques to poetry. Sidney and Shakespeare were the best writers of lyrics for music. Analyzes "Highway, since you my chief Parnassus be."

◄§ 615. YATES, FRANCES A. "The Emblematic Conceit in Giordano Bruno's *De gli eroici furori* and in the Elizabethan Sonnet Sequences." *JWCI*, 6 (1943), 101–21.
Sidney's sonnets were the first influential Petrarchan sequence. Even though Bruno attacked Petrarch, he used the Petrarchan conceit as an emblem. Sidney, Daniel, Greville, and Drayton used similar conceits. Sidney used the eye symbolism of Bruno, probably intending Stella's eyes to represent divine beauty. Sidney is often anti-Petrarchan in his use of conceits. Greville's sonnet sequence is metaphysical in style; Drayton's may be allegorical.

◄§ 616. YOUNG, RICHARD B. "English Petrarke: A Study of Sidney's *Astrophel and Stella*." In *Three Studies in the Renaissance: Sidney, Jonson, and Milton*, pp. 1–88. Yale Studies in English, 138. New Haven, Conn.: Yale University Press, 1958.
[Ph.D. diss., Yale University, 1953. *DDAAU*, 20 (1953), 263.]
The central issue of Sidney's poetry and criticism is the relationship between form and content. The sonnet sequence exploits

the Petrarchan content to form a whole. Astrophel's attitude toward love unites form and content. Divides the sonnets into three groups. The first sonnets are conventional and attempt to define the value of the experience. The next group, beginning with Sonnet 44, fuse convention and desire. The final group, beginning with Sonnet 85, are again conventional and show the lover accepting the necessary frustration implicit in the convention.

Rev.: John Buxton, *RES*, n.s., 11 (1960), 202–3; M. C. Bradbrook, *MLR*, 54 (1959), 84–85.

VI
Defence of Poesie

617. ABRAMS, M. H. *The Mirror and the Lamp; Romantic Theory and the Critical Tradition.* New York: Norton Library, 1953. xii, 406 pp.

Explores the shifts in relationships among the poet, reader, universe, and literary work. Considers Sidney's *Apologie* as an example of the pragmatic theory of poetry in which the work of art is the means to the end of instructing the audience.

Rev.: René Wellek, *CL*, 6 (1954), 178–81; Thomas M. Raysor, *MP*, 51 (1953–1954), 281–83.

618. ALI, S. M. MUHFUZ. "A Note on Aristotle's Theory of Imitation as Reflected in Shakespeare's Use of North's Plutarch." *Venture*, 3 (1963), 60–63.

Shakespeare followed Sidney's precept and transformed material from Plutarch.

619. ALLEN, DON C. *The Legend of Noah: Renaissance Rationalism in Art, Science, and Letters.* ISLL, 37. Urbana: University of Illinois Press, 1949. viii, 221 pp.

Studies reason and faith in the Renaissance to find their effect upon art. Sidney expressed a desire for "suprarational knowledge" in the *Defence* (p. 10). Sidney, Shakespeare, and Spenser were all doubtful concerning truth (p. 30).

Rev.: *JEGP*, 49 (1950), 581–83; S. Stein, *MLR*, 45 (1950), 526–28.

620. ALLISON, ALEXANDER W. "Poetry and Rhetoric: In Defense of Elizabethan Criticism." In *English Studies in Honor of James Southall Wilson*, pp. 203–10. University of Virginia Studies 4. Charlottesville: University of Virginia Press, 1951.

Critical views of a period provide insight into the period. During the Renaissance, poetry was considered as a part of rhetoric and one of the arts of persuasion. The Elizabethan period focused on the process by which something was accomplished.

◄§ 621. ARMSTRONG, WILLIAM. "*Damon and Pythias* and Renaissance Theories of Tragedy." *ES*, 39 (1958), 200–207.

A Renaissance theory held that tragedy performed a moral purpose by exposing the vices of tyrants. Sidney gave such a theory in the *Defence*, and Richard Edwards illustrated the doctrine in *Damon and Pythias*.

◄§ 622. ATKINS, J. W. H. *English Literary Criticism: The Renascence*. London: Methuen and Company, 1947. xi, 371 pp.

Contains an analysis of *Defence* (pp. 113–38). The last section, which treats of poetic art, is the most valuable. Jonson drew on Sidney for his theory of comedy (p. 191). The *Defence* may have been a reply to Gosson's *Plays Refuted* rather than to his *School of Abuse* (pp. 227–28).

Rev.: D. C. A., *MLN*, 63 (1948), 508; *TLS*, February 14, 1948, p. 91; F. R. Johnson, *QJS*, 34 (1948), 515 16.

◄§ 623. BAINE, RODNEY M. "The First Anthologies of English Literary Criticism, Warton to Haslewood."
SB, 3 (1950–1951), 262–65.

Lists reprints of literary criticism in the 17th and 18th centuries. The *Defence* was issued in 1752 by G. Robert Urie. Warton edited it for Nichols in 1787. It was reprinted by Thurlow in 1810.

◄§ 624. BAKER, HERSCHEL. *The Race of Time: Three Lectures on Renaissance Historiography*. Toronto: University of Toronto Press, 1967. 110 pp.

Contains three lectures: one on truth and history, one on the use of history, and one on the form of history. Sidney's view of the historian as a man who finds truth for the purpose of establishing a pattern of moral behavior was a typical Renaissance view (pp. 15–17).

Rev.: Eleanor Rosenberg, *RQ*, 21 (1968), 471–73.

◄§ 625. BARKER, ARTHUR E. "An Apology for the Study of Renaissance Poetry." In *Literary Views: Critical and Historical Essays*, Charles Carroll Camden, ed., pp. 15–43. Chicago: University of Chicago Press, 1964.

Lists six approaches to the study of poetry and suggests that the rhetorical approach is most active. The Renaissance appears now to have been a transition period, not a break with the Middle Ages. Sidney's *Defence* helped teach Spenser, Donne, and Milton what poetry might be. The *Defence* itself is an imitation spoken

by a persona who does not altogether understand what he is say-
ing. Sidney believed that poetry should exercise the mind and
enlarge the understanding. Sidney saw nature as God's art and
thought that poetry represented a creative force.

626. BATESON, F. W. *A Guide to English Literature*. New
York: Doubleday, 1965. xi, 254 pp.
Comments on Sidney's distinction between the illusion of love
in poetry, and poetry in which the illusion is lacking (p. 49). See
also Index.

627. BAUGHAN, DENVER EWING. "Swift's Source of the
Houyhnhnms Reconsidered." *ELH*, 5 (1938), 207–10.
Rejects Eddy's proposed models for the Houyhnhnms in favor
of the opening passage in Sidney's *Defence*. Such a source would
explain why Swift chose horses as a comparison to men.

628. BENNETT, A. L. "The Moral Tone of Massinger's Dramas." *PLL*, 2 (1966), 207–16.
Examines Massinger's plays in relation to Sidney's distinction
between delight and laughter. In his romances Massinger's moral
tone is blurred even though he preserves decorum, but in his
satires he evokes delight, not laughter, as Sidney recommends.

629. BENSON, DONALD R. "Idea and the Problem of Knowledge in Seventeenth-Century Aesthetics."
EM, 19 (1968), 83–104.
Traces the use of the philosophic term "ideas" from the
Renaissance through the 17th century to show that it retained its
place in aesthetic theory, although in epistemology, skepticism replaced it. The 17th century followed Sidney's theory that poetry
imitates "ideas." Aestheticians, such as Shaftesbury, specifically
attacked skepticism.

630. BIAGI, ADELE. *Sir Philip Sidney l'aeropage e la Difesa
della poesia*. Naples: Intituto universitario Orientale, 1958.
225 pp.
A first part assesses the evidence for the Aeropagus and gives
something of Sidney's life. A second part indicates the relation between the *Defence* and Aristotle, as well as various Italian writers.

◄§ 631. "The Bibliographical Jungle." *TLS*, August 5, 1949, p. 512.

[See 635.] Criticizes the current preference for first editions, writing that it is often hard to tell which edition is first, as in the case of Sidney's *Defence*.

◄§ 632. BLACKBURN, THOMAS H. "Edmund Bolton's *The Cabanet Royal*: A Belated Reply to Sidney's *Apology for Poetry*." *SRen*, 14 (1967), 159–71.

Contains the text of Bolton's work. Bolton intended to correct Sidney's treatment of historians. Bolton's answer to Sidney's argument that the historian is tied to truth is that adherence to truth is adherence to order. Bolton denies that the poet is free from nature; the poet is an imitator of nature. Bolton condemns the use of plot to attract attention and praises *Arcadia* primarily as a book that imitates the virtues praised by historians.

◄§ 633. BLOOM, EDWARD A. "The Allegorical Principle." *ELH*, 18 (1951), 163–90.

Studies the nature of allegory. Includes a historical survey, a survey of the function and rules of allegory, and a survey of the critics of allegory. Sidney believed allegory to be a method of making philosophy known.

◄§ 634. BLUNDEN, EDMUND. "Criticism: Sidney to Arnold." In *Addresses on General Subjects Connected with English Literature*, pp. 183–95. Tokyo: Kenkyusha, 1969.

Sidney's *Defence* is both "shrewd and attractive." It influenced the later criticism of John Dryden and Samuel Johnson.

◄§ 635. BOND, W. H. "The Bibliographical Jungle." *TLS*, September 23, 1949, p. 624.

[See 631.] Reviews the evidence for believing that the *Apologie* was printed prior to the *Defence*. An unauthorized edition of the *Apologie* was published by Olney prior to Ponsonby's authorized version of the *Defence*. Ponsonby then published the Olney edition with his own title page. Finally he published the authorized text.

ᴥᴥ§ 636. Boyd, John D. *The Function of Mimesis and Its Decline.* Cambridge, Mass.: Harvard University Press, 1968. 317 pp.

Sidney followed Horace in finding the function of poetry to be both pleasing and teaching. This position is more moralistic than Aristotle's view of poetry as "pleasurable contemplation" (p. 251).

ᴥᴥ§ 637. Bryant, Donald. "A Peece of a Logician." In *The Rhetorical Idiom: Essays in Rhetoric, Oratory, Language, and Drama. Presented to Herbert August Wichelns,* Donald Bryant, ed., pp. 293–314. Ithaca, N.Y.: Cornell University Press, 1958.

[See 817.] Investigates the rhetorical problems and methods of literary criticism in the 16th, 17th, and 18th centuries in England. Disagrees with Myrick's contention that the definition of poetry given in the *Defence* is the propositio of Sidney's argument. Sidney's plan was to defend poetry against three common arguments. The *Defence* is the first good critical essay in English.

ᴥᴥ§ 638. Chambers, Dwight. "*Deffensa de Poesia*: A Spanish Version of Sir Philip Sidney's *Defence of Poesie*." Ph.D. diss., University of Kansas, 1956. DA, 16 (1956), 2158.

Reproduces the Spanish version and compares it with the *Defence* and the *Apologie.* Concludes that the Spanish version is not a translation of either.

ᴥᴥ§ 639. Chatterjie, Visvanath. "Sidney and the Critical Tradition." *Essays and Studies.* Department of English, Jadavpur University of Calcutta.

ᴥᴥ§ 640. Clark, Earl John. "Spenser's Theory of the English Poet." Ph.D. diss., Loyola University of Chicago, 1956. *Index*, 16 (1955–1956), 141.

Spenser's theory of poetry is similar to Sidney's.

ᴥᴥ§ 641. Clemen, Wolfgang. *English Tragedy Before Shakespeare: The Development of Dramatic Speech,* trans. by T. S. Dorsch. London: Methuen and Company, 1961. 301 pp.

Finds no systematic treatment of tragedy in Elizabethan England. Sidney tried to extend the moral purpose of tragedy to comedy in the *Defence* (p. 39). See also Index.

❧§ 642. CRAIGIE, JAMES. "Sidney's King James of Scotland."
TLS, December 20, 1941, p. 648.
Identifies the King James of Scotland mentioned in *Defence* with James VI, not James I. The names seem to be in chronological order. If James VI is accepted, the *Defence* was probably written in 1584–1585, after Walsingham's visit to Scotland.

❧§ 643. DAICHES, DAVID. *Critical Approaches to Literature.* Englewood Cliffs, N.J.: Prentice-Hall, 1956. xiv, 404 pp.
Deals with the nature of literature, methods of criticism, and the relationship between criticism and other fields, such as psychology. Analyzes the arguments in the *Defence* (pp. 50–73). Concludes that Sidney sacrificed poetic independence by defending poetry as a method of teaching morality.
Rev.: René Wellek, *Yale Review*, 46 (1956–1957), 114–19; Leon Edel, *NYTB*, April 15, 1956, p. 3.

❧§ 644. DOWLIN, CORNELL M. "Sidney's Two Definitions of Poetry." *MLQ*, 3 (1942), 573–81.
[See 826.] Supports Irene Samuel's thesis [*MLQ*, 1 (1940)]. Sidney was defending poetry against Plato. Adds that the source of Sidney's second definition of poetry is drawn from Plato and then turned against him. Rejects Spingarn's suggestion that Minturno is the source.

❧§ 645. ———. "Sidney and Other Men's Thought."
RES, 20 (1944), 257–71.
While not denying Italian influence upon Sidney, questions the extent of that influence. Sidney's opinion regarding *Aethiopica* is original, not a quote from Scaliger.

❧§ 646. DUDEK, LOUIS. "Art, Entertainment and Religion."
QQ, 70 (1963), 413–30.
Sidney had to justify the existence of art, since for much of Western history, art has been subservient to religion, and entertainment has been given no ethical value.

❧§ 647. DUHAMEL, P. ALBERT. "Sir Philip Sidney and the Tradition of Rhetoric." Ph.D. diss., University of Wisconsin, 1945. University of Wisconsin, *Summaries of Doctoral Dissertations*, 9 (1947), 483–84.
Includes a study of the use of Ramistic theory and of Aristotelian theory of rhetoric. The remainder of the summary is a brief history of rhetoric from the Sophists to Bacon.

≈§ 648. DUNCAN-JONES, KATHERINE. "A Note on Irish Poets and the Sidneys." *ES*, 49 (1968), 424–25.

The reference to being rhymed to death in the *Defence* relates to a real practice in Ireland. Churchyard wrote that Sir Henry Sidney made it legal to take the goods of any "Rimar" in Ireland. These "rimars" swore to "rime" their enemies to death. To Sidney these men would have been abusers of poetry.

≈§ 649. EICHHORN, TRAUDL. "Prose und Verse im vorshakespeareschen Drama." *SJW*, 84/86 (1950), 140–98.

Sidney defended the Renaissance tendency to combine literary forms. Sidney based his opinions concerning criticism on Italian and classical writers, not on the practice of the Middle Ages. Sidney preferred verse to prose because it was more memorable and more difficult to write.

≈§ 650. ESTALL, H. M. "Philosophy's Dry Light." *QQ*, 71 (1964), 226–37.

Poetry and philosophy may be found together. Sidney is an example of a writer who mingled the two.

≈§ 651. EVANS, FRANK B. "The Concept of the Fall in Sidney's Apology." *RenP* (1969), 9–14.

Sidney is primarily a Christian thinker, and his concept of the Fall is important in his justification of poetry. The Fall is mentioned twice in the *Defence*. Sidney believed that since the Fall, Man has been degenerate; his will, not his thought, corrupt. Poetry affects the will and can make Man more moral.

≈§ 652. EVANS, MAURICE. "Guyon and the Bower of Sloth." *SP*, 61 (1964), 140–49.

The theme of Book II of *The Faerie Queene*, is Man's duty to love God. Guyon's temptations involve, not physical passion, but its effects on judgment. Concludes with a comparison between Spenser and Sidney. Sidney sees art as an incentive to virtue, but Spenser sees art in its dual nature: either as an aid to virtue or as a substitute for action.

≈§ 653. FLETCHER, JEFFERSON B. "Areopagus and Pléiade." *JEGP*, 2 (1898), 429–53.

Compares the literary theory of the Pléiade as it is given in Du Bellay's *La Deffence et Illustration de la Langue Françoise* with that of the Areopagus as given in E. K.'s glosses and in the

Defence. The English poets may have been influenced by the Pléiade. Both groups favored elevated syntax and style, but while Ronsard and Spenser approved of poetic diction, Du Bellay and Sidney did not approve of archaisms. Both groups advocated more varied use of rhyme and stanza.

✑§ 654. FLOWER, ANNETTE C. "The Critical Context of the Preface to *Samson Agonistes*." *SEL*, 10 (1970), 409–23.

Although this Preface is primarily neoclassical, parts are very like Sidney's *Defence*. Milton, like Sidney, stresses moral teaching over delight. But Milton takes the source of teaching to be in catharsis. Both Milton and Sidney justify by listing great men of the past who have written in the genre each is defending. Both argue against mixing comedy with tragedy.

✑§ 655. FRANTZ, R. W. [Note.] *ELH*, 6 (1939), 82.

[See 627.] Replies to Baughan that D. Nichol Smith has previously suggested the *Defence* as a source for the Houyhnhnms in *Gulliver's Travels*.

✑§ 656. FRASER, RUSSELL A. "Sidney the Humanist." *SAQ*, 66 (1967), 87–91.

Humanism is concerned more with function than with beauty for its own sake. Sidney, a humanist, designed his poetry for utility; he composed *Arcadia* to give moral instruction. The *Defence* indicates that poetry should impel the reader to action, that poetry is kinetic.

✑§ 657. FRIDEN, GEORG. *Studies on the Tenses of the English Verb from Chaucer to Shakespeare, with Special Reference to the Late Sixteenth Century.* Essays and Studies on English Language and Literature 2. Uppsala: A.-B Lundequistska Bokhandeln, 1948. 222 pp.

Studies the active tenses of the verb in the period from Chaucer to Shakespeare. Uses *Defence* as a source.

✑§ 658. GORDON, IAN A. *John Skelton: Poet Laureate.* Oxford: Oxford University Press, 1943. 223 pp.

Compares *Replication* with *Defence* and finds that Skelton anticipated Sidney in calling poetry inspired. Skelton, as Sidney, gives David as an example of the divine poet.

Rev.: *TLS*, July 8, 1944, p. 333.

৺§ 659. GREGORY, E. R. "Du Bartas, Sidney, and Spenser."
CL, 9 (1970), 437–49.
[See 665.] Does not believe, as Hamilton does, that Sidney's
and Spenser's poetic theory and poetry are opposed to du Bartas'.
All three poets consider poetry to have a serious purpose. Herbert,
Cowley, and Milton learned from du Bartas, as well as from
Spenser.

৺§ 660. HALIO, JAY L. "The Metaphor of Conception and Elizabethan Theories of the Imagination." *Neophilologus*
(Groningen), 50 (1966), 454–61.
Writes that the use of conception as a metaphor for the imagination indicates that the Renaissance viewed the imagination as
creative, not rational. Sidney saw imagination as invention, while
Shakespeare used the metaphor of conception frequently.

৺§ 661. HALL, VERNON. *Renaissance Literary Criticism: A Study
of Its Social Content.* New York: Columbia University
Press, 1945. viii, 260 pp.
Indicates the relationship between literary criticism and the
social and political ideas of the Renaissance. Includes sections on
Italy, France, and England. Sidney believed that the speech of the
aristocracy was standard English (p. 170).
Rev.: R. J. Clements, *NYTB*, October 21, 1945, p. 14; F. Mi-
chael Krouse, *MLN*, 61 (1946), 135–36; J. W. H. Atkins,
MLR, 41 (1946), 429–30.

৺§ 662. HALLAM, GEORGE W. "Sidney's Supposed Ramism."
RenP (1963), 11–20.
Compares the logical structure of the *Defence* with its content
to show that while Sidney accepted Ramistic logic, as a poet he
was aware of its limitations. The *Defence* is ironic in tone, for
while Ramistic logic suggests that nature is superior to poetry, the
Defence is based on the superiority of poetry.

৺§ 663. HAMILTON, A. C. "Sidney's Idea of the 'Right Poet.'"
CL, 9 (1957), 51–59.
Asserts that Sidney's third type of poet, the "right poet," is
original, not derived from Scaliger as J. E. Spingarn wrote.
Scaliger's division is based on age and inspiration, as well as
subject. Because the "right poet" imitates the ideal world, he
cannot be one of the poets Plato criticized. For Sidney the purpose
of poetry was to move postlapsarian man to virtuous action.

۶§ 664. ———. "Sidney and Agrippa."
RES, n.s., 7 (1956), 151–57.
Demonstrates the degree to which Agrippa is a source for Sidney. Sidney used Agrippa's charge that all the arts deal with sense experience to show that only poetry does not. Sidney answered Agrippa's charge that knowledge destroys faith by showing that poetry inspires faith.

۶§ 665. ———. *The Structure of Allegory in* The Faerie Queene. Oxford: Clarendon Press, 1961. 227 pp.
[Pp. 17–29 present material discussed in 663 and 664.] Suggests that Spenser was one of Sidney's "right poets."
Rev.: Joan Grundy, *MLR*, 57 (1962), 241–42; Michel Poirier, *EA*, 15 (1962), 73–74.

۶§ 666. HAMILTON, K. G. *The Two Harmonies: Poetry and Prose in the Seventeenth Century*. Oxford: Clarendon Press, 1963. vi, 218 pp.
Traces the separation of poetic discourse from other forms of discourse following the emergence of the scientific attitude. Sidney created a synthesis of the main poetic theories of the past (pp. 86–89). See also Index.
Rev.: *TLS*, October 11, 1963, p. 808.

۶§ 667. HATHAWAY, BAXTER. *The Age of Criticism: The Late Renaissance in Italy*. Ithaca, N.Y.: Cornell University Press, 1962. xii, 473 pp.
Deals with Italian literary criticism by tracing five ideas: imitation, universals and particulars, catharsis, poetic imagination, and divine influence upon poetic imagination. Sidney's description of poetic imagination is closer to Girolamo Fracastoro than to the Italians of Sidney's own age (pp. 326–27). See also Index.

۶§ 668. HERRICK, MARVIN T. *Comic Theory in the Sixteenth Century*. ISLL, 34. Urbana: University of Illinois Press, 1950. viii, 248 pp.
Commentaries on Terence indicate that comic theory was well established by the middle of the 16th century. Discusses Sidney's debt to Aristotle and Cicero for his theory of the risible (pp. 53–55).
Rev.: B. Weinberg, *MP*, 48 (1950–1951), 271–73; D. Bush, *JEGP* 50 (1951), 265–66; H. C. Lancaster, *MLN*, 46 (1951), 428.

◦§ 669. ——— *The Fusion of Horatan and Aristotelian Literary Criticism, 1531–1555*. ISLL, 31. Urbana: University of Illinois Press, 1946. 117 pp.

Renaissance theories of poetry grew out of the theories of Aristotle and Horace. Minturno and Scaliger followed Horace, Castelvetro followed Aristotle, Robortellis and Madius wrote about both men. Sidney followed Horace in finding art and nature as the bases of poetry (pp. 25–26). Sidney's theory held that to imitate was to create (pp. 37–38). Sidney's definition of the function of poetry was a fusion of Aristotelian and Horatian theories.

Rev.: F. S. Boas, *English*, 6 (1947), 313–14.

◦§ 670. ———. "Trissino's *Art of Poetry*." In *Essays on Shakespeare and the Elizabethan Drama in Honor of Hardin Craig*, Richard Hosley, ed., pp. 15–22. Columbia: University of Missouri Press, 1962.

Trissino is not, as Spingarn believed, the source for Sidney's remarks on comedy. Both men follow Aristotle, but both give different interpretations of what constitutes "comic delight." Both give similar definitions of poetry, but this definition was a Renaissance commonplace.

◦§ 671. HOLMES, CHARLES S., EDWIN FUSSELL, AND RAY FRAZER. *The Major Critics: The Development of English Literary Criticism*. New York: Alfred A. Knopf, 1957. 313 pp.

Includes excerpts and comments on *Defence* (pp. 45–70). The *Defence* is the best statement on the relationship between morality and literature.

◦§ 672. HYDE, MARY CRAPO. *Playwriting for Elizabethans: 1600–1605*. New York: Columbia University Press, 1949. ix, 258 pp.

Deduces a theory of Elizabethan drama from plays written between 1600 and 1605. Sidney misunderstood Aristotle's idea of realism; also, he failed to distinguish between dramatic techniques and principles (pp. 10–12).

Rev.: R. B. Sharpe, *MLR*, 45 (1950), 377–79; M. C. Bradbrook, *RES*, n.s., 3 (1952), 89.

◦§ 673. HYMAN, VIRGINIA RILEY. "Sidney's Definition of Poetry." *SEL*, 10 (1970), 49–62.

In Sidney's definition of poetry he summarized all the ethical values of previous definitions he had given in the narratio. Sidney followed Plato and the church fathers by stressing the rational aspect of poetry. He rejected the idea that the poet can show men a vision of divine truth but wrote that the poet can teach virtue.

❧ 674. ING, CATHERINE. *Elizabethan Lyrics: A Study in the Development of English Metres and Their Relation to Poetic Effect.* London: Chatto and Windus, 1951. 252 pp.

Considers Renaisance lyrics in relation to theories of meter from 1557 to 1633. Sidney subordinated meter to lyric in the *Defence* (p. 3).

Rev.: F. W. Sternfeld, *SQ*, 4 (1953), 79–83.

❧ 675. JENKINS, OWEN. "The Art of History in Renaissance England: A Chapter in the History of Literary Criticism." Ph.D. diss., Cornell University, 1954. *DA*, 15 (1955), 123–24.

Considers those Renaissance works, including the *Defence*, that contain criticism of history.

❧ 676. KELTY, JEAN McCLURE. "The Frontispiece of Ben Jonson's 1616 Folio: A Critical Commentary on the Elizabethan Stage." *TA*, 17 (1960), 22–35.

Jonson and Sidney held the same critical beliefs; Jonson's are demonstrated by the frontispiece of 1616 folio. This frontispiece contains representations of the pastor, the satyr, and Tragicomedy. Jonson may have been responsible for the design. Both Jonson and Sidney believed that poetry should teach and delight; both believed that comedy taught by criticizing human errors. Sidney taught that tragicomedy had been carried to absurdities; perhaps the frontispiece is a similar criticism by Jonson.

❧ 677. KISHLER, TH. C. "Aristotle and Sidney on Imitation." *CJ*, 59 (1963), 63–64.

Contrasts Aristotle's descriptive and analytic approach with Sidney's moral and synthetic one. Aristotle suggests imitation of things as they ought to be and as they are; Sidney, only of things as they ought to be. Sidney's poet tries to arrive at absolutes. Concludes that Aristotle's theory of imitation is more realistic than Sidney's.

❧ 678. KLEIN, K. L. "Rhetorik and Dischtungslehre in der elisabethanischen Zeit." In *Festschrift fur Theodor Spira*, H. Viebrock and W. Erzgraber, eds., pp. 164–83. Heidelberg: Carl Winter Universitatsverlag, 1961.

Sidney, with Richard Sherry, Leonard Cox, and Francis Bacon, advocated the middle style, a balance between words and matter.

Sidney believed that the function of rhetoric in poetry was to render the truth of reality, while in philosophy it functioned to delight the reader.

৵§ 679. KNOWLTON, EDGAR C. "Sir Philip Sidney on Italian Rhymes." N&Q, 16 (1969), 455–56.

Sidney was in error when he wrote that Italian poets have no masculine rhyme. A *tronco* verse has a stressed final syllable.

৵§ 680. KRIEGER, MURRAY. "Northrop Frye and Contemporary Criticism: Ariel and the Spirit of Gravity." In *Modern Criticism: Selected Papers from the English Institute*, Murray Krieger, ed., pp. 1–26. New York: Columbia University Press, 1966.

Frye makes less distinction between work, critic, and world than is made in traditional criticism. Frye's work is an extension of Sidney's, itself an extension of Plato's. Although Sidney saw the will as part of the fallen world, he saw the wit as capable of perfection; Frye follows him. But Sidney based his theory of imitation upon metaphysics; Frye does not. In this respect Frye is closer to Freud than to Jung.

৵§ 681. KROUSE, F. MICHAEL. "Plato and Sidney's *Defence of Poesie*." CL, 6 (1954), 138–47.

Suggests that Irene Samuel's thesis [*MLQ*, 1 (1940)] suffers because she fails to relate Plato's theory of myth to Sidney's theory of poetry. Sidney's idea of the function of poetry is Platonic, just as his definition of poetry is Platonic. Sidney is Aristotelian in his treatment of the formal aspects of poetry. Concludes that poetry, like myth, persuades through exciting the emotions.

৵§ 682. LEBEL, MAURICE. "Sir Philip Sidney (1554–1586) et son *Plaidoyer pour la Poésie* (1595)." PTRSC, 4th series, 1 (1963), 177–86.

Sidney was influenced by classical writers and by French and Italian Renaissance writers. The *Defence* is a record of these influences. These influences fashioned the new English poetry. Sidney wrote for all the people, not just the learned.

৵§ 683. LEVY, F. J. "Sir Philip Sidney and the Idea of History." BHR, 26 (1964), 608–17.

Early in the 16th century, history was believed to teach moral action; later in the century, to teach political action. Sidney's writings may have been instrumental in the change of attitude. When history becomes a way of teaching political action, it begins to search for causes.

⤳§ 684. McINTYRE, JOHN PATRICK, S. J. "Poetry as Gnosis: The Literary Theory of Sir Philip Sidney." Ph.D. diss., University of Toronto, 1969. *DA*, 31 (1970), 733A.
Relates Sidney's *Apologie* to the Northern humanistic tradition of *pietas litterata*. Sidney synthesized classical, Medieval, and Renaissance ideas to defend divine poetry. The divine poet can see the original pattern of creation, and he relates this pattern to existing institutions.

⤳§ 685. ———. "Sidney's Golden World."
   CL, 14 (1962), 356–65.
[See 817, 821.] The *Defence* is Christian and Platonic, not Aristotelian as Myrick and Spingarn have suggested. It is Neo Platonic in the assumption that poetry is inspired by God, in following the doctrine of decorum, and in the belief that the poet's inspiration will lead him to truth.

⤳§ 686. McKEON, RICHARD. "The Philosophic Bases of Art and Criticism." *MP*, 41 (1943–1944), 65–87, 129–71.
[Reprinted in *Critics and Criticism*, R. S. Crane, ed., pp. 191–273. Chicago: University of Chicago Press, 1957.] Examines the nature and philosophy of art through critical theories regarding the subject matter of art, such other fields as science and history, and the relation of critical judgments to the terms in which they are stated. Uses *Defence* as an example.

⤳§ 687. MacLEAN, HUGH N. "Greville's Poetic."
   SP, 61 (1964), 170–91.
Contrasts Greville's poetic theory with Sidney's to account for the difference between Greville's poetry and other Elizabethan poetry. In *Astrophel and Stella* the movement is from experience to philosophic observation. The audience is less obvious in Greville's poems than it is in Sidney's. Fewer of Greville's sonnets concern poetry as an art. These differences are the result of different poetic theory. For Sidney the end of poetry was to produce virtue; for Greville the function was to maintain the *status quo*. While Sidney believed that art imitated a higher nature, Greville held a more representational theory of imitation. Greville was more interested in utility and less interested in the "right poet."

∽§ 688. Mahl, Mary R. "A Treatise of Horsman Shipp."
    TLS, December 21, 1967, p. 1245.
[See 245.] A holograph manuscript of the *Defence* was bound in
Francis Blomefield's notes and indexed under the title of "a
treatise of Horsman Shipp." The manuscript is now part of the
Norfolk and Norwich Record Office Collection, and a facsimile
edition of it is in preparation.

∽§ 689. Malloch, A. E. "Architectonic Knowledge and Sidney's
    Apologie." *ELH*, 20 (1953), 181–83.
Sidney's claim that poetry promotes architectonic knowledge
unifies his claims that poets are "fathers in learning," that poetry
can teach men to find pleasure in mental activity, and that poetry
teaches virtuous action.

∽§ 690. Marks, Emerson R. *Relativist and Absolutist: The Early
    Neoclassical Debate in England.* New Brunswick, N.J.:
    Rutgers University Press, 1955. 171 pp.
Relativism in literary criticism began in the 16th century and
became frequent after the Restoration (p. 22). The *Defence* is
absolutist. See also Index.

∽§ 691. Muir, Kenneth. "Menenius's Fable."
    N&Q, 198 (1953), 240–42.
[See Maxwell, *N&Q*, 198 (1953).] Shakespeare's use of the
fable of the belly may have been influenced by Averell, Sidney, or
Camden, or by Holland's translation of Livy, as well as by Plutarch. Sidney used the fable in the *Defence*. Both Sidney and
Shakespeare begin with "There was a time"; both use the words
"mutinois," and "prettietales."

∽§ 692. Murrin, Michael. *The Veil of Allegory: Some Notes
    Toward a Theory of Allegorical Rhetoric in the English
    Renaissance.* Chicago: University of Chicago Press, 1969.
    224 pp.
Emphasizes the classical, rather than the Christian, tradition in
Spenser's allegory. Explains Renaissance critical theory. Sidney
belonged to the group of critics who saw the poet as a maker,
not to the group who molded historic truth to show cosmic truth
(pp. 168–69). Sidney envisioned a popular audience who would
be taught by poetry (p. 171). The poet would reform the morals
of the people (pp. 184–89).

◄§ 693. NELSON, T. G. A. "Sir John Harington as a Critic of Sir Philip Sidney." *SP*, 67 (1970), 41–56.

In various works Harington criticizes Sidney's writings. His reaction to Sonnet 18 and Sonnet 75 of *Astrophel and Stella* indicates that he took them literally, not as an attack on love. In what may be a parody of Sidney's *Defence*, Harington's *Tract on the Succession to the Crowne* defends love poetry as a harmless amusement. Harington preferred the satiric parts of *Arcadia*.

◄§ 694. NELSON, WILLIAM. "The Boundaries of Fiction in the Renaissance: A Treaty between Truth and Falsehood." *ELH*, 36 (1969), 30–58.

Fiction was often either defended in classical and Medieval times as allegorical truth or supported with false documentation. In the Renaissance the separation between history and fiction became firmer, with historians giving factual accounts and with writers of fiction dropping the pretense of truth to historic fact. Sidney's distinction between the two fields became standard.

◄§ 695. NEWELS, KLEMENS. "Eine spanische Übersetzung der *Defence of Poesie* von Sir Philip Sidney." *Anglia*, 72 (1954–1955), 463 66.

Describes the Biblioteca Nacional MS 3908, *Deffensa de la Poesia*, a translation of the *Defence*. Suggests that the translator may have been Juan de Bustamente, a philologist and grammarian. The handwriting of the manuscript is 16th century. Probably it was written after 1579.

◄§ 696. OGBURN, DOROTHY, AND CHARLTON OGBURN. *This Star of England: 'William Shake-speare,' Man of the Renaissance.* New York: Coward-McCann, 1952. xiii, 1297 pp.

Studies Shakespeare in relation to his times. Identifies the writer of Shakespeare's plays as the earl of Oxford. Describes Sidney and the Areopagus (pp. 173–92).

Rev.: Oscar James Campbell, *NYTB*, February 8, 1953, p. 7.

◄§ 697. ONG, WALTER J. "Oral Residue in Tudor Prose Style." *PMLA*, 80 (1965), 145–54.

Suggests that the interaction between the oral tradition and writing, particularly typography, can help define the Tudor style. *Defence* follows the organization of an oration, an oral form. Nashe and Lyly used a similar organization for narratives.

✍§ 698. Orwen, William R. "Spenser and Gosson."
MLN, 52 (1937), 574–76.

Even though Spenser indicates that Gosson was not rewarded for dedicating *The School of Abuse* to Sidney, he later dedicated *Ephemerides of Phialo* to Sidney and *Plays Confuted in Five Actions* to Walsingham. Suggests that Sidney may not have scorned Gosson.

✍§ 699. Osgood, Charles G. *Boccaccio on Poetry: Being the Preface and the Fourteenth and Fifteenth Books of Boccaccio's Genealogia Deorum Gentilium in an English Version with Introductory Essay and Commentary.* New York: The Liberal Arts Press, 1930. xlix, 213 pp.

The parts of Boccaccio's work translated in this book are those that deal with poetry and mythology. Some of these passages are similar to passages in the *Defence* (pp. xlv–xlvi). Probably Sidney did not use Boccaccio as a direct source (p. xlvi).

✍§ 700. Papajewski, Helmut. "An Lucanus sit Poeta."
DVLG, 40 (1966), 485–508.

The question of whether or not Lucan is a poet is tied up with the question of "truth" in poetry and the relationship of poetry to history. In the Renaissance, Scaliger and Sidney represent two different opinions: Scaliger believed that history and poetry should be separate; Sidney believed that although history should be used by the poet to give the appearance of truth, poetry should not be based on pure historical fact.

✍§ 701. Parker, M. D. H. *The Slave of Life: A Study of Shakespeare and the Idea of Justice.* London: Chatto and Windus, 1955. 264 pp.

Relates Shakespeare's thought to traditional Christianity rather than Bacon's new skepticism. Compares Sidney's more didactic concept of poetic justice with Aristotle's. Sidney did not understand Aristotle's distinction between the historian and the poet (pp. 199–202).
Rev.: Virgil K. Whitaker, SQ, 8 (1957), 108–12.

✍§ 702. Partee, Morriss Henry. "Plato and the Elizabethan Defence of Poetry." Ph.D. diss., University of Texas, 1966. DA, 27 (1966), 459A–60A.

Many Elizabethan critics were Platonists rather than Neo-Platonists or Christian Platonists. Sidney appeared to know Plato's original thought, as well as the Medieval tradition. Contrasts Sidney's concepts of inspiration and imitation with Plato's.

◄§ 703. ———. "Sir Philip Sidney and the Renaissance Knowledge of Plato." *ES*, 51 (1970), 411–24.

Sidney's knowledge of Plato indicates that Renaissance men were familiar with Plato's works. Sidney refers to Plato twenty times and to Socrates twice. Even though Sidney avoids answering the attack on poetry in Book 10 of the *Republic*, his interpretation of Plato's stand on poetry is consistent with the *Ion* and the *Phaedrus*.

◄§ 704. PERKINSON, RICHARD H. "Additional Observations on the Later Editions of *Nosce Teipsum.*" *The Library*, 5th series, 2 (1947–48), 61–63.

Notes that three passages in the Preface to the 1697 edition of *Nosce Teipsum* are similar to three in the *Defence*.

◄§ 705. PETTI, ANTHONY G. "Beasts and Politics in Elizabethan Literature." *Essays and Studies*, 16 (1963), 68–90.

The Elizabethans used inherited beast fables for analogy and allegory on political and religious themes. Gives examples from Churchyard, Shakespeare, and the satirists. Sidney approved the use of allegories although he criticized their abuse.

◄§ 706. PONTEDERA, CLAUDIO. "Poetica e poesia nell' *Apology for Poetry.*" *ACF*, 6 (1967), 125–47.

Traces the development of interest in poetic theory during the English Renaissance. Sidney's originality lies in his clarification of existing theories. Traces his sources and the publication history of the *Defence*.

◄§ 707. POPE-HENNESSY, JOHN. "Nicholas Hilliard and Mannerist Art Theory." *JWCI*, 6 (1943), 89–100.

Describes Hilliard's aesthetic theory given in *Arte of Limning*. Hilliard thought painting a gentleman's art. He elaborated his theory of proportion in the form of a conversation with Sidney. Hilliard's theory of art is more empirical than Sidney's.

◄§ 708. POTTS, L. J. "Ben Jonson and the Seventeenth Century." *ES*, n.s., 2 (1949), 7–24.

Contrasts Sidney's definition of poetry with Jonson's. Sidney interpreted Aristotle to mean that poetry represents what should happen, not what would probably happen. Concludes that Jonson is closer to Aristotle.

❧ 709. ROBERTS, MARK. "The Pill and the Cherries: Sidney and the Neo-Classical Tradition." *EIC*, 16 (1966), 22–31.

The *Defence* shows a concern with critical issues even though Sidney does not fully understand critical theory. Plato's argument that the artist represents reality at two removes is answered by Sidney's argument that the artist imitates ideas. Sidney borrowed from Horace the idea that the artist moves his audience to action through delight. The concept that poetry is a "pill" is Christian; that it is a "cherry" is Platonic. Even though the Elizabethans favored poetry used as propaganda, Sidney's concept is of truth giving delight. The ambiguity in *Defence* is the cause of delight.

❧ 710. ROBERTSON, D. W. "Sidney's Metaphor of the Ulcer." *MLN*, 56 (1941), 56–61.

Replies to G. G. Smith [*Elizabethan Critical Essays*, pp. 148–207]. Instead of being a reference to catharsis, the metaphor of the ulcer refers to content: tragedy exposes the criminal activities of the tragic personages and influences the audience to avoid them.

❧ 711. ROSSKY, WILLIAM. "Imagination in the English Renaissance: Psychology and Poetic." *SRen*, 5 (1958), 49–73.

The Elizabethan critics believed that imagination was a reflection of sensory impressions. Even though the imagination is the source of invention, the imagination may give a false impression. Sidney distinguished between the two forms of imagination in the *Defence*.

❧ 712. ROTHSTEIN, ERIC. "English Tragic Theory in the Late Seventeenth Century." *ELH*, 29 (1962), 306–23.

The *Defence* is the first English explanation of tragedy in terms of Aristotle's affective theory.

❧ 713. SACKELBERG, J. VON. *Humanistische Geistesvelt von Karl dem Grossen bis Philip Sidney*. Baden-Baden: Holte, 1956.

Studies European humanism. Reviews Sidney's life and translates the *Defence* (pp. 295–308). Suggests the extent of Sidney's knowledge (p. 300).

◄§ 714. SASEK, LAWRENCE A. *The Literary Temper of the English Puritans.* Louisiana State University Studies: Humanities Series, 9. Baton Rouge: Louisiana State University Press, 1961. 131 pp.

Studies Puritan attitutes toward various topics related to literature. Contrasts Sidney's beliefs with the beliefs of specific Puritans: Samuel Bolton wrote that his work would be profitable and would therefore please, in contrast with Sidney's dictum (p. 35). Puritans tried to find the ideal in the existing world; they did not, as Sidney recommends, try to create the ideal (p. 36). Many Puritans thought of fiction as falsehood (p. 64).

◄§ 715. SAUNDERS, J. W. "The Façade of Morality." *ELH*, 19 (1952), 81–114.

The professional poet had the problem of trying to write publishable poetry that would fulfill the middle class's demand for morality and at the same time please the court. Much poetry was unpublished because the two objectives were unreconciled. Sidney also demanded moral writing. Spenser, Daniel, Drayton, Churchyard, Gascoigne, Watson, and Warner tried to compromise. Mentions Sidney's objection to Spenser's language.

◄§ 716. SEWELL, ELIZABETH. *The Orphic Voice: Poetry and Natural History.* New Haven, Conn.: Yale University Press, 1960. 463 pp.

Uses the Orpheus myth to investigate the relations between language and mind, and poetry and biology. Compares Sidney and Sprat on the relationship between poetry and philosophy (pp. 72–74).

Rev.: F. W. Bateson, *Spectator*, February 17, 1961, p. 231.

◄§ 717. SMYTH, MARIAM. "The Ethical Conception of Literature in English Literary Theory." Ph.D. diss., University of Kansas, 1941. *Microfilm Abstracts*, 3 (1941), 17.

Examines the history of moral criticism of literature. Includes the *Defence.*

◄§ 718. SOENS, A. L., JR. "Criticism of Formal Satire in the Renaissance." Ph. D. diss., Princeton University, 1957. *DA*, 18 (1958), 593–94.

The Renaissance inherited both the classical satiric form and Medieval commentaries on it. Renaissance satirists imitated the classics directly, while the critics, with the exception of Sidney, were lost in the commentaries.

≤§ 719. STAFFORD, JOHN. "The Social Status of Renaissance Literary Critics." *UTS*, 25 (1945–1946), 72–97.

[See 661.] Modifies Hall's thesis that Renaissance criticism was primarily aristocratic and indicates that many critics were not aristocrats. Even though Sidney was, he was interested in bettering his position. Contains brief accounts of the social rank of such critics as Gascoigne, Spenser, King James, and Nashe.

≤§ 720. STARNES, D. T. "Purpose in the Writing of History." *MP*, 20 (1922–1923), 281–300.

Discusses the belief that the function of history was to teach virtuous action. This view persisted from Greek historians through such Renaissance historians as Elyot and Erasmus. Sidney accepted this view.

≤§ 721. STAUFFER, DONALD A. *The Nature of Poetry*. New York: W. W. Norton, 1946. 291 pp.

Sidney's narrow view of morality made his position hard to defend. Examines Sidney's definition of poetry in the *Defence* (pp. 95–98). See also Index.

≤§ 722. SYPHER, WYLIE. *Four Stages of Renaissance Style. Transformations in Art and Literature, 1400–1700*. New York: Doubleday and Company, 1955. 312 pp.

Relates the changing techniques of Renaissance painting, architecture, and sculpture to Renaissance literature. These changing styles produced literary changes. The *Defence* tends toward "academic paralysis" (p. 94). Compares the Renaissance structure of "My true love hath my heart . . ." with the manneristic style of Marvell's "To his Coy Mistress" (p. 118).

Rev.: Wallace K. Ferguson, *NYTB*, June 19, 1955, p. 3.

≤§ 723. THALER, ALWIN. *Shakespeare and Sir Philip Sidney: The Influence of the* Defence of Poesy. Cambridge, Mass.: Harvard University Press, 1947. 100 pp.

Indicates the influence of Sidney's poetic theory upon Shakespeare's poetry by pointing out parallels between the *Defence* and passages in Shakespeare. Finds that most of Sidney's ideas may be illustrated by Shakespeare's practice. Both men considered tragedy a means of illustrating tyranny. In *Henry* V Shakespeare may be defending "stage time" in reply to Sidney. Shakespeare had more faith in poetic imagination than Sidney, but Sidney had more faith in rules. Both men held the same view of philosophy and history. Compares their refutations of charges against poetry.

Rev.: M. T. Herrick, *JEGP*, 47 (1949), 193–96; *TLS*, February 28, 1948, p. 127.

724. THOMSON, P. "The Patronage of Letters Under Elizabeth and James I." *English*, 7 (1949), 278–82.

Discusses the social, economic, and political changes that affected patronage. Sidney's death became the occasion for such writers as Spenser to complain of lack of patronage. Poets writing after the *Defence* could assert their usefulness.

725. THORNE, J. P. "A Ramistical Commentary on Sidney's *An Apologie for Poetrie*." *MP*, 54 (1956–1957), 158–64.

[See 601.] Questions the value of criticizing Elizabethan poetry in terms of its logical structure. Ramus wrote very little about poetry. William Temple's commentary on the *Defence* indicates that a Ramist would disagree with most of Sidney's opinions. For a Ramist the most important part of a poem would be its dialectical element.

726. TILLYARD, E. M. W. "Sidney's *Apology*."
TLS, June 14, 1941, pp. 287–90.

Concerns a possible error in the printing of *Defence* for *World's Classics*. In the passage "when with a divine breath He bringeth things forth . . . ," *He* should not be capitalized. The referent is man, not God. The passage means that man is superior to all other works of nature and that man's ability to create poetry is an indication of his original virtue.

727. TURNER, ROBERT Y. "Pathos and the *Gorboduc* Tradition, 1560–1590." *HLQ*, 25 (1962), 97–120.

While Sidney and other critics were concerned with the significance of tragedy, the playwrights were interested in the feeling evoked by tragedy. Examines the rhetorical methods used to produce this feeling.

◆§ 728. TUVE, ROSEMOND. *Allegorical Imagery: Some Mediaeval Books and Their Posterity*. Princeton, N.J.: Princeton University Press, 1966. 461 pp.

Distinguishes between moral and allegorical interpretations of literature. Illustrates with Sidney's description of poetry picturing vice and virtue (p. 184). See also Index.

Rev.: *TLS*, September 8, 1966, p. 827.

◆§ 729. VANDERHEYDEN, JAN F. "De vertaling van Sir Philip Sidney's *Defence of Poesie* door Joan de Haes (1712)." *VMKVA* (1964), 315–51.

Gives biographical data for Joan de Haes. His translation of *Defence*, which was published in 1724, may have been written in 1711 or 1712. He seems to have used a 1666 text of *Defence*. Finds that he tones down Sidney's use of superlatives.

◆§ 730. VAN DORSTEN, J. A. "Arts of Memory and Poetry." *ES*, 48 (1967), 419–25.

Miss Yates's book *The Art of Memory* may be useful in interpreting Elizabethan writers, such as Sidney, who considered memory an art and who were familiar with the mnemonic techniques of translating abstractions into concrete images. Six passages in *Defence* indicate a connection between poetry and memory, and some of the sonnets may. The scene in which Musidorus sees Pyrocles disguised as Zelmane may serve as a mnemonic for the themes of love, honor, and responsibility.

◆§ 731. VICKERY, JOHN B. "William Faulkner and Sir Philip Sidney." *MLN*, 70 (1955), 349–50.

"Cataphracht of Nilus" in the *Defence* may be the source of "Momus' Nile barge Clatterfalque" in *Pylon*.

◆§ 732. WILSON, HAROLD S. "Some Meanings of 'Nature' in Renaissance Literary Theory." *JHI*, 2 (1941), 430–48.

Supplements Lovejoy's classification [*MLN*, 42 (1927)]. The term "nature" was used in various ways: as the object to be imitated (as Sidney used it in *Defence*); as a creative power of which literary activity is a part (as Sidney used it); as regulative power controlling literary activity (Sidney used it in this sense); and as a power regulating the audience's response. The Renaissance assumed that art was part of a uniform design.

733. WIMSATT, WILLIAM K., JR., AND CLEANTH BROOKS. *Literary Criticism, A Short History.* New York: Alfred A. Knopf, 1957. xv, 755, xxii pp.

Contains a description of the *Defence* (pp. 167–73). Reviews the evidence for considering the *Defence* a retort to Gosson (p. 169). Discusses the question of what Sidney meant by "goodness" of poetry (pp. 170–71). Compares Sidney's theory of imagination with Jonson's (pp. 181–82). Criticizes "Arcadian" rhetoric (pp. 224–25). Compares Shelley's *Defence* with Sidney's (p. 422).

Rev.: Harry Levine, *MLN*, 73 (1958), 155–60; Robert Marsh, *MP*, 55 (1957–1958), 263–75; Stanley Edgar Hyman, *KR*, 19 (1957), 647–57; Kenneth Burke, *Poetry*, 91 (1957–1958), 320–28.

734. WITSTEIN, S. F. "Bronnen en bewerkingswijze van de ontleende gedeelten in Rodenburghs *Eglentiers Poëtens Borst-weringh* (1619): Het Proza-betoog en de Emblemata." *Akademie van Wetenschappen, Afdeeling Letterkunde, Mededeelingen,* 27 (1964), 227–336.

The first forty-eight pages of Rodenburgh's *Eglentiers Poëtens Borst-weringh* is almost a direct translation of the *Defence.* The remainder of the book deals with rhetoric more than with poetry and is based on Sir Thomas Wilson's work.

735. ZOLBROD, PAUL GEYER. "The Poet's Golden World: Classical Bases for Philip Sidney's Literary Theory." Ph.D. diss., University of Pittsburgh, 1967. DA, 28 (1968), 5033A.

For Sidney the context was the most important part of a literary work. The "fore conceit" means universal idea and that which the poet is imitating. It is conceived in the poet's mind but is expressed in concrete terms to make it correspond to reality. Plato and Aristotle both influenced Sidney. From Plato, Sidney drew the idea of the "right poet"; from Aristotle he received the concept of a blend of golden and brazen worlds.

᪥ 736. APPLEGATE, JAMES. "Sidney's Classical Meters."
MLN, 70 (1955), 254–55.
"When to my deadly pleasure . . ." is an example of the
Aristophanic line, not the pseudo-Anacreontic line as Theodore
Spencer suggested. Lists other classical lines imitated by Sidney.

᪥ 737. BALD, R. C. "Will, My Lord of Leicester's Jesting
Player." N&Q, n.s., 5 (1959), 427–29.
[See 762.] Answers Mithal. Will Kemp was in the Netherlands
during the period in question.

᪥ 738. BAROWAY, ISRAEL. "The Accentual Theory of Hebrew
Prosody." ELH, 17 (1950), 115–35.
Investigates the accentual theory of English prosody and its
significance in the Renaissance. Sidney may have translated the
Psalms to demonstrate that accentual English verse is the best
medium for translating Hebrew verse.

᪥ 739. BOND, WILLIAM H. "A Letter from Sir Philip Sidney to
Christopher Plantin." HLB, 8 (1954), 233–35.
Prints an unpublished letter from Sidney to Christopher Plantin
that helps date Feuillerat's Letter 43 as March or April of 1586.
The letter refers to Sir Thomas Heneage.

᪥ 740. BRENNECKE, ERNEST. "Shakespeare's Singing Man of
Windsor." PMLA, 66 (1951), 1188–92.
In 2 Henry IV (II,i,79–80), Mistress Quickly mentions "the
singing man of Windsor." The line may refer to Sidney's epithet
("the singing man") for John Maudelen in A Discourse to the
Queenes Majesty. Shakespeare may be remembering the conspir-
acy, not the man.

᪥ 741. BROOKS, CLEANTH, JR., AND ROBERT P. WARREN. Understanding Poetry: An Antholgy for College Students. New
York: Henry Holt and Company, 1938. xxiv, 680 pp.
Explicates "Ring out your bells . . ." in relation to shifts of tone
(pp. 341–45). The first stanza is solemn, the second indicates self-
mockery, the third shifts to Petrarchan imagery used ironically,
and the fourth stanza shifts tone abruptly when the poet recog-

nizes that he is lying. With the final shift in tone, the refrain takes on a new meaning. The changes in tone are paralleled by changes in the persona's psychological state.

⊷§ 742. BUFORD, ALBERT H. "History and Biography: The Renaissance Distinction." In *A Tribute to George Coffin Taylor*, Arnold Williams, ed., pp. 100–112. Chapel Hill: University of North Carolina Press, 1952.

Plutarch distinguished between biography and history in relation to sphere of action. Biography deals with private action; history, with public. Sidney implied the same distinction in a letter to his brother. Sidney wrote that history is a "narration of things done" and that biography deals with virtue and vice.

⊷§ 743. CAMPBELL, LILY BESS. *Divine Poetry and Drama in Sixteenth-Century England.* Berkeley: University of California Press, 1959. 267 pp.

[See 777.] Relates Sidney's translation of the Psalms to his definition of the *vates* in *Defence*; writes that the Psalms are prophetic poetry. Supports Hallett Smith's explanation of the relationship between the Marot-Béza Psalter and Sidney's Psalms (pp. 50–54). Reviews the evidence for assuming a lost translation of du Bartas' *Divine Weeks and Works* (p. 98).

Rev.: Robert Weimann, *ZAA*, 10 (1962), 82–84; Robert Fricker, *Archiv*, 197 (1961), 200–201; G. R. Hibbard, *N&Q*, n s, 8 (1961), 316; K. M. Lea, n.s., *RES*, 11 (1961), 75–77; J. C. Maxwell, *DUJ*, 22 (1961), 85–86; Allan Holaday, *JEGP*, 60 (1961), 321–22.

⊷§ 744. DEMPSEY, PAUL K. "Sidney's 'And Have I heard her Say? O Cruell Painc.'" *Expl*, 25 (1967), Item 51.

The sonnet deals with the Christian belief that suffering may lead to ethical insight. The first quatrain deals with the physical pain felt by the mistress, the second quatrain compares physical and spiritual suffering, and the conclusion deals with the paradox of the lady who both feels pain and should rule pain.

⊷§ 745. DIX, WILLIAM S., ed. "Letters of English Authors: From the Collection of Robert H. Taylor." *PULC*, 21 (1960), 200–236.

Contains excerpts from letters in Robert H. Taylor's collection. Includes a letter from Sidney to his banker in 1573, a letter from Sir Henry Sidney, and one from Sir Fulke Greville.

◄§ 746. FABRY, FRANK J. "Sidney's Verse Adaptions to Two
Sixteenth-Century Italian Art Songs." *RQ*, 23 (1970), 237–
55.

Identifies two villanelles as models for three of Sidney's *Certain
Sonnets:* "The fire, to see my woes, for anger burneth," "The
nightingale, as soon as April bringeth," and "No, no, no, no, I
cannot hate my foe." Both villanelles are in a manuscript collection at Winchester College. Sidney adapted the melodic line of
his models to keep natural speech patterns. Analyzes the adaptation.

◄§ 747. FOGEL, EPHIM G. "A Possible Addition to the Sidney
Canon." *MLN*, 75 (1960), 389–94.

[Reprinted in *Evidence for Authorship*, David V. Erdman and
Ephim G. Fogel, eds., pp. 243–48. Ithaca, N.Y.: Cornell University Press, 1966.] Two sonnets—"Yeelde, yeelde, O yeelde . . ."
and "Allarme allarme . . ."—from Henry Goldwell's pamphlet
A Briefe Declaratio of the Shews should be added to those Ringler
suggested as possible additions to the Sidney canon. M. W. Wallace suggested them to be Sidney's. The style and rhetorical patterns are similar to the poems in *Arcadia*.

◄§ 748. FREER, COBURN. "The Style of Sidney's *Psalms*." *Lang&S*,
2 (1969), 63–78.

Explores Sidney's integration of stanza form, metrical pattern,
syntax, and meaning in the Psalms. In the Psalms, as well as in
Arcadia, Sidney developed new techniques for drama in poetry.

◄§ 749. FUCILLA, JOSEPH G. "A Rhetorical Pattern in Renaissance
Poetry." *SRen*, 2–3 (1955–1956), 23–48.

Studies the disseminative-recapitulative type of correlative
poetry practiced in the Renaissance. Writes that in Sidney's "In
wonted walks, since wonted fancies change," the disseminated
members are recapitulated in the final three lines. Traces the history of the artifice from Lucilius through the Renaissance. Concludes that this pattern was stimulated by the poets of the quattro-
cento, whose work should be separated from that of the Petrarch-
ists.

✑§ 750. HOFFMAN, DAN G. "Sidney's 'Thou Blind Man's Mark,' " *Expl*, 8 (1950), Item 29.

Explicates the seven metaphors of the first quatrain, all of which deal with the consequences of subjugation to desire. A man so subjugated is the agent of his own doom.

✑§ 751. HUTTAR, CHARLES ADOLPH. "English Metrical Para- phrases of the Psalms, 1500–1640." Ph.D. diss., Northwest- ern University, 1956. *DA*, 17 (1957), 631–32.

Deals with the reasons for and the characteristics of the metrical paraphrases of Psalms by Sidney, Gascoigne, Surrey, and others. Assesses their value as literature and as an influence.

✑§ 752. JENKINS, ANNIBEL. "A Second Astrophel and Stella Cycle." *RenP* (1970), 73–80.

"Other Sonnets of Variable Verse," from the 1591 edition, are a second sonnet cycle. These sonnets have a strong story line and show progressive emotional development. Sonnets 1, 3, 5, 7, and 9 are an emotional frame for the events of Sonnets 2, 4, 6, 8, and 10. Sonnet 11 is the conclusion. The sonnets end in an Eliot- like wasteland, with Stella unresponding and Astrophel unwilling to submit to her will.

✑§ 753. JUEL-JENSEN, BENT. "The Tixall Manuscript of Sir Philip Sidney's and the Countess of Pembroke's Paraphrase of the Psalms." *BC*, 18 (1969), 222–23.

This manuscript was formerly owned by Sir Talbot Constable and was sold at Sotheby's in 1899. It was part of a library originally formed by Sir Walter Aston, and it is possible that he was given the manuscript by King James I or by Prince Henry.

✑§ 754. KUERSTEINER, AGNES D. "A Note on Sir Philip Sidney." *N&Q*, 93 (1948), 268–69.

Writes that Sidney's letter of December 19, 1573, to Languet is incorrect in Stewart A. Pears's translation. This letter is the source for the hypothesis that Sidney was bad tempered.

✑§ 755. LEVY, C. S. "A Supplementary Inventory of Sir Philip Sidney's Correspondence." *MP*, 67 (1969), 177–81.

Lists letters from Sidney not included in Feuillerat's *Works* and summarizes those that have not been printed. Also lists all extant letters writen to Sidney, excluding those being edited by James M. Osborn and those at Christ Church, Oxford.

✠§ 756. ———. "An Unpublished Letter of Sir Philip Sidney."
N&Q, n.s., 13 (1966), 248–51.

Includes the text of a letter from Sidney to Peter Beutterich in April, 1585, that gives evidence that Sidney was interested in England's foreign policy in the Netherlands and in Queen Elizabeth's relations with James VI. Contains an analysis of the conditions surrounding both problems.

✠§ 757. McLane, Paul E. "Spenser's Political and Religious Position in The Shepheardes Calender."
JEGP, 49 (1950), 324–32.

The Shepheardes Calender is a protest against the Alençon marriage and against Elizabeth's and Burghley's policies. Reviews Sidney's opposition to the marriage.

✠§ 758. McMahon, A. Philip. "Sidney's Letter to the Camerarii."
PMLA, 62 (1947), 83–95.

Contains the text of Sidney's letter to the group, with an endorsement not found in Feuillerat's text. Recounts the relations between Philippus and Joachim Camerarius and Sidney.

✠§ 759. Martz, Louis L. The Poetry of Meditation: A Study in English Religious Literature of the Seventeenth Century. New Haven, Conn.: Yale University Press, 1954. xiv, 375 pp.

Finds that Herbert's The Temple and Sidney's Psalms are similar in line length, rhyme, and diction. Sidney's version of Psalm 6 is based on Coverdale but is more colloquial and idiomatic. Sidney attempted to use the Elizabethan lyric in psalmody (pp. 273–78).

Rev.: Hoxie N. Fairchild, MLN, 70 (1955), 445–48; TLS, June 3, 1955, p. 304; Perry J. Powers, CL, 8 (1956), 150–54; Helen C. White, JEGP, 55 (1956), 647–50; Rosemond Tuve, MP, 53 (1955–1956), 204–7.

✠§ 760. "Memorabilia." N&Q, 152 (1927), 326.

Notes that on May 31, 1927, Sotheby's is to offer an autograph copy of Sidney's Defence of Leicester for sale.

✠§ 761. Mesterton, Erik. [Correspondence.] London Magazine, 6 (1959), 60.

[See 769.] Rathmell is in error; the Psalter is incorporated in Feuillerat's Complete Works.

◄§ 762. Mithal, H. S. D. "Will, My Lord of Leicester's Jesting Player." *N&Q*, n.s., 5 (1958), 427–29.

[See 737.] Sidney refers to "Will" in his letter to Walsingham of March 24, 1586. Bruce has identified the man as William Kemp. Instead, the name may refer to Robin Wilson. Wilson was called "Wilsonus" by a fellow actor. He may have followed Leicester to Utrecht.

◄§ 763. Murphy, Charles D. "John Davies's Versification of Sidney's Prose." *PQ*, 21 (1942), 410–14.

Davies used Sidney's and Golding's translation of Mornay's *A Woorke concerning the trewness of the Christian Religion* as a source for his poem *Mirum Modum*. Davies took as a source passages on the names of God, on the Trinity, on the problem of evil, on the existence and power of God, and on providence. Cites parallel passages.

◄§ 764. Murphy, Karl M. "The 109th and 110th Sonnets of *Astrophel and Stella*." *PQ*, 34 (1955), 349–52.

Grosart's Sonnets 109 and 110 are not part of *Astrophel and Stella*. They change the moral tone of the sequence. Also, Sonnet 110 is an English sonnet, a form that Sidney did not use in the sequence.

◄§ 765. Orgel, S. K. "Sidney's Experiment in Pastoral: *The Lady of May*." *JWCI*, 26 (1963), 198–203.

In *The Lady of May* Sidney re examines the pastoral assumption that the life of contemplation is better than that of action. While the life of action, represented by Therion, seems to have the advantage, Queen Elizabeth follows tradition by choosing Espilus as the winner. Speculates that the Queen was left free to judge and missed the point of Sidney's drama.

◄§ 766. Osborn, James M. "New Light on Sir Philip Sidney." *TLS*, April 30, 1970, pp. 487–88.

Reports on the seventy-six letters to Sidney sold at Sotheby's. Most of these letters are from friends on the Continent, such as Jean Lobbet, Jean de Volcob, Wolfgang Zundelin, and Johann Conrad Brüning. These letters extend knowledge about Sidney's European tour.

⊷§ 767. Purdy, Mary M. "Political Propaganda in Ballad and Masque." In *Testament to Percival Hunt*, Agnes Lynch Starrett, ed., pp. 264–93. Pittsburgh: University of Pittsburgh Press, 1948.

Sidney used the pastoral for a political purpose prior to *The Shepheardes Calender*. In *The Lady of May* Sidney may be referring to Leicester's courtship of Queen Elizabeth, with Espilus as Leicester and Therion as Alençon. Bernard Garter refers to the same courtship in *Appelles and Pigmalion*.

⊷§ 768. Rathmell, J. C. A. "Exploration and Recoveries -I. Hopkins, Ruskin and the Sidney Psalter." *London Magazine*, 6 (1959), 51–66.

The Sidney Psalter is important in understanding the development of metaphysical poetry. Suggests that Ruskin, Hopkins, and Patmore were influenced by the strong accents of the Psalms. Points out parallel passages in Hopkins and Sidney. Both men were interested in Hebrew rhythm.

⊷§ 769. ———. [Correspondence.] *London Magazine*, 6 (1959), 60.

[See 761.] Only 43 of the 150 Psalms are reprinted in Feuillerat's *Complete Works*.

⊷§ 770. Ribner, Irving. "Machiavelli and Sidney's *Discourse to the Queene's Majesty*." *Italica*, 26 (1949), 177–87.

[See 409.] Machiavellian thought was not foreign to 16th-century English thought. Compares *A Discourse to the Queenes Majesty* with Machiavelli's writings: both show any change of government to be bad, both show friendship to be the basis for stable government, both warn against elevating potential enemies, both suggest that love and fear bind the people to the ruler, and both use history for verification. Both writers were utilitarians.

⊷§ 771. Ringler, William. "Poems attributed to Sir Philip Sidney." *SP*, 47 (1950), 126–51.

[Parts are reprinted in *Evidence for Authorship*, D. V. Erdman and E. G. Fogel, eds., pp. 229–42. Ithaca, N.Y.: Cornell University Press, 1966.] Of the 30 poems attributed to Sidney since his death, 17 are not his, 8 probably are not, 2 may possibly be, and only 3 should probably be added to the Sidney canon.

772. ROBINSON, FORREST G. "A Note on the Sidney-Golding Translation of Philippe de Mornay's *De La Verité De La Religion Chrestienne.*" HLB, 17 (1969), 98–102.

Sidney probably translated Chapter I; Golding, probably Chapter XV. Of the rest, not enough evidence exists to distinguish the parts each man translated. Feuillerat's claim for stylistic difference is hard to support.

773. RYKEN, LELAND. "Sidney's 'Leave me, O love, which reachest but to dust.'" *Expl*, 26 (1967), Item 9.

The source for the image of the yoke and the light may be Matthew 11:30. Sidney may have been punning on the word "light." Christ's yoke is light (i.e., visible light) in the sonnet.

774. SCHULZE, IVAN L. "The Final Protest against the Elizabeth-Alençon Marriage Proposal." *MLN*, 58 (1943), 54–57.

After warning Elizabeth against the proposed marriage in his letter, Sidney and his friends may have planned the symbolism of the tournament held in May of 1579 to warn the French ambassadors that the planned marriage would not take place.

775. SERONSY, CECIL C. "Another Huntington Manuscript of the Sidney Psalms." HLQ, 29 (1965–1966), 109–16.

A fifteenth manuscript of the Psalms has been discovered at the Huntington Library. Lists some variations between the new manuscript and the first printed copy.

776. "Sidney's *Defence of Leicester.*"
TLS, May 19, 1927, p. 360.

Notes the sale of an autograph manuscript of Sidney's *Defence of Leicester.* It was owned by Mrs. P. A. Russell.

777. SMITH, HALLETT. "English Metrical Psalms in the Sixteenth Century and Their Literary Significance."
HLQ, 9 (1956), 268–71.

Considers the motives and background for many metrical versions of the psalms in the 16th century. Older versions were in prose. Possibly Elizabethan psalms were translated into ballad stanza in order to compete with the "profane" lyrics of the courtiers. Classifies the translations into five groups, grouping Sidney's under those influenced by Marot. Of the 43 Psalms, 14 are imitations of the meter of a psalm in the Marot-Béza version. Sidney followed Marot by using a variety of meters in his Psalms.

~§ 778. Stevens, John E. *Music and Poetry in the Early Tudor Court*. London: Methuen and Company, 1961. xi, 483 pp.

Sidney's Psalms owe more to the French versions of Marot than to the English tradition (p. 85).

Rev.: R. L. Greene, *Medium Ævum*, 31 (1962), 220–22.

~§ 779. Summers, Joseph H. *George Herbert. His Religion and Art*. Cambridge, Mass.: Harvard University Press, 1954. 246 pp.

Herbert was influenced by Sidney (p. 148). Sidney's experiments with contrapuntal rhythm in the Psalms resemble Herbert's experiments. See also Index.

Rev.: Geoffrey Bullough, *MP*, 53 (1955–1956), 277–78; K. Williamson, *SN*, 27 (1955), 165–66; Jackson I. Cope, *MLN*, 70 (1955), 55–57; Rosemond Tuve, *JEGP*, 54 (1955), 284–85.

~§ 780. Thomas, W. K. "Sidney's 'Leave me, O Love, which reachest but to Dust.'" *Expl*, 28 (1970), Item 5.

[See 773.] Follows Ryken's suggestion and looks for Biblical allusions in the sonnet. "Which" in line 7 may have as its referent "humble all thy might./To that sweet yoke." If so, the allusion may be to Ecclesiaticus 35:16–17. Line 9 may allude to Matthew 18:2–4, and "light" may be a metaphor for Christ.

~§ 781. Wilson, Harold S. "Sidney's 'Leave me, O love, which reachest but to dust.'" *Expl*, 2 (1944), Item 6.

Suggests that the poem yields best to a Christian, rather than to a Petrarchan, interpretation. The poem contrasts earthly and heavenly things. Matthew 11:29–30 and John 8:12 are sources for lines 6–8. The closing couplet is a prayer to God.

VIII
Foreign Studies

⊷§ 782. ALMON, LISELOTTE. "Die Staatsidee in Sidneys *Arcadia*, Barclays *Argenis* und Anton Ulrichs *Aramens*." Marburg, Phil. F., Diss. v. 14 Febr. 1944. 187 gez. Bl. 4° [Maschinenschr.]. Listed in *Jahresverzeichnis der deutschen Hochschulschriften*, 60 (1944–1945), 6432, and in Lawrence F. McNamee, *Dissertations in English and American Literature: Theses Accepted by American, British and German Universities, 1865–1964*, 196.

⊷§ 783. ANDERSON, D. M. "Characterisation in Sir Philip Sidney's *Arcadia*." B.Litt., Magdalen College, Oxford University. Listed in *Index to Theses Accepted for Higher Degrees in the Universities of Great Britain and Ireland*, 6 (1955–1956), Item 159.

⊷§ 784. BIEDRZYCKA, HALINA. "Elementy Kalsyczne w 'Obronie Poezji Filipa Sidney.'" *Roczniki Humanistyczne*, T. 6. 1957, pp. 105–95.

⊷§ 785. CHALLIS, L. M. "A Study of Sidney· *Arcadia* and *Astrophel and Stella* in the Light of Contemporary Rhetoric and Literary Convention." M.A., 1962, University of London. Listed in University of London, *Theses, Dissertations and Published Works Accepted for Higher Degrees: A Classified List with Author and Subject Indexes*, 1 October 1961–30 September 1962, 5.

⊷§ 786. DUNDAS, OENONE J. "The Concept of Wit in English Literary Criticism, 1579–1650." M.A., 1951, University College, University of London. Listed in University of London, *Theses, Dissertations and Published Works Accepted for Higher Degrees: A Classified List with Author and Subject Indexes*, 1 October 1950–30 September 1951, 16.

≈§ 787. Eisig, K. T. "Moral Criteria in Renaissance Literary Criticism With Special Reference to Milton." M.A., 1951, University of London. Listed in University of London, *Theses, Dissertations and Published Works Accepted for Higher Degrees: A Classified List with Author and Subject Indexes,* 1 October 1950–30 September 1951, 16.

≈§ 788. Gaines, Lily. "The Heroic Ideal in Sidney and Spenser." M.A., 1958, University College of Wales. Listed in *Index to Theses Accepted for Higher Degrees in the Universities of Great Britain and Ireland,* 9 (1958–1959), Item 155.

≈§ 789. Glasscoe, M. "Sidney's Treatment of the Theme of Virtue in *Arcadia*." M.A., 1964, Bedford College, University of London. Listed in University of London, *Theses, Dissertations and Published Works Accepted for Higher Degrees: A Classified List with Author and Subject Indexes,* 1 October 1963–30 September 1964, 8.

≈§ 790. Huesgen, Hildegardis. *Das Intellectual Feld der deutschen Arcadia und in Ihrem Englischen Vorbild.* Münster, 1936.

≈§ 791. Mainusch, Herbert. "Die Dichtungstheorie Sir Philip Sidneys." Münster, Phil. F., Diss. v. 3. Nov. 1956 (Nichtf. d. Aust.). o. O. 1956. 159 gez. Bl. 4° [Maschinenschr. vervielf.]. Listed in *Jahresverzeichnis der deutschen Hochschulschriften,* 72 (1956), 7490.

≈§ 792. Owen, L. J. "Chivalric Friendship and its Survival in the Sixteenth Century English Versions of Medieval Chivalric Romance." Ph.D. (Arts), 1958, University College, University of London. Listed in University of London, *Theses, Dissertations and Published Works Accepted for Higher Degrees: A Classified List with Author and Subject Indexes,* 1 October 1957–30 September 1958, 6.

≈§ 793. Rathmell, J. C. A. "A Critical Edition of the Psalms of Sir Philip Sidney and the Countess of Pembroke." Ph.D., 1965, Christ's College, Cambridge University. Listed in *Index to Theses Accepted for Higher Degrees in the Universities of Great Britain and Ireland,* 15 (1964–1965), Item 251.

◆§ 794. RIVERA, MARIA ANGELICA HINOJOSA DE. "Traduccion de *An Apologie for Poetrie* de Philip Sidney." Thesis, 1965, Instituto Tecnologico y de Estudios Superiores de Monterrey. Listed in *National Union Catalogue*, 1963–1967, p. 591.

◆§ 795. ROSE, M. A. "A Study of Sir Philip Sidney's *Old Arcadia*." B.Litt., Merton College, Oxford University. Listed in *Index to Theses Accepted for Higher Degrees in the Universities of Great Britain and Ireland*, 14 (1963–1964), Item 207.

◆§ 796. SAGE, L. "Poems on Poetry from Sidney to Milton." M.A., University of Birmingham. Listed in *Index to Theses Accepted for Higher Degrees in the Universities of Great Britain and Ireland*, 17 (1966–1967), Item 341.

◆§ 797. SCANLON, P. A. "Elizabethan Prose Romance." Ph.D., 1966, Trinity College, Dublin. Listed in *Index to Theses Accepted for Higher Degrees in the Universities of Great Britain and Ireland*, 17 (1966–1967), Item 365.

◆§ 798. SCHINDL, ERIKA. "Studien zum Wortschatz Sir Philip Sidney: Neubildungen und Entlehnungen." Wien, Phil. Diss. 25 Mai 1955. 141 Bl. 4° [Maschinenschr.]. Listed in *Oesterreichische Bibliographie: Verzeichnis der Oesterreichischen Neuerscheinungen*, 14 (1955), Item 58.

◆§ 799. SCHON, HILDA. "Catulls Epithalamion und Seine Englischen Nachahmer bis 1660." Ph.D., 1940, University of Vienna.

◆§ 800. WALMSLEY, J. M. "Types and Techniques of Elizabethan Prose Fiction." M.A., 1960, Queen Mary College, University of London. Listed in *University of London, Theses, Dissertations and Published Works Accepted for Higher Degrees: A Classified List with Author and Subject Indexes, 1 October 1959–30 September 1960*, 5.

◆§ 801. WETZEL, GUNTER. "Die Literarische Kritik in England von Sidney bis Dryden." 168 gez. Bl. Kiel 2.7 1941. Bock. Kiel UB. Listed in *Anglia*, "Bibliographie der an Deutschen und österreichischen Universitäten 1939–1951 angenommenen anglistischen dissertationen," 71 (1953), 382.

IX
Reprinted Works

&‍§ 802. AUBREY, JOHN. *Brief Lives,* Oliver Lawson Dick, ed. London: Secker and Warburg, 1949. 408 pp.
[First published, 1813, as *Lives of Eminent Men.*] Gives an account of Sidney's life based on Greville (pp. 278–80).

&‍§ 803. ———. *Brief Lives and Other Selected Writings,* Anthony Power, ed. New York: Scribner's, 1949. 410 pp.
[See 802.] For Sidney's life, see pages 34–37.

&‍§ 804. BALDWIN, CHARLES SEARS. *Renaissance Literary Theory and Practice: Classicism in the Rhetoric and Poetic of Italy, France, and England, 1400–1600.* Gloucester, Mass.: Peter Smith, 1959. xvi, 251 pp.
[First published, 1939.] Relates literary theory and practice in the Renaissance to the classical and Medieval periods.

&‍§ 805. DANIEL, SAMUEL. *Poems and A Defence of Ryme,* Arthur Colby Sprague, ed. Chicago: University of Chicago Press, 1965. xxxviii, 216 pp.
[First published, 1930.] Mentions Sidney's influence upon Daniel, and Daniel's relations with the Sidney circle (i–xxxvii).

&‍§ 806. DRINKWATER, JOHN. "Sir Philip Sidney." In *Prose Papers,* pp. 74–93. Freeport, N.Y.: Books for Libraries Press, 1969.
[First published, 1917.] While *Astrophel and Stella* is sincere, the object of love may be more an ideal than a physical woman. Traces the evolution of the sonnet from Petrarch to Shakespeare.

&‍§ 807. EMPSON, WILLIAM. *Seven Types of Ambiguity.* Meridian Books. Cleveland, Ohio: The World Publishing Company, 1955. 298 pp.
[First published, 1930.] Analyzes Sidney's "Ye goatherd gods . . ." as an example of one of the seven ways in which a poet can achieve multiple meaning. The poem plays on a repetition of the words "mountaines," "vallies," "forrests," "musique," "evening," and "morning." Sidney's repetitions build a cumulative emotion.

808. Fuller, Thomas. *The Worthies of England,* John Freeman, ed. London: George Allen and Unwin, Ltd., 1952. 716 pp.

[First published, 1662, as *The History of the Worthies of England.*] Concentrates on Sidney as a statesman and soldier. Praises Sidney's learning. He was well educated in England and increased his knowledge by foreign travel. *Arcadia* is evidence of his mastery of both content and language (p. 277).

809. Gebert, Clara. *An Anthology of Elizabethan Dedications and Prefaces.* New York: Russell and Russell, 1966. 302 pp.

[First published, 1933.] Includes Sidney's Preface to *Arcadia* (p. 65), Thomas Nashe's to the 1591 edition of *Astrophel and Stella* (p. 71), and Olney's to the 1595 *Apology* (p. 112).

810. Greg, W. S. *Pastoral Poetry and Pastoral Drama.* New York: Russell and Russell, Inc., 1959. xii, 464 pp.

[First published, 1905.] Reviews the publication of the New *Arcadia* and the revisions in the text (pp. 147–50). Finds its style little better than euphuism (pp. 150–54).

811. Harrison, John Smith. *Platonism in English Poetry of the Sixteenth and Seventeenth Centuries.* New York: Russell and Russell, Inc., 1965. 235 pp.

[First published, 1903.] Interprets "Leave me, O love . . ." as an expression of the soul's desire to seek heavenly love (pp. 84–85).

812. Hunt, Leigh. *Leigh Hunt's Literary Criticism,* Lawrence H. Houtchens and Carolyn W. Houtchens, eds. New York: Columbia University Press, 1956. 732 pp.

Reprints Hunt's criticism of Sidney. Sidney's writing is over-intense (p. 110). Hunt also comments upon Hazlitt's criticism of Sidney (p. 258).

813. John, Lisle Cecil. *The Elizabethan Sonnet Sequences: Studies in Conventional Conceits.* New York: Russell and Russell, 1964. 278 pp.

[First published, 1938.] Traces the relationship between the Petrarchan sonnet sequence and the Elizabethan sequence. Lists conceits. The sun and star imagery in *Astrophel and Stella* gives it unity (p. 152). Describes Sidney's use of the convention in which Cupid wages war on the poet (p. 62). Sidney was skillful in adapting traditions (p. 71). Discusses Sidney's use of the theme of sleep (p. 87), the theme of the exchange of hearts (p. 96), and the theme of despair (p. 104).

᪐§ 814. JUSSERAND, J. J. *The English Novel in the Time of Shakespeare.* London: Ernest Benn Limited, 1966. 433 pp.

[First published, 1890.] Studies Lyly, Sidney, and Nashe in relation to the novel as a form. Concludes that Sidney wrote *Arcadia* to please his sister, not, as Greville believed, for a moral purpose (p. 234). The subject matter of *Arcadia* is love, not politics (p. 245). The prose style of the *Defence* had more influence on later novelists than did the style of *Arcadia* (p. 403). Traces the works for which *Arcadia* is a source (pp. 260–83).

᪐§ 815. LANCASTER, HENRY CARRINGTON. "Sidney, Galaut, La Calprenede: An Early Instance of the Influence of English Literature upon French." In *Adventures of a Literary Historian: A Collection of His Writings Presented to H. C. Lancaster,* pp. 177–86. Baltimore: Johns Hopkins Press, 1942.

[First published, *MLN*, 42 (1927), revised.] *Arcadia* was the source of Galaut's *Phalante,* which was the source of La Calprenède's *Phalante.* Includes a note answering Osborn [*MLN,* 48 (1933)]. Suggests that Galaut may have read *Arcadia* in English.

᪐§ 816. LONGFELLOW, HENRY WADSWORTH. "The Defence of Poetry." In *The Achievement of American Criticism: Representative Selections from 300 Years of American Criticism,* Clarence Arthur Brown, ed., pp. 102–38. New York: Ronald Press Company, 1954.

[First published, *North American Review,* 34 (1832).] Defends the study of poetry, writing that nothing is useless that contributes to happiness. Poetry cannot be false. Relates literature to national character. The pastoral mode was never very important in English poetry. *Arcadia* was popular because of its author's popularity. Concludes that American writers follow British modes instead of developing an original literature.

◄§ 817. MYRICK, KENNETH. *Sir Philip Sidney as a Literary Crafts-man.* Lincoln: University of Nebraska Press, 1965. 362 pp.

[First published, 1935; 2d ed. includes additional footnotes and a critical bibliography of studies since 1935 prepared by William L. Godshalk.] Sidney was a more serious writer than his remarks concerning his works would indicate (pp. 5–6). The *Defence* is a classical oration following the rules of Quintilian (pp. 53–61). *Arcadia* follows Minturno's rules for the epic: it begins *in medias res,* includes dramatic narration, and avoids interruptions in important scenes (pp. 125–46). The New *Arcadia* shows more artistry than the Old (p. 146). It is not an allegory; it is an imitation of what human action should be (p. 251). The sonnets may be autobiographical but also are artistically pleasing (pp. 310–15).

◄§ 818. OSGOOD, CHARLES GROSVENOR. *The Voice of England: A History of English Literature.* New York: Harper and Brothers, 1952. 627 pp.

[First published, 1935.] Contains a section on Sidney's life and work (pp. 158–64). See also Index.

◄§ 819. PEARSON, LU EMILY. *Elizabethan Love Conventions* New York: Barnes and Noble, Inc., 1966. 365 pp.

[First published, 1933.] Considers Petrarchism and anti-Petrarchism in England. Believes that the biographical matter of the sonnets is less important than the psychological analysis of love and the use of conventions; Stella may be a symbol of spiritual love (pp. 84–86). The sequence is a battle between physical desire and spiritual love (pp. 95–99). Contrasts Sidney's Platonism with Spenser's Petrarchism (pp. 162–63).

◄§ 820. SHEAVYN, PHOEBE. *The Literary Profession in the Elizabethan Age,* revised by J. W. Saunders. Manchester: Manchester University Press, 1967. 248 pp.

[First edition, 1909.] Explains in a series of seven essays the effects of social, economic, and legal conditions upon professional writers. The first essay, "Authors and Patrons," deals with the patronage of the Sidney family. Sidney was the ideal patron (p. 13).

821. SPINGARN, JOEL E. *Literary Criticism in the Renaissance*. New York: Harcourt, Brace and World, 1963. 227 pp.

[First published, 1899.] Traces the development of the theory of literature from Italy to France and England. The *Defence* is the epitome of Italian Renaissance literary criticism.

822. SYMONDS, J. A. *Sir Philip Sidney*. The Gale Library of Lives and Letters: British Writers Series. London: Macmillan and Company, Limited, 1968. 205 pp.

[First published, 1886.] Includes criticism with a life of Sidney. *The Lady of May* has neither good dialogue nor good lyrics (p. 54). A *Discourse to the Queenes Majesty* is eloquent and courageous; outlines the arguments (pp. 70–76). *Arcadia* is without serious purpose (p. 82). *Astrophel and Stella* expresses sincere emotion (p. 126). Explicates many sonnets (pp. 124–54). The *Defence* is Sidney's most mature work (p. 156).

823. TAYLOR, HENRY OSBORN. *England*. Vol. II of *Thought and Expression in the 16th Century*. New York: Ungar Press. 1959. 2 vols.

[First published, 1920.] Weighs Sidney's use of Plato and Aristotle in the *Defence*; criticizes Sidney's failure to appreciate romantic literature (p. 222). Considers Sidney's use of French and Italian sources for *Astrophel and Stella* (pp. 224–26) and the use of repetition and animism in *Arcadia* (pp. 226–30). Concludes that *Arcadia* is not didactic (p. 230).

824. THOMPSON, FRANCIS. *The Real Robert Lewis Stevenson and Other Critical Essays by Francis Thompson*, Terence L. Connolly, S.J., ed. New York: University Publishers Company, 1959. 409 pp.

[First published, *Athenaeum*, August 27, 1898.] Reviews Gray's edition of Sidney's sonnets. Writes that the sonnets are sincere, not conventional.

825. WALLACE, MALCOLM WILLIAM. *The Life of Sir Philip Sidney*. New York: Octagon Books, Inc., 1967. 428 pp.

[First published, 1915.] Gives full details of Sidney's life drawn from Elizabethan documents. Adds to the known sources Thomas Marshall's Book of Accounts, which records Sidney's expenses for part of 1565 and 1566. This account book is printed in an appendix (pp. 406–23). Assesses the conclusions of earlier biographers and of traditions about Sidney by weighing them against documentary fact. Finds a reference to a lost translation of Aristotle's *Rhetoric* in John Hoskyns' *Figures of Rhetoric* (p. 327).

⏴§ 826. WARREN, CLARENCE HENRY. *Sir Philip Sidney: A Study in Conflict.* New York: Haskell House, 1967. 240 pp.

[First published, 1936.] Relates Sidney's life to his poetic ability and his religious nature rather than to his accomplishments as soldier and courtier. Believes Stella may be a composite picture of Penelope Rich and an unknown woman (p. 131).

⏴§ 827. WHITE, HAROLD OGDEN. *Plagiarism and Imitation During the English Renaissance.* New York: Octagon Books, Inc., 1965. 209 pp.

[First published, 1935.] Develops the thesis that what is now called plagiarism was by the Elizabethans called imitation. In the *Defence* Sidney distinguished copying from imitation (pp. 60–64).

⏴§ 828. WILSON, MONA. *Sir Philip Sidney.* London: Rupert Hart-Davis, 1950. 328 pp.

[First published, 1931.] Emphasizes Sidney's role in Elizabethan literature and his role in politics. Takes the Aeropagus seriously (p. 125). Writes that each edition of *Astrophel and Stella* preserved the same ordering of poems; probably this ordering is Sidney's (p. 169). Finds a three-part division in the sonnets (pp. 179–97). The Appendix traces the history of Sir Henry Sidney's service in Ireland (pp. 290–300) and describes the style of *Arcadia* based on a book by John Hoskyns (pp. 304–9).

⏴§ 829. WOLFF, SAMUEL LEE. *The Greek Romances in Elizabethan Prose Fiction.* New York: Burt Franklin, 1961. ix, 520 pp.

[First published, 1912.] Suggests that Mary Sidney is responsible for the changes in Books IV and V of *Arcadia* (pp. 345–46). Describes the difference between the Old and New *Arcadia* (pp. 348–52). Indicates imitations of Heliodorus and Achilles Tatius in *Arcadia* (pp. 353–66).

⏴§ 830. WOOLF, VIRGINIA. "The Countess of Pembroke's *Arcadia.*" In *The Common Reader Second Series*, pp. 38–49. New York: Harcourt, Brace and Company, 1948.

[First published, 1932.] Because Arcadia lacks direction, it becomes dull, but it still contains all the seeds of English fiction.

The prose is generalized, but the poetry is more particular and realistic.

❧ 831. ZANDVOORT, R. W. *Sidney's* Arcadia: *A Comparison Between the Two Versions*. New York: Russell and Russell, 1968. 215 pp.

[First published, 1929.] Finds the New *Arcadia* superior to the Old in style and characterization (pp. 198–99). Old *Arcadia* does, however, present a more coherent story (p. 118).

Bibliography of Sources

Abstracts of Dissertations Approved for the Ph.D., M.Sc., and M. Litt. Degrees in the University of Cambridge. (1940–1941—1961–1962). Cambridge: University Press, 1942–1962.

Abstracts of English Studies. Vols. 1–14. Boulder, Colo.: National Council of Teachers of English, 1958–1970.

Anglia. "Bibliographie der an deutschen and österreichischen Universitäten 1939–1951 angenommenen anglistischen Dissertationen." 70 (1952), 454–60; 71 (1952), 127–28; 71 (1953), 249–56, 376–83, 498–515.

ARMS, GEORGE, AND JOSEPH M. KUNTZ. *Poetry Explication: A Checklist of Interpretation since 1925 of British and American Poems, Past and Present.* New York: Swallow Press, 1962.

ASSOCIATION OF RESEARCH LIBRARIES. *A Catalogue of Books Represented by Library of Congress Printed Cards. Issued to July 31, 1942.* Ann Arbor, Mich.: Edwards Brothers, 1942–1946. 167 vols.

———— *Supplement. Cards Issued August 1, 1942–December 31, 1947.* Ann Arbor, Mich.: J. W. Edwards, 1948. 42 vols.

BALDENSPERGER, FERNAND, AND WERNER P. FRIEDERICH. *Bibliography of Comparative Literature.* University of North Carolina Studies in Comparative Literature 1. Chapel Hill: University of North Carolina Press, 1950.

BATESON, F. W., ED. *The Cambridge Bibliography of English Literature.* New York: Macmillan, 1941. 4 vols.

BESTERMAN, THEODORE. *A World Bibliography of Bibliographies,* 4th ed. Laussane: Societas Bibliographica, 1966. 5 vols.

Biblio. Bibliographie des Ouvrages Parus en Langue Français dans le Monde Entier. Vols. 8 (1941)–37 (1970). Paris: Service Bibliographique de la Librairie Hachette, 1942–1971.

Bibliografia Nazionale Italiana. Nuova Serie del Bollettino delle Pubblicazioni Italiane Ricevuto per diritto di Stampa. Vols. 1 (1958)–11 (1969). Florence: Biblioteca Nazionale Centrale, 1958–1969.

Bibliographic Index: A Cumulative Bibliography of Bibliographies. Vols. 1 (1937–1942)–10 (1970). New York: H. W. Wilson, 1945–1970.

Bibliographie der deutschen Literaturwissenschaft. Vols. 1 (1945–1953)–8 (1967–1968). Frankfurt: Vittorio Klostermann, 1957–1969. Hanns W. Eppelsheimer, ed., Vol. 1; Clemens Köttelwelsch, ed., Vol. 2.

Bibliographie der deutschen Zeitschriftenliteratur. Vols. 78–120. Leipzig and Osnabruck: Felix Dietrich Verlag, 1940–1964. [Vols. 95 and 96 not published.]

Bibliographie der fremdsprachigen Zeitschriftenliteratur (1939–1962). Leipzig and Osnabruck: Felix Dietrich Verlag, n.d. [Vol. 26 not published.]

Bibliographie internationale de l'Humanisme et de la Renaissance. Vols. 1 (1965)–4 (1968). Geneva: Librairie Droz, 1967–1970.

Biography Index: A Cumulative Index to Biographical Material in Books and Magazines. Vols. 1 (1946)–8 (1970). New York: H. W. Wilson, 1949–1971.

BRADNER, LEICESTER. "The Renaissance: 1939–1945." *Medievalia et Humanistica,* 5 (1948), 62–72.

British Humanities Index (1962–1970). London: Library Association, 1963–1971.

British National Bibliography Annual Volume (1950–1970). London: Council of the British National Bibliography, 1951–1971.

COLUMBIA UNIVERSITY, GRADUATE FACULTIES. *Masters' Essays and Doctoral Dissertations* (1952–1960). Morningside Heights, N.Y.: Columbia University Libraries, 1952–1962.

CORNELL UNIVERSITY. *Abstracts of Theses Accepted in Partial Satisfaction of the Requirements for the Doctor's Degrees* (1941–1947). Ithaca, N.Y.: Cornell University Press, 1942–1949.

Cumulative Book Index: A World List of Books in the English Language (1941–1971). New York: H. W. Wilson, 1942–1971. [Supplements *The National Union Catalog,* 4th ed.]

Deutsches Bücherverzeichnis (1940–1960). Leipzig: Borsenverein der deutschen buchhändler, 1942–1960. 38 vols.

Dissertation Abstracts. Vols. 12 (1952)–31 (1970). Ann Arbor: Mich.: University Microfilms, 1953–1970.

Doctoral Dissertations Accepted by American Universities. Compiled for the Association of Research Libraries. Vols. 8–21. New York: The H. W. Wilson Company, 1940–1954.

ENGLISH ASSOCIATION. *The Year's Work in English Studies* (1940–1968). Oxford: University Press, 1941–1970.

Essay and General Literature Index. Vols. 3 (1941–1947)–7 (1965–1969). New York: H. W. Wilson, 1941–1971.

FORDHAM UNIVERSITY. *Dissertations Accepted for Higher Degrees in the Graduate School.* Vols. 8 (1941)–29 (1962). New York: Fordham University Press, 1942–1962.

GOLDEN, HERBERT H., AND SEYMOUR O. SIMCHES. *Modern French Literature and Language: A Bibliography of Homage Studies.* Cambridge, Mass.: Harvard University Press, 1953.

GUFFEY, GEORGE ROBERT. "Sir Philip Sidney: 1941–1965." In *Elizabethan Bibliographies Supplements* VII. London: The Nether Press, 1967.

HARVARD UNIVERSITY, GRADUATE SCHOOL OF ARTS AND SCIENCES. *Summaries of Theses Accepted in Partial Fulfilment of the Requirements for the Degree of Doctor of Philosophy* (1941–1945). Cambridge, Mass.: The University, 1945–1947.

HARVARD UNIVERSITY AND RADCLIFFE COLLEGE. *Doctors of Philosophy with Titles of Their Theses* (1945–1946—1952–1953). Cambridge, Mass.: The University, n.d.–1953.

Index to American Doctoral Dissertations. Vols. 16 (1955)–29 (1969). Ann Arbor, Mich.: University Microfilms, 1957–1970.

Index to Theses Accepted for Higher Degrees in the Universities of Great Britain and Ireland. Vols. 1 (1950)–17 (1968). London: Association of Special Libraries and Information Bureaux [Aslib], 1953–1970.

International Index to Periodicals: A Quarterly Guide to Periodical Literature in the Social Sciences and Humanities. Vols. 10 (1941)–19 (1965). New York: H. W. Wilson, 1942–1966.

Internationale Bibliographie der Zeitschriften Literatur aus allen Gebieten des Wissens (1965–1968). Osnabruck: Felix Dietrich Verlag, n.d.

Jahresverzeichnis der deutschen Hochschulschriften. Vols. 59–81. Leipzig: Deutschen Bucherei, 1943–1965.

Libri d'Italia (1947–1952). Florence: Sansoni, 1948–1959.

McNamee, Lawrence F. *Dissertations in English and American Literature: Theses Accepted by American, British and German Universities, 1865–1964.* New York: R. R. Bowker Company, 1968.

Microfilm Abstracts. Vols. 4 (1941)–11 (1951). Ann Arbor, Mich.: University Microfilms, 1942–1952.

Modern Humanities Research Association. *Annual Bibliography of English Language and Literature.* Vols. 21 (1940)–44 (1968). Cambridge: University Press, 1942–1971.

———. *The Year's Work in Modern Language Studies* (1940–1968). Cambridge: University Press, 1941–1971.

Modern Language Association. "American Bibliography." *Publications of the Modern Language Association of America,* 56 (1941)–70 (1955). [Issued annually.]

———. "International Bibliography." *Publications of the Modern Language Association of America,* 71 (1956)–84 (1969). [Issued annually.]

The National Union Catalog: A Cumulative Author List Representing Library of Congress Printed Cards and Titles Reported by Other American Libraries. 1953–1957. Ann Arbor, Mich.: J. W. Edwards, 1958. 28 vols.; 1958–1962. Ann Arbor, Mich.: J. W. Edwards, 1963. 54 vols.; 1963–1967. Ann Arbor, Mich.: J. W. Edwards, 1969. 65 vols.; 1968. Washington, D.C.: Library of Congress, 1969. 12 vols.; 1969. Washington, D.C.: Library of Congress, 1970. 13 vols.

NORTHWESTERN UNIVERSITY, GRADUATE SCHOOL. *Summaries of Doctoral Dissertations Submitted to the Graduate School of Northwestern University in Partial Fulfillment of the Requirements for the Degree of Doctor of Philosophy.* Vols. 9 (1941)–20 (1952). Chicago and Evanston, Ill.: Northwestern University, 1942–1953.

Oesterreichische Bibliographie: Verzeichnis der Oesterreichischen Neuerscheinungen (1945–1965). Vienna: Oesterreichischen Buchhändler.

Readers' Guide to Periodical Literature. Vols. 12 (1939–1941)–30 (1970–1971). New York: H. W. Wilson Company, 1941–1971.

SCHUTZ, ALEXANDER H., ed. *The Sixteenth Century.* Vol. 2 of *A Critical Bibliography of French Literature.* Syracuse, N.Y.: Syracuse University Press, 1956.

Shakespeare Association Bulletin. "Bibliography of Shakespeare and his Contemporaries." 16 (1941) 23 (1948). [Issued annually.]

Shakespeare Quarterly. "An Annotated World Bibliography." 1 (1950)–21 (1970). [Issued annually.]

Social Sciences and Humanities Index. Vols. 19 (1965) 23 (1970). New York: H. W. Wilson, 1967–1971.

STANFORD UNIVERSITY. *Abstracts of Dissertations for the Degrees of Doctor of Philosophy and Doctor of Education with Titles of Theses Accepted for the Degrees of Master of Laws, Engineer, Master of Education and Master of Arts.* Vols. 17 (1941)–27 (1952). Stanford, Cal.: Stanford University Press, 1942–1952.

Studies in English Literature. "Recent Studies in the English Renaissance." 1 (1961)–11 (1971). [Issued annually.]

Studies in Philology. "Literature of the Renaissance." 38 (1941)–66 (1969). [Issued annually.]

THOMSON, S. HARRISON. *Progress of Medieval and Renaissance Studies in the United States and Canada.* Nos. 15 (1940)–24 (1957). Boulder, Colo.: University of Colorado Press, 1940–1960.

University of Iowa Doctoral Dissertations, Abstracts and References. Vols. 4 (1940)–10 (1952). Iowa City: University of Iowa Press, 1940–1954.

UNIVERSITY OF LONDON. *Subjects of Dissertations and Theses and Published Works Presented by Successful Candidates at Examinations for Higher Degrees from 1937 to 1944.* London: The University, n.d.

————. *Theses, Dissertations and Published Works Accepted for Higher Degrees: A Classified List with Author and Subject Indexes* (1944–1964). London: The University, 1944–1964. [Title varies.]

UNIVERSITY OF NEBRASKA. *Abstracts of Doctoral Dissertations Presented to the Graduate College in Partial Fulfilment of the Requirements for the Degree of Doctor of Philosophy.* Vols. 1 (1940)–14 (1953). Lincoln: University of Nebraska Press, 1940–1953.

UNIVERSITY OF SOUTHERN CALIFORNIA, LOS ANGELES. *Abstracts of Dissertations for the Degree of Doctor of Philosophy with the Titles of Theses Accepted for Masters Degrees* (1941–1958). Los Angeles: University of Southern California Press, 1942–1958.

UNIVERSITY OF WASHINGTON. *Abstracts of Theses, Faculty Bibliography and Research in Progress.* Vols. 6 (1941)–10 (1949). Seattle: University of Washington Press, 1941–1949.

UNIVERSITY OF WISCONSIN. *Summaries of Doctoral Dissertations.* Vols. 6 (1940)–16 (1955). Madison: University of Wisconsin Press, 1942–1956.

VANDERBILT UNIVERSITY. *Abstracts of Theses.* Bulls. 41 (1940)–59 (1959). Nashville, Tenn.: Vanderbilt University, 1941–1959.

WATSON, GEORGE, ED. *Supplement. The Cambridge Bibliography of English Literature.* Vol. 5. Cambridge: University Press, 1957.

Yearbook of Comparative and General Literature, Werner P. Friederich, *et al.,* eds. Vols. 1 (1952)–19 (1970). Chapel Hill: University of North Carolina Press, 1952–1960; Bloomington: University of Indiana Press, 1961–1970.

Index

About the Author

Mary A. Washington is Assistant Professor of English at Utah State University in Logan, Utah. She is the compiler of *An Annotated Bibliography of Western Manuscripts in The Merrill Library*, published in 1971 by the Western Text Society, Utah State University. Professor Washington attended the University of Texas, where she received a B.A. in 1956, and the University of Missouri—Columbia, where she received an M.A. in 1961 and a Ph.D. in 1969. It was during her studies at the University of Missouri—Columbia that she began the project that has led to the present publication.